WISE ENOUGH
TO PLAY THE FOOL

This fellow is wise enough to play the fool,
And to do that well, craves a kind of wit:
He must observe their mood on whom he jests,
The quality of persons, and the time,
And like the haggard, check at every feather
That comes before his eye. This is a practice
As full of labour as the wise man's art:
For folly that he wisely shows is fit;
But wise men, folly-fall'n, quite taint their wit.

Shakespeare, *Twelfth Night*, III, i

WISE ENOUGH TO PLAY THE FOOL

A Biography of Duncan Macrae

PRISCILLA BARLOW

Foreword by Stanley Baxter

JOHN DONALD PUBLISHERS LIMITED
EDINBURGH
IN ASSOCIATION WITH
THEATRE STUDIES PUBLICATIONS
UNIVERSITY OF GLASGOW

First published 1995

The publisher acknowledges subsidy from
the Scottish Arts Council towards
the publication of this volume.

A catalogue record for this book is available
from the British Library.

ISBN 0 85976 418 4

Printed and bound in Great Britain by
Redwood Books, Trowbridge, Wiltshire

— FOREWORD —

If Duncan Macrae is not the greatest actor Scotland has ever produced, most Scots would probably accord him this accolade if questioned on the subject. There is no doubt he was certainly the most colourful.

He had a small holiday home in Millport and when I went to visit him there to discuss a forthcoming pantomime we were to do together he met me at the 'Old Pier'. The boat was edging its way to its moorings and I saw no sign of him as yet. Suddenly the turnstile flew round and with quite alarming histrionic stride he appeared — using a walking stick as if to demonstrate its theatrical potential — first as an aid to locomotion then as a sort of flag to wave his recognition of my wife and me who were still on board. By this time shipboard arrivals and those meeting them — not to mention the crew and pier employees — were riveted at the sight he made. As we strolled towards his little flat in Kames Bay he vouchsafed the information that he liked the island so much because 'I keep a low profile here and just merge into the background'!! You know I think he might even have believed that. He had a wonderful gift of self deception. When we eventually got round to rehearsing the aforementioned panto I gave him the moves required for a slapstick sketch I had devised. He balked at my direction. I said, 'This is where you go to the sideboard and get a mixing bowl.' 'Ah!', said John (nobody but strangers called him Duncan), 'that kind of direction is no good to me. I have to work out how I get to the table. Do I turn on my left foot or my right? If you drew my movements in chalk on the stage it would be the same each performance.' I was duly impressed until on the first night and thereafter I discovered his uniquely eccentric choreography got him all over the stage every night.

The truth is he was a most undisciplined performer. He often didn't know how his laughs were achieved and would burl round to discover what actor to his rear was slipping in comic movements. The bemused rearguard players couldn't believe he didn't realize it was his performance that was convulsing the house. This meant that often he would change magical moments and lose his laughs and retreat to the 'wings' growling 'rotten house the night'.

All right — that gets the failings of a great man out of the way. What were the virtues? Oh so many! As an artist his great roles were truly great. Indeed unforgettable. His *Jamie the Saxt, Gog and Magog* and Oliphant in *Let Wives Tak Tent* will be remembered by all who had the joy of witnessing them, and fortunately for posterity he registered well on film. As a man I am very grateful for the very real kindness towards me in my first year at Citizens' when I was a new boy to the profession.

A biography of Macrae is long overdue. Priscilla Barlow is to be congratulated on remedying this gap in the Scottish theatre story.

Stanley Baxter

— ACKNOWLEDGEMENTS —

This book could not have been written without the co-operation and goodwill of John Duncan Macrae's daughters, who made available private documents and letters and gave so much of their time. My thanks and appreciation are unreservedly due to them. Their invaluable memories, coupled with those of Macrae's late sisters, made beginning possible. I also acknowledge the generous help of other family members and of his many friends.

To Stanley Baxter and the countless actors, actresses, stage and film directors, too numerous to list, in Scotland, England and America, who shared their recollections so willingly, I am greatly obliged. They will each recognize their individual contributions and will, I trust, know how much these are appreciated by me.

I wish to thank the staffs of the following institutions, whose courteous assistance made research so much easier; the Manuscripts Room of the National Library, Edinburgh; Glasgow City Archives; Glasgow University Archives; Jordanhill College of Education; the Theatre Museum, London; Edinburgh Festival Society; Manders & Mitchison; Arts and Recreation Division, Central Library, Aberdeen; Perth City Archives; and the Scottish Theatre Archive; also Mrs Margaret Wilson for allowing me access to the papers of Dr Tom Honeyman, and the Scottish Equity Headquarters for access to minutes of meetings. In particular, I acknowledge the unfailingly knowledgeable help of Elizabeth Watson at the Scottish Theatre Archive.

I am indebted to my editors, Claude Schumacher and Brian Hannan, for their patient advice — in particular to Claude Schumacher for his preparation of the final script — and to David Fergus and my husband who, occasionally reading the manuscript, encouraged me to keep going. Further thanks are due to Karen Marshalsay for her sharp-eyed proofreading.

I thank the Duncan Macrae Memorial Trust for the generous financial support which aided my research and the publication of this book.

Material from the Macrae Collection and Dr Tom Honeyman's papers is cited and reproduced by courtesy of the Trustees of the National Library of Scotland.

Hugh MacDiarmid's 'Cranks never make good democrats', originally published in the Duncan Macrae Memorial Trust Appeal Brochure, is reprinted by kind permission of Michael Grieve.

Finally, I wish to record my gratitude to the late Dr Alasdair Cameron who had faith.

Priscilla Barlow, 1995

Contents

— ILLUSTRATIONS —

Cover picture: Publicity photograph for *Loot* — 1965 (© *Lewis Morley / Akehurst Bureau*)

1. The Macrae Family — 1910 (*Courtesy of Ann Caldwell and Christine Macrae*)
2. Cast list for *Emergency Call* (*Courtesy of Scottish Theatre Archive*)
3. Publicity still for The Curtain Theatre — 1930s (*Courtesy of Mrs Annabel Kirk and Miss Ann Macrae*)
4. Wedding photograph — John and Peggy Macrae — 1943 (*Courtesy of Ann Caldwell and Christine Macrae*)
5. *The Forrigan Reel* — Sadler's Wells (*Courtesy of National Library of Scotland*)
6. Playbill for *The Holy Isle* — 1943 (*Courtesy of Scottish Theatre Archive*)
7. *Let Wives Tak Tent* (*Courtesy of Scottish Theatre Archive*)
8. Macrae as 'The Pardoner', *The Three Estates* — 1948 (*Courtesy of Scottish Theatre Archive*)
9. A page from Macrae's earnings record (*Courtesy of Ann Caldwell and Christine Macrae*)
10. Principals in Alhambra pantomime (*Courtesy of National Library of Scotland*)
11. Pantomime poster — 1951 (*Courtesy of National Library of Scotland*)
12. *Tartuffe* (*Courtesy of Scottish Theatre Archive*)
13. *Gog and Magog* (*Courtesy of Scottish Theatre Archive*)
14. Still from the film *The Kidnappers* (© *The Rank Organisation Plc*)
15. At Millport (*Courtesy of Ann Caldwell and Christine Macrae*)
16. Empire review — 1956 (*Courtesy of National Library of Scotland*)

Back cover: (Left to right) Macrae as — Tartuffe, Tammas Biggar, Harry Magog, Mr Oliphant, Para Handy, Lord James Stuart

For Jonathan

— PROLOGUE —

NOT JUST A SPARROW

The revival of interest in Scottish drama in the 1940s occurred at precisely the right moment for John Duncan Macrae. Until then, the popular image of the Scottish stage to the world beyond, with virtually no exceptions, was the tartan one of the music hall comedians. Macrae's energies, in common with anyone with a desire to act in plays or who cherished any hopes for a Scottish national drama, were largely confined to the activities of a thriving amateur movement. Scottish actors with serious aspirations to a career in legitimate professional theatre either had to lose their regional accents on the journey south or be forced into character parts there. This did not necessarily inhibit the Scots from taking to the boards. By 1939 both Perth and Dundee had modest repertory theatres and by 1941 Wilson Barrett had taken the place of the Brandon-Thomas Players. But with the birth of a more ambitious Scottish-based theatre enterprise in 1943 in the shape of the Glasgow Citizens' Theatre Company, a new set of circumstances was created in which the professional Scottish actor could begin to take his place at home. The flow of talent was then partially reversed and Scotland began to be a place in which English directors and actors thought it was advantageous to work.

In many ways the Macrae story is a reflection of amateur and professional Scottish theatre history, mirroring the fortunes of these two branches of the stage over a period of some forty years. When Macrae eventually turned professional, he was one of the select band of actors who made the transition from the legitimate to the variety stage and back look effortless. These switches, however, were not without their price. If Duncan Macrae is

1

mentioned to the average Scot of a certain generation, even twenty years and more after his death, the response will almost invariably be to associate him with the song, 'The Wee Cock Sparra'.

The claims made for knowing Macrae's source for this song, or being present at his first ever performance of it, are legion. They are made with the kind of proprietorial pride reserved for eager identification with historical events. He is credited with 'stealing' it from a multitude of people who ranged from the legendary Scots comedian Tommy Lorne to an obscure backstage crew member at the Curtain Theatre who allegedly liked to think of it as his own party piece. He is also reported to have learned it in 1939 from a small boy in the class he taught at Finnieston School.

While these tales — all of them unquestionably reliable according to the memory of the various tellers — lend colour to the myth of 'The Wee Cock Sparra', the irrefutable fact is that his rendering of the song on BBC television, on 31 December 1959, brought him popular recognition on a scale far in excess of any he had hitherto enjoyed in pantomime, film or legitimate theatre.

But with the passing of time it was fame of a kind that he came to resent for he believed it devalued his more serious work. Despite the precious publicity, the wretched bird became like an albatross around his neck which he could never quite shake off. It was not how he would have cared to be remembered.

There was so much more to the art of Duncan Macrae than the pawky performance of the song about the jaunty wee bird. His face will be familiar to those who have perhaps seen him only on the large screen in films like *The Brothers*, *Whisky Galore*, *The Kidnappers* and *Tunes of Glory*. There may be television viewers who remember *Para Handy*, or even the advert for porridge. But for those who have never seen him live on stage, this story introduces them to memorable characters like Jamie the Saxt, Polly at the Pally, The Queen of Crossmyloof, Flatterie, Donald MacAlpin and Harry Magog, that he created with the indefinable, spellbinding and elusive magic which graced so much that he did.

— 1 —

FIRST ENTRANCES

The early years - university and college -
a career in teaching - the amateur actor

Duncan Macrae made an inconspicuous beginning on the professional stage at the Westminster Theatre in London in 1943. Not surprisingly, as Alastair Sim's understudy in *Mr Bolfry*, he passed unnoticed and unpublicized. But Sim believed there was a future in the theatre for his fellow Scot and he made an inspired suggestion. If Macrae intended to make a career in theatre, he should adopt his second name, Duncan, in preference to John. He thought it had a more theatrical ring. Macrae found the idea attractive. And so began the career of Duncan Macrae, the actor whose style and personality were destined to pass into the myths and legends of Scottish theatre history.

The notion of donning a mask and becoming somebody else is fundamental to the actor's art. How much more significant is the act of changing one's given name and creating an entirely new persona. 'Duncan Macrae' did not exist until John Macrae adopted that name at the age of thirty-eight. It was only the mask of Duncan Macrae that was familiar to the theatre-going public. To anyone who knew the man behind the mask, in or out of the theatre profession, he remained always John.

John Duncan Graham Macrae was born in Glasgow in 1905, the fifth child of James and Catherine Macrae. His grandfather owned a croft at Culkeine in Sutherland where, in common with most crofters, he supplemented his living with other employment, finding work as a 'preventiveman' with the Customs and Excise Service. Until he was twenty, his father, James, worked on a farm earning on average thirteen shillings a week. But the hard subsistence life of the Highland croft offered

3

few prospects and in July 1891 James became part of the great migration from rural to urban Scotland and left home for Glasgow. He found lodgings at 8 Govan Street, on the south side of the River Clyde, and was recruited as a probationary constable in the 'A' division of the Glasgow Police Force. By August he achieved routine promotion to the rank of third-class constable, at a weekly wage of twenty-three shillings and ten pence and moved to new lodgings in Burgess Lane.

Over the next three years he progressed uneventfully through the ranks and in May 1894 he was promoted to first-class constable with the princely wage of twenty-eight shillings and tuppence.

Like James Macrae, Catherine Graham left the countryside to seek employment in the city. Her parents, Jane and Dugal, a journeyman joiner, lived in the Stirlingshire village of Kippen at the foot of the Gargunnock Hills, a village that was to become very much a part of the Macrae family life. On 4 November 1897, twenty-eight year old Catherine married James, two years her junior, and set up home in a room and kitchen at 118 Kirkland Street in Maryhill. Their first child, Kenneth, was born in August 1898, Jane in June 1900, Annabella in October 1901, Katherine in November 1902 and, on 20 August 1905, at three o'clock in the morning, John Duncan Graham made his first entrance.

By then James Macrae was a well-established family man with promotion to third-class sergeant, and a weekly wage of thirty-four shillings and eight pence. The Macraes were numbered amongst the 'respectable' who paid their way. (In 1905 approximately twenty-one shillings a week was the average sum spent on food by a family with three or four children; there would be little left for luxuries after attending to heating and clothing.) By the time John was three the family had moved south of the river to 21 Hutcheson Square in the Gorbals district. Ann was born in December 1908. Two years later yet another transfer took the family back across the river. James had achieved the rank of first-class sergeant enabling him to move his family to relative prosperity in a three-room-and-kitchen flat, 'two up', at 139 Berkeley Street where the children grew up. At that time two-thirds of Glasgow's total population still lived in one or two-roomed houses.

Berkeley Street sits behind Glasgow's imposingly domed Mitchell Library, parallel to Sauchiehall Street and runs west from Charing Cross to Finnieston. It is a long broad road which, at the turn of the century, swept from the large elegant residences of the tobacco lords in Blythswood Square, St Vincent Street and Bath Street, to the fringes of the thriving, teeming dockland area of the Clyde. There would still be tall, funnelled ships plying their trade on the river when Macrae was a child, with trams and even hansom cabs in the streets. The hazard to a childhood game of rounders on the road outside the house would not be the risk of passing traffic but the fear of being trampled underfoot by a herd of cattle, unloaded from a boat at Yorkhill Quay, being driven along Berkeley Street to market. The flat was just before the road bends into Argyle Street. A walk of barely ten minutes in one direction could take you right into the heart of the city or, in the other, to Kelvingrove Art Gallery and Museum and the green and pleasant slopes of Kelvingrove Park, dominated by the gothic bell tower of the University on Gilmorehill.

In 1910, the five-year old John made an inauspicious start to schooling. The first day at Kent Road Primary School, only two hundred yards away from the house, was memorable for its brevity. Duly delivering the new pupil at the gate in the care of his older brothers and sisters, his mother returned home and, to her surprise and the subsequent amusement of the family, found the reluctant scholar waiting at the front door. Clearly unimpressed by the prospect of education — a stance he certainly did not retain in later life — and convinced of the superior attractions at home, he had promptly left by the back exit of the playground and taken the short cut to Berkeley Street!

In the same year the young Macrae was initiated into the mystery of acting — an enterprise much more congenial than the rigours of the schoolroom. Two worthy ladies, the Misses McDonald, daughters of the minister of the Highland Memorial Church in Kent Road, took a keen interest in 'theatricals' and organized playlets on subjects ranging from scriptural themes to folk tales, for the children in the congregation to perform. The

Macrae children were eager participants in these productions which were treated very earnestly, meticulously rehearsed and costumed and performed with considerable pride. When John was a little older he showed a flair for pantomime in the title role in *Puss in Boots*.

Life at 139 Berkeley Street was happy and secure. James and Catherine Macrae created a warm and loving atmosphere which resulted in the children enjoying a loyal and lasting affection for each other when they grew to adulthood. In the heart of the city, their mother managed to keep alive the essential family spirit of village life, carrying on the links with Kippen through the regular and welcome visits of the children's grandmother Graham who was always on hand. Birthdays were celebrated with a prized 'cloutie dumpling' and at Christmas the dolls, always amongst the little girls' presents, were solemnly and ceremoniously named. One of the children's pleasures was to gather round the piano to listen to their mother play and join in her favourite songs, *The Rowan Tree* and *Land of the Leal*. Their father's skill on the bagpipes was less popular. But from him they acquired a strict set of moral standards, strong religious values, a sense of duty, a love of learning and an abiding devotion to their native culture. James was President of both the Sutherland Association and the Clan Macrae Association and spoke fluent Gaelic. That the children were not Gaelic speaking was one of the regrets of his life, for the only occasions on which the mother tongue was heard in the house was on his sisters' rare visits. One of the most striking and attractive features of the actor, Duncan Macrae's arresting voice, was the characteristic half-tone lilt and fall of the musical inflections of the Highland accent which were etched in his consciousness when he was a boy.

James and Catherine Macrae inherited the Calvinist legacy of disapproval of theatre. This attitude notwithstanding, the Macrae children rarely missed the annual pantomime outing to the Royal Princess's Theatre in the Gorbals, where they must have seen Tommy Lorne, the comedian with whom Macrae was to be so often compared. During Macrae's formative years there was sufficient theatre activity in Scotland for him to be aware of the place it held in the cultural life of the community. By 1910 there were fifteen theatres in Glasgow and fifty-three throughout Scotland. These mainly hosted variety shows and visiting professional companies.

Films, however, were regarded with less reservation, for the youngest child, Dugal, who was born in 1913, was often left in the care of his older brothers and sisters while their parents indulged in the weekly visit to the local cinema.

Before the First World War holidays were a luxury undreamed of by the average city dweller. The annual ration of sea air was more often than not confined to a day's outing sailing 'doon the watter' of the Firth of Clyde to Largs or Dunoon. The Macraes, no exception, joined in the exodus dressed in their holiday best, starched collars, crisp caps and gleaming ringlets in all their innocent glory, recording the occasion for posterity with a sepia-tinted framed photograph taken by the ubiquitous photographer on the pier. But the Macraes were fortunate to be able to spend many idyllic summers at the family croft in Sutherland. The adventure, for to the children it was nothing less, began with the thrill of the cab ride to the station at Charing Cross. Laden with hampers containing not only the clothes but also the family supply of linen, cutlery and dishes which were quite the normal part of holiday luggage, they set off. It was a journey of ever increasing excitement, first by train to catch the boat and then the long sail up the west coast, past landscapes of great mystical beauty, to Lochinver. From there the winding and climbing road took them north, up rocky braes, past reed filled lochans, the distant mountains of Suilven, Sutherland's 'shrouded ghosts', Cul Mor, Cul Beag and Stack Polly dominating the view to the south, and then suddenly dipping down into the bay of Stoer with its dazzling expanse of white sands, home to Culkeine, amidst the rugged grandeur of Wester Ross.

The Macraes continued to prosper. In 1914, Sergeant Macrae was not called to military service as members of the police force were exempted. When the war ended he was earning sixty-five shillings plus one shilling and four pence for 'Boot Money' and was in a position to consider seriously the aspirations he held for his children. True to the ethics of his upbringing he had never failed to instil in them the values of learning and the ability to earn a living. His most earnest ambition was that his sons should be engineers. Kenneth, the oldest, did eventually became an engineering draftsman, and the girls worked as bookkeepers and secretaries. When the second son, John, began to show promise at Woodside School, it was decided that he should attend Allan Glen's fee-paying school for boys in North Hanover Street which enjoyed a reputation for encouraging budding scientists and engineers. The school records for the period immediately after 1918 were destroyed by fire, so the precise date of John's entrance there is not known, nor is it known if the fees were assisted by scholarship. His father was promoted to Inspector, a position of considerable status, earning £320 per annum in April 1919, making a private education affordable. The headmaster at that time, James Steel, was a graduate in the arts and the cultural and recreational pursuits of the boys were not neglected. In 1921 the school spent £2 on the Dramatic Club compared with £122 10s on rugby. Even so, in that year it paid the £40 expenses of putting on a Greek play.

Macrae acquitted himself creditably at Allan Glen's. In the summer of 1923 he took up a place in the Engineering Department of the Faculty of Science at the University of Glasgow. It was a sensible choice for there was no indication that he had aspirations in any other field. The strict Presbyterian background would have forbidden serious contemplation of acting. The fees of £26 12s 6d, plus laboratory and individual class fees, were within the scope of a police inspector's salary, whether or not the new student had won a bursary.

Undergraduate life in the early 1920s was provocative, exciting, depressing and inspiring with social, economic and political upheavals, especially in a heavily industrialized city like Glasgow. In the 1922 General Election, Glasgow returned ten Independent Labour Party members to Parliament including James Maxton, Campbell Stephen and David Kirkwood. It was the era of the great outdoor orators and before the right to assemble on Glasgow Green was withdrawn in 1922, it was estimated that up to 100,000 people gathered there of a Sunday between the hours of 10 a.m. and 10 p.m. to hear impassioned speeches on politics or theology, indeed on anything and everything under the sun. Macrae himself tried his hand at soap-box oratory and was to be found 'Shouting the odds' on behalf of the Scottish National Party on many a Saturday night at draughty corners as far apart as Cowcaddens and Knightswood. He reported to his family that on one wet and windy sortie he drew a crowd of 'a drunk man, two auld wives and two snottery-nosed weans who should have been in their beds'. He achieved the dubious distinction of being thrown out of election meetings for heckling too vociferously.

Reflecting the increasing agitation for home rule, the post-war period saw an upsurge of interest in fostering a native Scottish literature. Publications specifically Scottish in origin began to proliferate. In 1922, for instance, C.M. Grieve (Hugh MacDiarmid) published the first edition of *Scottish Chapbook*, a journal with very ambitious national and international literary aims. Neil Munro created Para Handy and the adventures of the Clyde puffer skipper were immortalized in a series of stories which were dramatized for television some thirty years later with Macrae in the title role.

The theatre was equally alive to the resurgence of this interest in native culture and was working on principles, aims and ideals very similar to those which were to preoccupy Macrae for a considerable part of his life. The launch of the British Drama League in 1919 paved the way for the fertile years of the amateur movement during the thirties when Macrae began to be recognized as an actor of considerable talent. In 1921, inspired by the example of the Abbey Theatre in Dublin, the challenge of forming a national theatre for Scotland was taken up by a group of theatre enthusiasts including D. Glen Mackemmie, Robert B. Wharrie, Tom Honeyman and the playwrights James Bridie and Gordon Bottomley. With the aid of funds remaining from the defunct Glasgow Repertory Theatre they laid the foundations of the Scottish National Theatre Movement which, with the Scottish National Players, gave first expression to the long cherished dream. It was the obvious outlet for Scottish writers, actors and producers and anyone with a commitment to native drama. The

Movement's first production at the Royal Institute in Glasgow was a triple bill of plays, C. Stewart Black's *Chatelard*, J.L. Waugh's and A.P. Wilson's *Cute McCheyne* and J. Brandane's and A.W. Yuill's *Glenforsa*. In 1923 another field of immense possibilities for Scottish writers and performers opened up when SC5, Scotland's first radio station, made its inaugural broadcast from a studio in Bath Street. The first broadcast of a full length drama was, appropriately, *Rob Roy*. Like many amateur actors, Macrae, who was by that time deeply involved with the amateur movement, was often called on to play supporting roles in these pioneering productions.

At University Macrae stepped into a cultural tradition fostered by a group of exceptionally gifted and creative undergraduates who had preceded him: Bridie, Walter Elliot, James Maxton and Tom Honeyman, all of whom were to be major influences in his life. Academically, he was a satisfactory student. His marks in mathematics were above average and while he was not as reliable in the written chemistry exams, the results in the practical classes were excellent. His regular attendance at laboratory sessions is on record.

In the 1920s when professional legitimate theatre in Glasgow was still being supplied by visiting English companies led by the great actor-managers of the day like John Martin Harvey, Henry Baynton, Brandon Thomas and Esmé Percy who played everything from Shakespeare to the latest 'West End' comedies, touring companies used to engage local amateurs to take on walk-on parts. Macrae spent most of his free time in this way with an undergraduate friend, James P. Kennedy. An evening spent covered in greasepaint, behind the footlights, watching some of the finest actors of the time at close quarters, was to them far more attractive and profitable than poring over a problem in mathematics or chemistry. They would often be joined by another starry-eyed hopeful, the budding Glasgow journalist and theatre critic, Jack House.

There is no record to show that Macrae either passed or failed the degree examinations at the end of that first year, but by the end of the summer there was no doubt in his mind that he would not be an engineer. He never returned as a student to Gilmorehill. But before the university connection was finally severed in 1924 he attended a Student Theatre Summer School in Bath during the vacation, where he and Kennedy wrote and performed a sketch in a Gaelic gibberish that the English students assumed to be authentic. By all accounts they had an uproarious reception. The only recorded association Macrae had with the University's dramatic club was in November 1930, when he was invited, with Ian Fleming, to work on the sixth annual *College Pudding* show, which ran for five nights at the Lyric Theatre in Sauchiehall Street. Macrae stage-managed and appeared as a reporter in a sketch called 'The Daily Gale'. He also helped Fleming build and paint the set representing Glasgow tenements in, according to Fleming, 'a rather dingy place below the Bute Hall'.

Still uncertain about the future Macrae spent the next year employed in a shipyard. Then, in an unpredicted change of direction, he enrolled in the autumn of 1925 on a two-year course at Glasgow's Jordanhill College of Education to train as a primary school teacher. He excelled in English, History, Phonetics, Nature Study, Drawing and Handwork. Singing was marked only 'Fair'! Part of the course entailed practical teaching and he was seconded to Washington School in the Finnieston district and to Harmony Row in Govan. He made good progress with favourable although not outstanding reports from the headmasters at the end of every term.

Studying at Jordanhill involved long hours in classes, quite unlike the more 'voluntary' nature of attendance at university lectures. But he still found time to take advantage of the first real opportunity to learn about the stage in a constructive and disciplined fashion. Macrae came under the spell of Anne McAllister, a small, slender and attractive woman with a plait of dark hair wound around her head. About thirty years old, with a seemingly boundless supply of energy, she taught Phonetics and Voice Production. Fired with her enthusiasm and under her guidance, a nucleus of students, including Macrae, his friend Kennedy, Ernie Mace and Ralston P. M'Kell, formed the Torch

Theatre Club. In *Who's Who in the Theatre* Macrae stated that he was 'trained by Anne McAllister' and he never failed publicly to acknowledge his debt to her.

With the formation of the Torch Club, the twenty-one year old, adopting the fashionable practice of using initials, J.D.G. Macrae came into his own. Fellow students recall him as 'difficult' or 'awkward' and his gaunt, gangling appearance bestowed on him an air so sinister that most of the women students were more than a little wary of him. But on stage the transformation was magical. He became filled with a glowing confidence and an authoritative majesty which offset a tendency to overact.

The Torch soon gained recognition at the Scottish Community Drama Association Festivals, earning praise for plays chosen with 'a skill unusual among amateurs'. In 1926 the club presented four one-act plays at the annual festival in the Athenaeum Theatre: *Rory Aforesaid* (John Brandane), *The Three Games* (Earnest Dawe), *Umbrellas* (anon.), and *Half-an-Hour* (J.M. Barrie). Barrie's play was singled out as the most challenging. Not all the notices were generous and one in particular delivered Macrae a resounding broadside:

> Mr. J.D.G. Macrae repeated his fault of the first piece and consistently overdid everything. The doctor was badly made up, and made the strongest part the poorest performance.

In spite of such opinions, the time with the Torch was a happy one and he continued to work with them until 1931.

Macrae graduated from College in 1927, with an average mark in the theory of teaching but with a praiseworthy and auspicious 70+ in the skill. By then his father had retired from the Police Force and a small holiday cottage was purchased at Burnside in Kippen, the village where his mother was born. At the age of twenty-two, Macrae was at the centre of a clique of young men who spent most weekends there, walking in the hills and earnestly arguing, usually about theatre and politics. It was a very important period of the young Macrae's life.

His first teaching appointment at Wolsley Street School in Anderston, lasted from February to May 1928. He then moved to Rosevale Street School in Finnieston where he worked till 1934. The following year he taught for only brief periods at four different schools. In October 1935 he was appointed to Finnieston School.

He brought to teaching the charisma that became his hallmark as an actor. His approach was very different from that of other teachers, adopting unconventional methods to arouse the curiosity of his pupils in the days when the schoolroom was a place of monotonous regimentation. A gifted and dedicated schoolmaster, he earned the lasting affection and respect of his pupils, many of whom came from underprivileged backgrounds. The departures from the rigours of a strictly programmed curriculum meant that for the first time in their young lives they were exposed to someone who treated their opinions seriously. The children were stimulated to question, as he delighted in making them aware of their environment. He might freeze suddenly in the midst of a lesson, urging the children to listen, in a new way as if to music, to the familiar rhythmic clanking of the riveters' hammers, drifting into the stilled classroom from the shipyards on the nearby Clyde, or show films, or take his classes to concerts conducted by Beecham or Barbirolli. Surprised colleagues, coming to talk to him in his classroom, would find him reading Shakespeare to thirty hushed, captivated boys. At Rosevale Street, because of its location adjacent to the school supply room, his classroom was known as the 'Store Room'. It was common knowledge that the 'Store Room' would frequently be locked from the inside, boxing gloves would be fetched and, to the boys' delight, 'a wee match' would be set up. Despite his off-beat attitude to education his reputation was that of a strict disciplinarian. No unwary miscreant or inattentive pupil would escape the sharply flicked piece of chalk from the endless supply he carried in his pockets. The yard at Cranstonhill Fire Station was regularly commandeered by boys for extramural fights at lunch time in the popular misapprehension that they could not been seen by the masters. But the first glimpse of Macrae's long

13

loping figure looming on the horizon could clear that yard within five seconds.

All the while he was 'hammering wooden pegs into brass skulls', as one colleague described teaching, the essential Macrae was coming to life after school hours, acting and directing on the Glasgow amateur stage. During this period he affirmed and reaffirmed not only his fervent commitment to the formation of a national drama for Scotland but also his belief in the necessity of fostering a native acting style. Macrae was in the right place at the right time at the blossoming of the amateur dramatic movement.

The Scottish Community Drama Association was founded in 1926 and in the first season, 1926-7, no fewer than thirty-five plays were entered in the one-act play festival. The first decade (1926-36) was the most fertile and creative in the history of the amateur stage in Scotland. G.W. Bishop, the editor of *The Amateur Theatre Dramatic Yearbook* described the phenomenon as nothing less than 'a dramatic renaissance unequalled since Elizabethan times'. The press was quick to pick up on this and for the first time, newspapers, albeit mainly provincial ones, were running special weekly columns devoted to local amateur players. Reviews often expressed surprise at the rising standards. The drama critic was rapidly becoming a household name and in Glasgow the opinions of 'Jingle', 'Mask' or 'J.Mc.N.R.' were eagerly awaited by a rapidly increasing audience. A vigorous element in the movement which appeared to take all aspects of production with a scholarly seriousness was documented in well-informed articles on lighting, directing, or designing in *The Amateur Stage*.

Significantly, the amateur movement had generated sufficient public interest to justify publishing the pertinent controversies over the amateur ethos and in particular over the dearth of good new Scottish plays. In this way, the dilemma was raised that persistently bedevilled the definition of Scottish culture, namely the apparent confusion of sentimental nostalgia with a genuinely historical heritage.

The Glasgow amateurs took up the challenge presenting a stimulating alternative to the more pedestrian fare of the professional theatre where audiences were being offered the familiar mix of London musicals and drawing-room comedies, a selection of classics produced by English companies on tour and Scottish comics. The week beginning 21 May 1929 was fairly typical. The London actress Lillian Braithewaite was starring in *The Silver Cord* at the King's theatre; at the Alhambra the constant favourite, Jack Buchanan, was packing the house in *That's a Good Girl* with Debroy Somers and his Band; the Empire was showing, 'direct from London Palladium', the C.B. Cochrane revue, *One DamnThing After Another*; the local attraction at the Pavilion was the comedian, Will Fyffe, billed 'Direct from his Big American Tour Success Supported by an All-Star Vaudeville Programme'; and at the Royal another touring English company was presenting *The Good King*.

But the same week also saw the opening at the Lyric Theatre (24 May) of the Moscow Art Theatre Company in a short season of twelve performances, 'direct from the Garrick Theatre London'. The programme changed nightly, with matinées on Tuesdays and Saturdays and the seats cost from 1s 2d to 5s 9d. There is a certain indictment of the intelligence and taste of Glasgow audiences implicit in the wording of the advance publicity, to say nothing of the apparent lack of confidence in the Russian company's ability to attract an audience in its own right. The assumption was that only if a production had come 'directly from London' was it likely to be of good entertainment value.

About that time Macrae penned his own manifesto for Scottish theatre, entitled *Drama as a Separate Art,* in which he comments on the Scottish attitude to the art of acting:

> In Scotland where nearly all professional shows are English, it is very difficult indeed to realize that nearly every other nation sets a stamp upon its acting, as surely identified with it as the play itself. So little do we appreciate style in acting that a recent visit of Maurice Schwartz's company was a miserable failure here. Scarcely anybody knew that a company from the Comédie-Française was in Scotland lately. And a short time ago the Moscow Art Theatre, visiting the Lyric, Glasgow, was well received as approximating very closely to the English

naturalistic treatment when actually the playing represented the last word in virtuosity. (I had the dismal privilege of recovering a few days ago, from the rubbish can in the Lyric, a show-card of the Moscow Art Theatre bearing photographs of some of greatest actors in the world.) Dramatists, so dogmatic about the primary importance of the text, are failing consistently to realize a satisfactory form. May not this be due to the lack of a conscious and progressive system of acting, designed to merge finally with the words of the authors in a Scottish Art of the Theatre?

The Art of the Theatre is the art of conceiving a play as acted in a particular style in a particular place. Without this approach Scottish Drama will continue to waver indeterminately following the lead of the West End in a vicious Piccadilly Circus.

John Duncan Macrae's banner was thus well and truly nailed to the flag pole. But he was also becoming involved in the flowering of amateur drama on a political stage.

As early as 1925 groups like the Clydebank I.L.P. Players and the Labour College Group composed from all Labour and Socialist organizations in the city had formed themselves into the Glasgow Federation of Socialist Players, performing plays like Chekhov's *The Bear*. This union was the prelude to the foundation of the original Tron Theatre Club in 1930, where Macrae first began to make any real impact on the consciousness of both critics and public.

On Saturday 17 March 1928, Glasgow opened the doors of the new 300-seat Little Theatre in the premises of the Keir Hardie Institute at 228 Renfrew Street, the meeting place of members of the local Independent Labour Party, where Macrae now spent a great deal of time. Funded and equipped by the Institute, The Little Theatre was designated for the use of Labour and Socialist dramatic societies. The Clarion Players launched the theatre with their production of Shaw's *Man and Superman*. The new venture was not initially interested in establishing native drama. A certain dichotomy in the amateur ethos now seems to have appeared. Socialist working-class theatre groups like the St George's Co-operative Players, Glasgow Workers' Theatre

Group, Glasgow Corporation Transport Players, the Clarion Players and the Jewish Institute Players, tended to produce drama with a socially conscious message by writers like Ibsen, Chekhov and Shaw. It was left to the other groups, in particular those outside the city, to experiment with the output of locally bred writers and continue the tradition of performing the more sedate drawing-room comedies.

Donald Sutherland writing 'A Critical Review of the Scottish Dramatists', in *The Scottish Stage* in December 1930, put his finger on the continual problem of the amateur which is crucial to any explanation of the lack of good Scottish writing:

> Localized experience and local accent debar most of the new born dramatic clubs from the presentation of 90 per cent of existing drama. A demand has been created for Scottish plays in the vernacular, which in turn is creating its own supply. At the moment the younger dramatists have been writing more with the object of satisfying that demand than to express any original views. The result is that Scottish Drama, a true and natural expression of Scottish life, has yet to be written. Nor is the future without hope. The younger school owe very little to the past... When the man comes bringing the true Scots play he will reap a rich reward.

R.F. Pollock now made his first appearance on the public scene. The son of a dye works manager in Balloch, on Loch Lomond, he had been fascinated by the theatre from his earliest years when he had taken part in 'Christie Minstrel' shows. By the time he was thirty-one in 1927, he was absorbed in the so-called 'Scottish Renaissance', counting amongst his close friends writers and poets like G.R. Malloch, Alexander McGill and C.M. Grieve.

Pollock had been to Moscow and seen at first hand, the followers of Stanislavsky and Komissarzhevsky working in their native context. He began to expound and publish his theories on the practice of theatre arts, laying particular emphasis on attention to detail. In 1927 he produced four Scottish plays at Alexandria which eschewed the Highland tartan cliché. They were *The Flower*, by Reston Malloch, *Tribute*, by Alexander

M'Gill, *The Wind*, by Margaret Sackville and *The Baby Who Spoke*, by Pollock himself.

In this climate, he formed a group with high hopes of building a club with professional standards. And so the scene was set for the founding of the Tron Theatre Club. Its development paved the way for a lasting and significant place for the amateur movement of the 1930s in the history of the theatre in Scotland. It was with the Tron that Macrae's budding talents first gained real recognition.

The initial meeting of the Club was called on 7 November 1930 at the Keir Hardie Institute. Pollock had gathered together some of the 'faithful' from the clubs around the city. The first company included Ernie Mace, May Edwards (Pollock's wife), Winnie Rough, Mary (Molly) Urquhart and Macrae. Despite limited public support, it was proposed to establish what was being hailed as 'Glasgow's first experimental theatre'. The company would adopt and follow Pollock's theories of production and acting, which included reading and close study not only of the play in rehearsal but of other plays too. New one-act plays of Scottish character would be sought and encouraged. Although lack of funds restricted the original intention of renting and equipping premises of their own, the scope and purpose of their work would go on unhindered.

The highlight of the first season was the first production in Glasgow of Ibsen's *The Master Builder* (April 1931), and the season as a whole was judged overall to be a success to the extent that it was decided to reduce the membership subscription for the following year.

In 1932 the club's 'A team' gave Glasgow another first with Pollock's production of Chekhov's *The Three Sisters*. J. McNair Reid, reviewing for the *Glasgow Herald*, doubted that the play was a suitable choice for 'experiment by Scots people ostensibly out to explore the unspoken and to communicate the emotional and spiritual intensity there by stagecraft'. He found that although the setting was 'surprisingly effective' and the play well performed by a 'well-trained' cast, the overall results were cold and artificial. Macrae however was singled out in the role of

Captain Soliony as giving 'an immaculate picture of that weird character'.

That year the club went from strength to strength. While the main group, including Macrae and Molly Urquhart, was rehearsing upstairs with Pollock, the subsidiary members were meeting weekly to discuss, read and rehearse short plays. Pollock published a series of articles in *The Scottish Stage* on 'The Theory and Practice of Play Production' and two members had plays accepted by the professional theatre — Dr Graham Buchan's *The Call* was to be produced at the 'Q' Theatre in London and Paul Vincent Carroll's play, *Things That Are Caesar's*, had been taken up by the Abbey Theatre in Dublin.

As events turned out, the club was not functioning as harmoniously as had been imagined, and rumours of the emergence of a splinter group were beginning to circulate. The rift was made public in a report in *The Scottish Stage* when it was revealed that not one but two 'new and separate groups' were being formed. The article implied that the Tron might cease to function altogether. Conflicts in personalities, policies and ambitions had precipitated such a crisis that some form of personal collision between Grace Ballantine and Pollock made continuing impossible. Grace Ballantine and Norman Bruce, a local amateur drama critic, withdrew from the club because they believed that no serious efforts were being made to find a Scottish Ibsen or Chekhov.

And so the 'battle lines' were drawn. Macrae's preference for plays with a 'leftish' bias was well-known. He had quietly joined forces with Fred Grant, one of the Kippen cottage circle of theatre enthusiasts, to form the first breakaway group, The Project Theatre. Other friends rallied round and they were joined by the painter Ian Fleming and by Tom Smith who had worked in the Torch Club, Rosina McCulloch, Alexina Reid, Neil Bruce Mohr, Winifred Sinclair, Margaret Gourlay, Betty McPherson and Arline Anderson. They were already in rehearsals for their first production at the end of December when *The Scottish Stage* gave specific intimations of the second company, The Curtain, whose founders included Norman Bruce, Grace Ballantine and Paul Vincent Carroll.

Most people who were closely involved in the split believed that Macrae's real reason for leading what could be interpreted as a desertion of Pollock was to enable him to produce the kind of play that interested him most. The continuing mutual respect and admiration Macrae and Pollock held for each other suggest that, for these two men at least, it was a matter neither of personalities nor of the realization of personal ambition. For Pollock it was a clean break and the Tron died out. For Macrae the dissension became the opportune moment for him to lead his own company.

The Project's first presentation in the Keir Hardie Institute, at the end of December 1932, was a triple bill, produced by Macrae: *Dark Earth*, by Paul Vincent Carroll, *The Cobble Hole*, by Cormac Simpson and *Aye, Son*, by Emilio Coia. *The Scottish Stage* reviewer gave the productions his serious attention, singling out the director for specific praise:

> The honours of the evening undoubtedly went to the producer, Mr J.D.G. Macrae. He achieved about all that was possible on such a tiny stage. The lighting, particularly in the last play, was effectively handled. With this debut the Project Theatre can be said to justify its existence.

They quickly followed up this initial success in January 1933. By then, there were sufficient members to have formed an affiliated group in neighbouring Clydebank who offered two of the four productions that were put on at the Institute. The Glasgow section, under Macrae, produced *Nesbitt*, by Hugh MacDiarmid, and *Secret Passions*, by Charles Delaney. *The Needle's Eye*, by T.M. Watson, and *Molly Crone*, by J. Melville Thomson were produced by the Clydebank section. Macrae's production was criticized as needing 'tightening up'.

Meanwhile, Grace Ballantine's venture, The Curtain Theatre, was underway. She had been given some old scenery 'flats' from the Queen's Theatre in Watson Street and a pair of beautiful front curtains which were the inspiration for the name of the new company. But it was not until the end of the year that a long L-shaped room was leased in 15 Woodside Terrace and converted to a small and well-equipped theatre space, seating seventy people. 'Active' membership was courted and The Curtain opened in January 1933 with a double bill, *X=O* and Chekhov's *The Bear*. The company aimed to provide a stage, equipment and experience for both actors and dramatists in addition to building a team of experienced actors and technicians.

With astonishing drive, Macrae swiftly, in February, put on a double bill of new Scottish plays at the Institute: *The Record*, by Christine Orr, and *Whirligigs*, by W. Orr. Nevertheless, he was not immune to criticism and certain aspects of his producing judgement were questioned. However, still carrying on with the momentum of their initial success, he ambitiously tackled Maeterlinck's *Pelleas and Melisanda* which was described in *The Scottish Stage* as 'at once a striking success and a sad failure'.

But the premature death in May 1934 of one its founders, Fred Grant, aged only thirty-three, hit The Project and its activities gradually faded out. Inspired and encouraged by Gordon Inglis and Paul Vincent Carroll, the members regrouped in September 1935 with the formation of the Glasgow Theatre Arts Club. The new club's aims were to invite local amateur groups who were concerned with the production of the more 'intellectual' plays, to perform in the Metropole Theatre in Stockwell Street on Sunday evenings, to raise the status of the theatre in Glasgow, to encourage people to acquire the repertory habit and thereby to pave the way for a Glasgow Repertory of distinction. The idea was attractive to Macrae and he threw in his lot with them. The extent of his involvement is unclear, but it was likely to have been in an executive producing capacity which meant he could wield considerable power and influence in the choice of productions. The atmosphere of this Club would certainly have been congenial to him as many of his old friends, like Ian Fleming, became involved in one way or another.

The honour of the first invitation to perform on Sunday 1 September fell to the Clarion Players. Their production of Shaw's *Arms and the Man* was followed on successive Sundays during that month by The Renfrew Exchange Players with R.C. Sherriff's *Journey's End*, The Corporation Transport Players with Galsworthy's *The Skin Game*, The Glasgow Players with Ibsens's *Ghosts*, the Adelphi Players production of O'Casey's *The Plough and the Stars*, and the Clarion's production of Eugene O'Neill's

Diff'rent. In October, the club was forced to leave the Metropole and a month later its activities were suspended. There was a brief attempt to carry on but the concept of a Sunday night repertory theatre was premature and it became impossible for the organizers to sustain the effort. Production under the G.T.A.C. banner ceased and so yet another abortive attempt at stimulating native drama once again deprived Macrae of an immediate stage for his developing ideas as a director. Over the next few months he worked as a guest director with companies like the Erskine Players while he waited for the right opportunity that would permit him to follow his instinct and inclinations.

It was not until 1936 however that it seemed to Macrae that The Curtain, in its uncontested position as Glasgow's leading amateur company, would provide a viable and more permanent platform for his particular gifts. Curbing his own pioneering urge, he joined the company as an actor.

—2—

'CUTTING THE PAINTER'

The Curtain Theatre - Jamie the Saxt
the outbreak of war - Peggy - Molly Urquhart's theatre -
going professional

Grace Ballantine, the wife of a prominent Glasgow lawyer, was an attractive woman who enjoyed the reputation of being able to charm most people into agreeing with her about practically anything. Presiding over the theatrical alchemy of The Curtain with matriarchal authority — she always referred to the men in the company as 'her boys' — she commanded and earned the respect of everyone who worked with her. Opinionated and self-willed she may have been but her vision of Scottish theatre was singularly clear. Macrae was cast in a very similar mould. It would have not been the least surprising if these fiery elements had combined to be destructively explosive but the chemistry proved to be just right and their respective artistic aims, personal ambitions and natural temperaments combined to form a creative, if sometimes stormy, partnership.

By the time Macrae joined in October 1936, The Curtain had established the pattern for its annual programme with an opening production in October, one in December, one in February and one in April. The schedule consisted of three or four weeks of rehearsal followed by one week of performance. The month intervening between each production was devoted to readings and planning meetings. With productions occupying over half the year, this routine demanded commitment and a great deal of volunteered time, after a full day's work.

In his decision to join The Curtain, Macrae displayed again his uncanny knack of being the right man, in the right place at the right time. His association with the company marked the real beginning of his acting career. Wavering for a while towards directing, he at last seemed to be committed to acting. He played in ten productions, directed one and stage-managed another. Almost all his Curtain parts were leading roles. If these roles were typical of the stereotyped characters common to plays of the 1930s, they were none the less testing in terms of experience. To Grace Ballantine's credit almost the entire repertoire was made up of new plays by local Scottish writers.

The 1936-7 season opened with Macrae cast as Cardinal Beaton in George Malcolm's historical costume drama, *A Letter from Rome*, set in sixteenth-century Scotland. Macrae made an instant impact as the powerful and cunning manipulator, giving a masterly display of pathos in the final scene. The company demonstrated its versatility in December, with Owen Davidson's comedy thriller, *The Crime at Balquhidder*. Macrae played the hero, Desmond Duncan, 'an impressive man of 40 years, a trifle artistic in his dress', an author/sleuth in the Sherlock Holmes tradition who knows about everything from cooking to anatomy. It was a part that could easily have sunk into melodrama but Macrae was fully in control, successfully 'keeping nonsense on the edge of credibility'.

He followed this with the leading role in *There's Money in It*, a sentimental piece about an acquisitive family, by the local journalist and critic Robins Millar. While the roles Macrae took were satisfyingly varied, the plays themselves were not of any lasting significance. Entertaining as they might have been, none of them was of the calibre necessary to pass into the professional repertoire. But that changed with Robert McLellan's *Jamie the Saxt*. McLellan's earlier work had caught James Bridie's attention and his *Toom Byres* had been hailed as an outstanding contribution to Scottish drama. But there was still no professional platform to absorb and nurture the work of Scottish playwrights writing for a native audience.

When the script, written in Doric and originally entitled *English Siller*, arrived, Grace Ballantine told McLellan that 'Jock' Macrae was the only actor in the company capable of playing the lead. McLellan had reservations, mainly because Macrae did not speak Scots. Mrs Ballantine retorted that Macrae would have to learn, and as always she had her way. The play went into rehearsal. By this time Macrae's work was consistently recognized as 'one of the outstanding features of the season in Glasgow'. Consequently, everyone had high expectations of his 'Jamie' and the company was convinced that the play would be a significant Scottish milestone. They were not disappointed. Followers of amateur drama were unanimous in their acclaim. Clyde Irvine wrote:

> In all the years in which I have peered at amateur drama I have never seen a performance that comes within miles of Mr Macrae's work. It lived, breathed, reflected in every facet the character of 'the wisest fool in Christendom', but it also showed the unsuspected reserve of talent which this actor-producer possesses.

The honours were shared with McLellan's vigorous language and characterizations, Douglas N. Anderson's atmospheric sets and Grace Ballantine's production, which was sensitive in every detail to the spirit of the play. Pearl Colquhoun, Jamie's Queen, recalled that the company had 'worked with love and excitement on the play and that is what shone out. All of us had put all our hearts into this play and it showed.'

Macrae, McLellan, the play, the company — even the year itself — all slipped into their rightful place in the history of Scottish theatre and the season ended on a note of triumph. *Jamie the Saxt* was the only Curtain play ever to be published or revived in the professional theatre. It would be difficult to follow the outstanding success of McLellan's play.

Nothing daunted, The Curtain opened the 1937-8 season with George Malcolm Thomson's *Moonlight Flitting*, a slice of 1920s Glasgow socialist realism, set in the tenement kitchen of a poor working-class district. The lead part was a strong one with plenty of opportunity for histrionics. Macrae acquitted himself as the idealist, Rob Elliot, with customary flair. The play was followed in December by a production of *Miracle at Morn*, Norman Bruce's satire on the behaviour of artists and the Scottish landed gentry. Set in the village of Morn, the action moves back to Roman times and returns to the present day. The critics were cautious about the play but they approved Grace Ballantine's direction, Douglas Anderson's design and the cast's 'zealous' acting. Macrae played the dual roles of Checko Breingan, 'a dissatisfied schoolmaster rebel' and a philosopher seer. Once again the role could have been tailor-made to Macrae's specifications, for Breingan's character was written in terms of the kind of magnetism that became Macrae's hallmark. Many of The Curtain plays were in fact written to accommodate the skills and characteristics of the current company. *Emergency Call*, by Robins Millar, was the February offering. The season closed in April with a return to the history play. Margaret Monro's *The Winnock*, a poignant play set in thirteenth-century Scotland, was written in the vernacular, which caused problems for audiences and critics alike. They were not alone. With the meticulous attention to detail that he brought to the study of everything he did, Macrae carefully marked his script, translating the difficult vocabulary for all the parts throughout the entire text.

Family life continued at Berkeley Street. The Macrae brothers and sisters were settled in their careers. Kenneth and Annabel had married, Ann continued to work as a secretary and Dugal had become a piano tuner. In 1938 shortly after the death of their mother, Catherine, the family moved from 139 Berkeley Street when the tenement was demolished to make way for the new Woodside School. The short cut which had been so attractive to the five year old Macrae became the site of the janitor's house. A spacious five apartment flat was found at 778 Anniesland Road near the busy junction at Anniesland Cross. The new house was large enough to accommodate Annabel and her child Catherine who moved back to live with the family after the premature death of her husband. It was at this flat that, to the astonishment of the neighbours, Macrae perfected his individual method of learning lines, marching around in the garden on the square of grass, apparently muttering to himself, stopping at each corner to kick his height. His eccentricity was fast becoming a byword.

In 1938-9, breaking with their own established tradition of providing a platform for new Scottish writing, The Curtain opened in October with a 'welcome excursion into the field of

European masterpieces'. Whether the decision to produce *Hedda Gabler* prompted the choice of Macrae to direct, or whether Macrae was assigned to direct and then chose his preferred play, is immaterial to the resulting resounding success. Confident in the return to the classics Macrae displayed sensitive insights, eliciting 'flawless performances' from his cast. The production was judged to be 'brilliant'. Then in December, for the first time in their six years, The Curtain revived a production, *There's Money in It*.

At the turn of the year Robert McLellan presented the company with another script, this time one set in the fashionable and artistic circles of Glasgow's 'bohemian' West End. *Portrait of an Artist* discussed the Scottish taste for the sentimental in art and the persistent rejection of anything modern. In contrast to the overwhelming praise enjoyed by *Jamie the Saxt*, the press reviews were less than enthusiastic. The chief criticism was that the 'Great Art Debate' was too 'wordy' and consequently the pace was too often slowed to a virtual halt. Macrae's performance on the other hand as the intense sculptor, Duncan Macaulay, was deemed by some critics to be the best thing he had done with The Curtain, apart from the celebrated Jamie portrayal. He was praised for his spontaneity and for bestowing significance on each and every movement. It was a fine demonstration of everything he had learned at the feet of R.F. Pollock, building the character, in accordance with the dictates of Stanislavsky, to create a portrayal of the artist in uncanny depth.

By April 1939 when the season's last play was due for production, events in Europe and the possibility of Britain's involvement in war were the concerns uppermost in people's minds. Courageously, The Curtain took issue in the pacifist debate and presented Tom Allen's play, *Man of Peace*. Jack House, 'Jingle' of the *Evening Times*, said that the play's only disadvantage was that it made people think, and that was 'an awful crime these days'. Macrae played the pacifist minister, John Geddes. *Man of Peace* examines the dilemma of a gentle but strong man, who, pilloried by his own congregation and the Church, is ultimately brought to question his own faith, but finally reaches a personal solution. 'This heart and brain can never resign, never!' It was a part with which Macrae could genuinely identify. The sincere intensity of his interpretation was greatly admired.

By the end of the year it was obvious that The Curtain could no longer remain a viable proposition. The call-up, combined with straitened finances, forced the cessation of productions. The Curtain's legacy to Scottish theatre and its influence on subsequent events was not trivial. It had proved there was a following for home-produced drama and the plays of local playwrights. If the writers they encouraged had succeeded in making a name for themselves in mainstream theatre — Robert McLellan was the notable exception — the combination of enthusiasm, ambition and talent might well have given earlier birth to a more permanent truly Scottish theatre.

Macrae was with The Curtain for three of its six years, sharing the dreams, the successes and the disappointments. However reluctantly, he was drawn into the small charmed circle of regular members. No matter how cynical observers of the amateur scene mocked the social element which was integral to the structure and, indeed, the survival of the movement, it was an undeniably attractive feature of that period in his life. Amongst the happiest times were weekends spent at the Gairloch cottage of Ian Sandler, a member of the company, idling away the days walking, eating and talking endlessly about theatre. More often than not the conversations would be frivolous or light-hearted but Macrae would invariably lapse into the most earnest discussion on theories or methods, talking late into the night — insistent, single-minded and passionate in his devotion to the art. His sincerity was never doubted and he was respected for it. Although at times he could be irritatingly dogmatic, the theme that punctuates all descriptions of him during these years was that of integrity.

But the creative energy that went to building The Curtain was not entirely dissipated. By the end of the thirties, more than one thousand amateur clubs were established throughout Scotland in a surge of resourceful enterprise that was nothing short of miraculous. Between 1938 and 1943, when Scotland's first all professional company was inaugurated in Glasgow, the foundations were laid of several companies which later became professional, including the repertories at Dundee and Perth. These were to be the springboards for many Scottish professional acting careers.

However, by 1939 the strongly rooted ideals and ambitions of certain individuals in the amateur movement, which had in the past led to constant grouping and regrouping of companies, were surfacing again. Jack Stewart, a man of independent means, had been The Curtain's house manager. In June that year he had put forward proposals to establish a small permanent theatre, to be called 'The Park Theatre Club', at 16 Woodside Terrace, next door to The Curtain's home at number 15. Stewart made it clear in the speech he made to mark the formal conclusion of The Curtain's activities, that the new club would be organized quite differently from The Curtain and all pettiness and individual glorification would be avoided. Those members of the old club who were prepared to follow the new policies would be welcome 'to enjoy and explore for many years to come that which we set ourselves resolutely to serve and uphold — the art of the Theatre'.

For the first time in many years Macrae was no longer the linchpin of any company. But the pattern of grouping, splitting and reforming that had begun with the establishment and subsequent break up of the Tron Theatre Club in the twenties, was once again picked up by Molly Urquhart. In the face of the stiffest odds she declined to join The Park and successfully set up her own repertory theatre in a disused church in Rutherglen. Using her own initials, she named it the M.S.U. Theatre.

Flourishing in its custom-built playhouse, The Park Theatre broke from The Curtain's tradition of fostering local playwrights with a more conventional programme of Priestley, Houseman and Masefield. Macrae joined neither Park nor M.S.U. At the time it was alleged that he was sceptical about the wisdom of the Urquhart enterprise and rumour had it that the ethos of the embryo Park club was far removed from his socialist principles.

In the years that preceded the war Macrae gradually evolved into being a 'character'. In appearance he was strikingly tall, lean and muscular. The publicity photos of the thirties reveal a figure that was unashamedly and elegantly suave. Dapper coat, large brimmed soft felt hat worn with the fashionably rakish tilt, sleek hair, piercing eyes and enigmatic smile — all the trappings of a 'star'. He had a certain flamboyance and eccentricity of movement that marked him out in a crowd. This image certainly conflicted with that of the intense, intellectual, caring man who had chosen to make his life in teaching.

The years between leaving Jordanhill College and the outbreak of war were very full. Teaching, acting and involvement with an ever widening circle of friends, whose cultural and political interests matched his own, left little time for what were considered by Macrae to be more superficial pursuits. Girls had not featured largely in his earlier years although his sisters remembered that their friends took more than a passing interest in their tall, saturnine — oblivious — brother. He never formed any attachments. He did however join in the social activities and dances at the Highlanders' Institute in Renfrew Street, only just mastering the foxtrot. Walking remained his favourite recreation and in 1934, wearing the kilt, he went on a walking tour in Germany with another teacher, Arthur Young.

The outbreak of war in September 1939 had two immediate consequences for Macrae. First, the amateur movement was abruptly if temporarily disrupted. Second, the theoretical dilemma of conscientious objection to military conscription became a reality. Already thirty-four years old, Macrae was unlikely to be amongst the first to be called up. Nevertheless, he chose to adopt the stance of conscientious objection, not in terms of this particular conflict but based on his belief that to take arms against one's fellow men was wrong under any pretext. In common with many like-minded friends, he appeared before the tribunals set up to establish the validity of the wave of claims to exemption which surged throughout the country. In Scotland the issue frequently took on a more political undertone. The nationalists declared their willingness to fight — but only under a Scottish flag in a Scottish army. Macrae's call-up was deferred. In his case the board was convinced of his deeply held personal convictions. He was granted permission to remain in teaching.

This resulted in his immediate involvement in the evacuation programme that was devised following the initial panic reaction to the prospect of bombing.

City parents were offered the option of sending children individually or in small groups to the safety of the countryside. Quite commonly teachers, with their entire classes, were transported to residential schools hastily set up in commandeered country houses. Gatherings of forlorn little figures, gas masks in cardboard boxes slung across their shoulders, clutching beloved teddy bears or favourite dolls were a commonplace sight at railway stations and bus depots all over the country.

As things turned out, evacuation was not at all unpleasant for Macrae. His first assignment was to accompany two twelve-year old boys from Finnieston School to Rosehearty in the north of Scotland. There was a tradition that to toss a coin from the train crossing the Forth Bridge would bring good luck. One of boys fell silent as the train approached the bridge. He had no money. That child never forgot the threepenny piece Macrae gave him.

In October 1940 Macrae was delegated to Southpark, a residential school set up in Ascog House on Rothesay in the Kyles of Bute. By a stroke of good fortune his friend Paul Vincent Carroll was also on the staff. As for the children, although separated from their families, the excitement of being in the country — the first time for many of them — was an experience to be remembered for the rest of their lives. Macrae was an inspired and popular mentor and companion. Under his guidance nature rambles turned into adventures for the boys, scrambling over fields, down lanes, running to keep abreast of the long Macrae legs. Many of his modest acts of thoughtfulness, like buying an old bicycle, transformed evacuation into an enriching experience for those lucky enough to be in his care. In spite of the tension it was a surprisingly fulfilling period in his life.

After some months Macrae returned to his post at Finnieston. But within a few weeks, in 1941, he was sent with a party of handicapped children to the village of Parton about twenty miles west of Dumfries. There, they joined other evacuees in Aird's

House, a large rambling country home which had been taken over to accommodate their needs. Unbeknown to him his old friend and walking companion Arthur Young had been evacuated to a school in nearby Castle Douglas. They met quite by chance walking round Loch Ken. It was a happy reunion.

Amongst the children at Aird's House was a group from Allen Glen's School, in the charge of a young woman teacher whose background was not dissimilar to Macrae's. Peggy Scott, the third of five children, was born in Paisley on 13 May 1907, to Thomas Scott, a bakery clerk with the Co-operative Society and his wife Janet. The family moved to Govanhill in Glasgow where the children grew up. Peggy, a bright intelligent girl, graduated from Glasgow University. Her ambition was to become a secondary school teacher. As a student she soon earned something of a reputation for being outspoken, usually to be found at the centre of debate and argument as she developed strong political affiliations with a distinct bias towards Communism. She was part of a small group of girls labelled 'The Library Set', who remained her friends for the rest of her life. After graduation, when it was becoming increasingly difficult to obtain a teaching post in Glasgow, she led a militant march to the Education Headquarters in Bath Street in protest against the shortage of work for Scottish teachers. Quite soon after that she found an appointment.

There was another side to Peggy Scott that perhaps unfairly did not enjoy the public currency attracted by the more forceful streak in her character. She made no capital from her innate capacity for caring and self-sacrifice. A university education had meant certain financial deprivation for her parents as they were bringing up two young cousins in addition to their own five children. When Peggy began to earn her own living, she provided the luxuries for these youngsters and for several years rented a holiday house on the Cumbrae island of Millport.

None of this dedication, however, detracted from Peggy Scott's sociable inclinations. It was during these early teaching years that she met the first real love of her life. She was in a group of teachers supposedly attending a needlework course at the Glasgow School of Art on Saturday mornings. But after signing in for the class, Peggy and her friends joined a gathering of other young people in the café at the Regal cinema in Sauchiehall Street. Harry Whitely, a divinity student, was one of the 'regulars'. Peggy and Whitely were very attracted to each other and for a time their friends thought of them as a couple. But Whitely, who later became minister at St Giles in Edinburgh, met and married another girl.

According to her friends, Peggy was 'quite heart-broken'. Then the opportunity arose in 1939 for her to participate in a teaching exchange scheme to Canada. With financial help from friends, George and Margaret Brown, she managed to go to Canada. She worked there for several months but was forced by her mother's illness to return to Glasgow.

Peggy Scott was nothing if not resilient. By 1940 she had returned to teaching in Glasgow, fully recovered from the recent trauma. At that time countless allied troops, American, Canadian, French and Polish were based in Scotland. She met a Canadian, 'Bill', and before long they were informally engaged. Their courtship was not destined to last for, in 1941, Peggy was evacuated with her pupils at Allen Glen's School to Aird's House in the village of Parton, Dumfriesshire. She was impressed to find John Macrae there for, as a keen follower of theatre in Glasgow, she had heard a great deal about him. Naturally, they were introduced. Nothing was to be quite the same for either of them again. Much later she told her family that from the moment she first saw Macrae's conspicuous figure coming up the driveway, she knew he was the man for her! And so he was. Loch Ken became a very special place for Peggy Scott and John Macrae.

They came back to Glasgow to continue their friendship in a city of blackouts, air raid sirens, ration cards and clothing coupons. Not many months passed before friends noticed that the Canadian figured less and less in Peggy's conversation and John Macrae's name began to occur with increasing regularity. Peggy enjoyed being seen in Macrae's company as he was recognized as a personality. She admitted to friends that it was as good as being seen with the Prince of Wales! Then, as years later Macrae confessed himself, she, characteristically, took the initiative. By the summer of 1942 they were engaged.

At the outbreak of war many British people who had been travelling, studying or working on the Continent were forced to return home. Their return and the influx of European refugees transformed Glasgow into something of a cosmopolitan cultural centre. Amongst those coming back were the artists William Crosbie and J.D. Fergusson and Fergusson's wife, the dancer Margaret Morris. They decided to find a communal meeting place. MacEwan's Dance Studio at 388 Sauchiehall Street was commandeered and re-named 'The Centre'.

The Centre soon became the meeting place for the Polish refugee groups and the Anglo-Polish, Anglo-Russian and Anglo-French Associations. Into this melting pot of nationalities, spicing the intellectual life of the city, there poured an exciting, stimulating exchange of ideas and ideals. Reunited with old friends and exploring new horizons, Macrae was in his element.

William Crosbie had been painting in France since 1936. At his parents' insistence he returned to Glasgow, renting a studio in the lane behind the houses at Ruskin Terrace. The nineteenth-century terrace, one of the many which line the wide tree-bordered Great Western Road in its majestic sweep out of the city to the north west, was then, as it still is to some extent, very much at the heart of fashionably artistic Glasgow. At the turn of the century No. 12 was the home of the painter D.Y. Cameron who had built the studio in the lane behind the house. Macrae and Crosbie were introduced by a mutual friend, Robert Blair Wilkie, another reluctant teacher with a penchant for theatre and politics.

Macrae's integration into the small community of writers and artists was immediate. He began to spend the off-duty weekends from Rothesay, not with his family at Anniesland but at the Crosbie studio, bedding down amidst the canvas and clutter. In those years, Crosbie by his own admission was a young man 'with a desire to be sociable' and a flair for throwing parties. Macrae joined heartily into this conviviality, arguing and drinking, but with a strong inclination to the more serious aspects of life than to the frivolous. The preoccupation of this clique was with Scottish nationalism, but it was cultural nationalism rather than political. Regardless of the legitimacy of claims to an already existing cultural tradition in Scotland, Crosbie and friends saw themselves as champions of a 'truly Scottish culture'. It was the desire to correct this perceived contradiction, that informed many of Macrae's ambitions to establish a flourishing theatre for the Scottish people.

According to Crosbie, Macrae was 'a fellow of sterling character, a companionable, loveable and trustworthy fellow'. Their friendship flourished and Crosbie added a portrait of Macrae to the gallery of friends he had painted. Macrae was comfortable in the company of his familiars of the early 1940s. They were amongst the strongest influences in his entire life: Douglas Young, a classics lecturer at St Andrews University who was in the forefront of the conscientious objection movement, spending long periods in Saughton Jail for his beliefs; the Hannah brothers, one a poet, one a painter who never obtained the identity card necessary to the proof of genuine deferment from the army; the mysterious and glamorous Isa Gourlay who maintained some kind of 'underground cell' in the Garnethill area, near the Art School where she is alleged to have given refuge to those dissenters without identity cards; the poet Hugh MacDiarmid and McCall, a high-profile kilted Scottish Nationalist who arrived in Glasgow from London with a 'vast cartload of books'. It was indeed the worst and the best of times.

By 1942 the situation had stabilized and many children returned home regardless of the continuing risk of air raids. Macrae took up a position at Rosevale School. He was now able to assess what the amateur theatre could offer. There were three possibilities. He could join The Park Theatre Club, the M.S.U. Repertory Theatre or the interesting new venture, Glasgow Unity Theatre.

Unity had been born in 1940, the offspring of the amalgamation of the clubs in the city with a left-wing bias; Glasgow Workers' Theatre, Glasgow Transport Players, the Clarion Players and the Glasgow Jewish Institute Players, all of whom found themselves greatly depleted both in manpower and resources when war was declared. Unity took over 'The Centre' in Sauchiehall Street from the Refugee Association as its base, but performed in the Athenaeum and the Lyric, and quickly established a reputation for worthy productions of the classics of world drama, with an emphasis on the Russian. The Unity ethos had none of the frivolity which was the charge regularly levelled at so many of the amateur clubs in the late 20s and 30s. With its serious-minded artistic attitudes and high standards in both acting and production, painters and sculptors like Tom McDonald and Helen Biggar were attracted to design for them. A host of impressive acting talents were recruited, including Archie Duncan, Russell Hunter and Ida Shuster, all of whom went on to build successful professional careers. To all intents and purposes its philosophy should have been attractive to Macrae. There was one reservation. Unity had no commitment to encouraging native drama. He did not join.

Molly Urquhart was obviously running her Rutherglen company very professionally. As she continued to fulfil her promise to promote Scottish drama, Macrae chose to join her company and return to the local stage after an absence of nearly two years. He had remained on the sidelines partly from the contingencies of his responsibilities to the teaching profession and partly from the uncertainty of the ever changing amateur scene. Macrae now seemed prepared to jettison some of his more intellectual idealism in favour of serving the cause of Scottish drama. In March 1942, the *Rutherglen Reformer* reported that M.S.U. was happy to introduce to Rutherglen two well-known actors, Mr J.D.G. Macrae and Mr John Titterton.

In the days when formal training was non-existent, at least in Scotland, repertory companies like M.S.U. provided the vital training ground for aspiring actors. With her husband Willie McIntosh acting as the financial manager, Molly Urquhart's creative force attracted many young actors like Gordon Jackson, Nicholas Parsons, Eileen Herlie and Andrew Crawford. Conditions at Rutherglen were anything but luxurious. Regular audiences knew to come furnished with cushions, rugs and even hot water bottles. Deterred neither by discomfort nor the fear of air raids the enthusiastic company built a loyal following. The programmes announced:

In the event of an air raid the performances will continue. Those who wish could leave the building but are advised against doing so.

Governed by budget constraints on the production side, everyone pitched in to help, actors and stage crew alike. Scenery was feverishly prepared and when a play closed, the paint would be scraped off in readiness for the painter to work on the set for the next production — conditions very familiar to everyone who worked in weekly rep., amateur or professional. Backstage was acknowledged to be the territory of the company 'treasure', Mrs Mary McGuiness. Above all she was the company's *confidante*; she could turn a hand to anything from making costumes to coaching Irish accents. There were many dark, bleak, winter evenings when, despite Molly Urquhart's disapproval, Mary McGuiness would light up the old cooker in the gents' dressing-room, to dry out a damp, cold Macrae, weary after the day's teaching, and brew the tea he so enjoyed when he arrived at the theatre.

At M.S.U. Macrae was re-united with many old friends who had been roped in by the infectious Urquhart enthusiasm. The attraction of working once again with people like Paul Vincent Carroll, Robert Blair Wilkie, Rosina McCulloch and Molly Urquhart herself, was a major influence in his decision to go to Rutherglen.

In contrast to The Curtain's policy of supporting local writers, Molly Urquhart's selection of plays was altogether more eclectic. Her professional management was nothing but beneficial to Macrae's development. Although it was difficult to avoid type-casting an actor of his distinctive physique, Macrae was given every opportunity to extend his range. If the repertoire was not exclusively Scottish, there was a distinct bias towards writers with Scottish associations. Macrae played in two plays by Paul Vincent Carroll, two by James Bridie, three by J. M. Barrie, one by St John Ervine, one adaptation of Priestley, one by John Titterton, one by Joe Corrie and one by Walter Ellis. Of the last three local writers, only Corrie had an established reputation.

Robert's Wife, although styled a comedy, addressed both the contemporary issue of a pacifist's son's inability to distinguish between the just and the unjust war, and the married woman's dilemma — the choice between a having career or being a wife and mother. Cast as the Reverend Robert Carson opposite Molly Urquhart as Carson's second wife, Macrae's introduction to the Rutherglen audience received excellent reviews. In May, he continued to broaden his experience in Titterton's tight and amusing thriller, *See the Holly Bush* and in Corrie's *A Touch of Nature*. The season ended in June with Carroll's *Things That Are Caesar's*. Macrae only played the supporting role of Peter Hardy, the ex-schoolmaster fighting for his daughter's intellectual freedom, but he won the lion's share of praise.

In August he was free to accept an invitation from Charles Marford at the Byre Theatre, St Andrews, to stage-manage and play in a comedy, *Just Like Judy*, by Ernest Denny. First produced at St Martin's Lane in London in 1920, it is a pedestrian drawing-room comedy in which the main action springs from untangling a series of mixed-up relationships. The part taken by Macrae, of Hugh Crauford, a handsome, well groomed, enigmatic roué, is not the leading one, but it is central to the plot. According to the actor/politician, Andrew Faulds, who was in the St Andrews company at the time, Macrae's performance was not very good in a role that did not suit him. Macrae returned to Glasgow in time for the autumn school term and the new season at Rutherglen.

From time to time repertory companies — even those amateur ones with a brief life span — produce plays which stand out in the memory of audience and actors. One such was M.S.U.'s production of Paul Vincent Carroll's *The Strings My Lord Are False*. It acquired a reputation reminiscent of that won by The Curtain's production of *Jamie the Saxt*. The play, although dated by its subject matter and its pawky, patriotic sentimentality, strongly depicts communal unity in the face of adversity. It peddles a lucid sermon on religious, racial and social tolerance. Canon Courtenay, parish priest of St Bride's Church in Port Monica on the Clyde — a latter day saint —, was a role totally sympathetic to Macrae's brand of personal magnetism. Dominating the entire play right up to the final curtain which leaves him in a single shaft of light, bearing the dead child in his arms, Macrae brilliantly rescued the play from mawkish emotion with his uncannily instinctive sense of timing. The play was so popular that the run was extended to a second week. The production was something of a triumph, with the company reaching 'new and high standards of histrionic merit'.

Throughout his career, both amateur and professional, Macrae played in four of Carroll's plays. There is no evidence that Carroll wrote with his friend in mind, but the characters, especially Canon Courtenay, were suited both to Macrae's physical appearance and his particular gift for comedy and pathos. The plays, either set in Ireland or with the leading character Irish in origin, are thoughtful, well-observed studies of human nature operating in the context of the opposition of social, political and religious idealism to hypocrisy.

Helen Murdoch states in her biography of Molly Urquhart, *Travelling Hopefully*, that Macrae's presence in the company enabled Molly Urquhart to embark on a more ambitious programme. The popular Urquhart-Macrae partnership, which had operated intermittently since The Curtain days, showed every promise of becoming a formidable team as they tackled the more challenging roles of established writers like J.M. Barrie. Macrae played Shand to Urquhart's Maggie in the October production of *What Every Woman Knows*.

During November a controversy blew up over Joe Corrie's *Dawn* which the censor banned because its theme was too sensitive in war time. This meant a change of schedule and Macrae was not cast in the alternative play. Faced with this gap in his programme, he accepted Unity's invitation to play the chief engineer in Vishnevsky's *The Optimistic Tragedy*, at the Athenaeum. It was the first of the three occasions he played with them.

The year drew to a close with a Christmas show, Walter Ellis's farce *Good Men Sleep Alone*, which was praised for the skilful playing of ideal seasonal fare. One review remarked on Macrae's excellence in 'an unusual role to that in which he has always been seen, namely comedy', expressing with some surprise that he seemed 'equally at home as in the more serious forms of the art'. This surprise illustrates the pitfalls into which the unwary or unadventurous actor can be trapped. The error of being lulled, by the expectations of press and public, into the restrictions of predictable casting in unchallenging parts, can be treacherously destructive to an actor's development. Macrae was often guilty of falling into that trap and, in some respects, this limited his potential.

Encouraged by the critical and popular success of the Carroll and Bridie plays in 1942, Molly Urquhart confidently planned the first production for 1943. Her choice of Bridie's *A Sleeping Clergyman* was to be instrumental in setting up the chain of events which culminated in Macrae turning professional. As Dr Marshall, Macrae was supported by a very strong cast of M.S.U. stalwarts: Robert Wilkie, Guy Muir, who had been with The Curtain, Elsie Russell who was Grace Ballantine's daughter, Rosina McCulloch, who had acted in The Project group, and Urquhart herself in the triple role of the three Cameron women.

In the company at the time was Nicholas Parsons, a young inexperienced actor who, at the last minute, had been asked to join the cast of *The Strings My Lord Are False*. Like Macrae, Parsons had started engineering studies at Glasgow University. His time there was equally short-lived. The inspiration of Macrae's patient guidance at Rutherglen, encouraged him to make a career in theatre. Parsons played young Cameron in Bridie's play. As Cameron dies in the first scene, Parsons had time to watch Macrae make-up, gradually ageing as the play proceeded, and time to listen to the man he so admired talking about acting. The advice, 'I think you should look in the mirror occasionally — study your face and realize what you can do with it', was absorbed, stored and treasured. Macrae practised what he preached. The mobility of his own craggy features was one of the most singular trademarks of his art.

The season continued with Macrae playing the resourceful butler in Barrie's *The Admirable Crichton*, in February, Dr Knox in Bridie's Burke and Hare thriller, *The Anatomist*, in March, and Peter McSorley in James Woodburn's adaptation of Priestley's *When We Are Married*, in April. Molly Urquhart had achieved her artistic goal. The calibre of her productions did not go unnoticed by the more knowledgeable of Glasgow's critics and audiences who readily trooped over to Rutherglen where they were guaranteed an evening of satisfying theatre. Bridie always went to see the production of his own plays. He was delighted by what he found and was immediately struck by the quality of Macrae's performances. Macrae was already known to him through the intellectual and cultural network in Glasgow. It was at this point that Bridie began seriously to persuade Macrae that he should no longer squander his talents, but turn professional. But for Macrae the time was not ripe. Going professional on any significant scale was still synonymous with going south of the Border. Refusing to be seduced by flattery, he steadfastly resisted all temptations until such times as there was a Scottish company to join. This obstacle would soon be removed.

By 1942, the demand for some form of civic playhouse was being discussed in the columns of the *Glasgow Herald*. The urge for a more permanent platform for Scottish playwrights and professional actors could no longer be resisted. James Bridie was the only person in the debate with any real theatrical clout but, despite his private hopes, he was publicly sceptical. It fell to Winifred Bannister, a local journalist with a keen interest in theatre, to galvanize the first moves towards forming a new company. Dr Tom Honeyman, the director of Kelvingrove Art Gallery, was unreservedly enthusiastic from the outset and Bridie, despite his reservations, agreed to lend his name to the venture. Mrs Bannister's initial effort to find a venue failed and Bridie was, to say the least, disparaging. But Mrs Bannister was undaunted and enlisted the support of George Singleton who owned the Cosmo cinema, (now the Glasgow Film Theatre). Singleton's reaction to the idea of creating a brand new theatre enterprise in the middle of a world war was, 'How daft can you get.' However, in December 1942, Bridie joined the council of C.E.M.A., (Council for the Encouragement of Music and the Arts — the wartime subsidizing equivalent to the Arts Council), in order to put himself 'in a strategic position' to secure financial aid, should the opportunity arise.

Four months later Tom Honeyman invited Norman Duthie, Guy McCrone, George Blake, Paul Vincent Carroll and Bridie to dinner at the Glasgow Art Club in Bath Street, to 'indulge in the preliminary investigation of the matter of a civic theatre for Glasgow'. The result was the formation of a committee with Bridie as chairman. He set about raising funds.

Macrae yet again was in the right place at the right time. Eager to be involved in the new venture, he now wrote to Bridie offering his help in any capacity. Bridie's reply was guarded and non-committal, avoiding the issue by saying, 'I think we must start with Pros — even if many of them are English.' He ended more reassuringly promising, 'at the proper stage, I'll certainly call on your help', and urged Macrae to be patient.

In June, now firmly supported by Peggy Scott's faith and her resolute encouragement, Macrae wrote to Bridie again, tentatively seeking advice about going professional. Characteristically, he asked for certain assurances before making any public commitment. A great deal, after all, was at stake. It would have been imprudent for a man contemplating marriage to abandon the relative security of teaching in favour of the uncertainty of an acting career. Additionally it would have been unwise to prejudice deferment from call-up without further guarantees.

Bridie who had been negotiating with Alastair Sim about his latest play, replied with a proposition that was only negotiable under certain conditions:

> 3 Camstradden Drive East
> Bearsden
> Dumbartonshire
> 25 vi 43
>
> Dear Mr Macrae,
>
> This letter probably does not make sense. I don't know what your present occupation and commitments are. But I gathered, more or less between the lines of your letter, that you had some sort of idea of cutting the painter and going into the theatre professionally.
> ONLY IF THIS IS A FIRM DECISION, I have to make the following proposal to you:
> I have a play coming on in London during the first fortnight in August. Rehearsals begin in a week or so. It is

really an interesting play. It is a Comedy about theology. The cast will include Alastair Sim (who hopes to escape through it from a barren period of clowning), Charles Goldner, a very brilliant Hungarian Jew, Sophie Stewart and Ellis Irving. Sim will produce and he wants, as his is the leading part, the best understudy available. As the part is that of an intellectual Highland Minister, you can understand that actors who can play it don't grow on every bush. If it would interest you to study the part with a really crack company, the job is yours for the taking. I don't know what they pay star understudies but it is certain — more than a living wage.

Now, as to the follow-up. The play is pretty subtle and tough and will probably only have a limited run. In any case, you would be needed mainly to hold the fort until they have settled down and you wouldn't need to hang about for more than two or three weeks after the opening. Then I would be prepared to offer you an engagement in the new Glasgow Theatre which is getting underway. As certain delicate negotiations are still going on, I can't give you the details I promised, but you can take it that a professional company will be functioning in Glasgow this winter and that they will do nothing that is not worthwhile.

Could you let me know by telephone whether at least the first proposal is within the bounds of probability ?

I should like to know during this weekend, as I have to go to London on Tuesday.

Yours sincerely
O.H. Mavor

James Bridie.

Macrae was decided and lost no time in writing directly to Sim. The correspondence which ensued was typical of his caution and concern over the financial aspects of being an actor. Sim confirmed the offer.

56 Wellbeck St.,
W 1

30 June 43

Dear Mr Macrae

Thank you for your letter. I am very pleased to hear you would like to join our company to understudy for me. This would be your main task but I'd also like you to cover one of the other parts too, if you would? I don't know what your views are as regarding salary. If you have any, perhaps you will let me know? We should, of course, pay your fare down & there is the standard £2 10/- per week during rehearsals. These start on Monday 12th July & I hope to open on the 3rd or 4th of August at the Westminster for a 3 or 4 weeks try out. Please return my greetings to Paul Carroll if you see him.

All good wishes till we meet
Sincerely
Alastair Sim

There followed a brief exchange of letters showing that Macrae, cautious as ever, was concerned over the terms of the contract, as he understood it. Bridie hastened to clarify the situation:

21/2 guineas is the flat rate at present; but the management can spread the weekly fee back to include ten 3 weekly rehearsal fees. E.g. if you ask eight guineas they could make it 41/2 guineas for rehearsal & six for 3 weeks after the play opened.
I think you should ask for eight gns. That takes you over the 'Insurance' pay & is a good fee for a West End understudy for a leading part. It goes up, of course, for extra matinees; after a certain run ... & so on; & if you have to play the part, I think for a number of nights.
If you would like to ask for 6 gns a week, including rehearsals to go up to eight when the sum above the flat rate has been taken off they will pay for it.

Superficially, acceptance of this London-based contract, which did not even guarantee an appearance on stage, might well have been interpreted as a compromise of ideals. It was however a realistic method of breaking into the strictly professional and commercial side of the business in the days before the existence of a strong actors' union could prevent amateurs from easily crossing the professional barrier. Macrae was neither capitulating nor betraying his Scottish loyalties, nor was he lapsing into uncharacteristic humility. The fact that the play, *Mr Bolfry*, was by a Scotsman, set in Scotland, the leading character was Scottish and he was to understudy a fellow Scottish actor, allowed Macrae as far as any pangs of conscience were concerned, to preserve his personal integrity, and to defend it in the face of any challenge. At the bottom of Bridie's fateful letter, Macrae pencilled a note that unequivocally indicates that such a contract was to be nothing more than a means to an end:

> Only interest in London to lead to Rep. Contract in spec. terms for Manpower Board. Can influence be use.

He was laying the foundation for further deferment from military conscription by supplying the necessary evidence of professional employment. This was crucial. Macrae had to be in a position to take up any contract Bridie might offer in the increasing likelihood of there being a professional company in Glasgow.

Bridie's good offices prevailed and, reassured that Macrae was not causing unnecessary difficulties, Sim wrote the very next day with a firm offer of £6 a week and on 11 July 1943, Macrae set off for London.

In the meantime, back in Glasgow the civic theatre project, now named the Citizens' Theatre Company, was running into some difficulties. The Athenaeum Theatre was finally approved as the most suitable venue, but finding the best available producer was proving difficult. This in turn held up the engagement of a company, as only a reputable producer would attract any noteworthy actors and actresses to a new venture. Additionally, there was some disagreement about the choice of the first play. Macrae, in London, was concerned about the security of a Citizens' contract. His fears were in some measure justified as Honeyman and Bridie had been engaged in further debate about the constitution of the proposed company. Honeyman had gone so far as to state that he believed they should not employ any

Glasgow actors other than in very minor roles or as 'extras'. Bridie wrote to Macrae, confirming that there were problems, but reassuring him that:

> We have an excellent cast (which includes you) and we hope to be in a position to make some of the contracts before September. I shall see that you are offered one.

The next step was to ensure that the deferment from military service still held. A series of formalities was concluded with some urgency. The official termination of his employment by the Education Authorities and the subsequent transfer to the payroll of the Citizens', which was also technically under local authority control, guaranteed continuing military exemption. Macrae had cut loose the painter and he was now officially a professional actor.

CITIZENS' AT THE ATHENAEUM

Early successes - marriage -
The Forrigan Reel - the European tour

In 1943, the Athenaeum Theatre was still part of the Scottish National Academy of Music. For decades it had been host to countless Glasgow amateur productions and when Macrae returned to Glasgow to take up his contract with the newly-established Citizens' Theatre Company, he was immediately at home in familiar surroundings. The stage area was well equipped, but low doorways were a problem to designers and stage crews and the backstage facilities for actors left much to be desired. However, despite the limitations, it was a theatre brimful of atmosphere. Years later, when the Royal Scottish Academy of Music and Drama moved to custom-built premises, there were many people who lamented the departure from the old theatre with its own sense of history and its own ghosts.

The Citizens' teething problems were resolved. Bridie's *Holy Isle* had been chosen to launch the venture and a producer, Jennifer Sounes, had been engaged. She, unfortunately, had little relevant experience and, despite their love of the theatre, neither Bridie nor Paul Carroll knew much about the mechanics of getting a play on the stage. So on the advice of Tyrone Guthrie, Elspeth Cochrane from the Old Vic was signed up as stage-manager. The nucleus of a company began to take shape. Denis Carey and Yvonne Coulette were first to be contracted as leading actor and actress. Then, piecemeal, other actors joined until at last a full working company, which included Anna Burden, Betty Dixon, Una Dysart, Lesley Anderson, Betty Temple, James Anderson, Antony Baird, Philip Desborough, Geoffrey Edwards, Michael Martin-Harvey, Kenneth Miles, Nicholas Parsons,

Walter Roy and Duncan Macrae, was ready to go into rehearsals. Macrae's contract was for £10 a week.

The momentous first night of *Holy Isle* on 11 October was an appropriately glittering occasion, in the presence of such local dignitaries as the Lord and Lady Provost and the Principal of Glasgow University endowing the adventure with both respectability and publicity. The production was destined to be a resounding critical and popular success. The play was described as 'Intelligent ... Bridie at his best' — a marked contrast to the verdict of 'ancient tosh disinterred' expressed by the more sophisticated, or perhaps more jaded, critics many years later when the play was revived at the Edinburgh Festival in 1988. The parable on the more dubious values of 'civilized' society, set on a remote mythical Hebridean island in 500 BC, is not sophisticated. But the play has a certain naive charm. In 1943, the *Daily Express* described it as 'hovering uneasily between fun and philosophy'. Typical Bridie but none the less entertaining. In the minor role of Friar Innocent, the archetypal proselytizing priest, Macrae had the ideal vehicle for his innate talent for deriving comedy from the juxtaposition of his appearance with the character's circumstances. He made the most of it. The *Evening Citizen* critic singled him out as giving 'one of his best performances that I remember'.

The play ran until 23 October, with nightly performances and matinées on Saturdays. Tickets ranging in price from 1s 6d to 5s were bookable in advance at Patersons', the music shop in Buchanan Street, and the specially designed programme, emblazoned with the new logo, a knight on horseback, cost 2d. The company was safely launched and on course for a fair passage. In a matter of weeks a thriving Theatre Society formed the basis of a loyal and enduring audience.

In contrast, the second production, Goldsmith's *The Good Natured Man*, was not universally popular. The general feeling was that the company had overstepped itself and the houses were not good. The *Evening Citizen*, uncompromisingly critical, asserted that the company should 'cut its coat according to its cloth and contain its literary ambitions until ampler space and lighting and decor are available for its purposes'.

Macrae played Sir William Honeywood, the moralizing but understanding father of the wayward hero in this eighteenth-century comedy of mistaken identities and disguises. Any approval of his performance was submerged in the faint praise for the production which was judged to be nothing more than 'worth seeing'.

This cool reception, combined with the general dissatisfaction with Jennifer Sounes, began to undermine the confidence of the Board. The administration was involved in endless meetings and rows. Actors and technicians were, on occasion, reluctantly drawn in. Eventually, following delicate negotiations in November, Jennifer Sounes and the designer Riette Sturges Moore resigned after the third production, Carroll's *Shadow and Substance.*

The appointment of a new producer, Eric Capon, and a new designer, Peggy Pilling, heralded a period of greater stability and harmony. Capon came to Glasgow with admirable references. During the 1930s he had taught at a German refugee school, helping to build a theatre which produced an avant-garde Continental repertoire. In 1939 he had been assistant director to Herbert Marshall using Stanislavky rehearsal methods. He published articles on a Marxist approach to theatre and, in 1943, he was appointed as the first full-time director of drama at the Guildhall School of Music and Drama and deputy principal. Invalided out of the army in 1943, he restarted the Unity Theatre School of Drama. With this background, one which was likely to have gained Macrae's approval, Capon soon gained the confidence of the company and became both popular and respected.

Macrae was now beginning to attract a larger share of press coverage, even in minor roles. Nevertheless, ambitious as always, he hoped to play the title role in the Christmas play, *Noah*. When he was passed over in favour of Morland Graham he made something special of a minor character, 'The Man'. The *Glasgow Herald* reported his 'few telling minutes' on-stage. However, for the English actors, Macrae was just another unknown Scot — whose amateur reputation was of no consequence to them. But before long his very idiosyncratic personality began to make an

49

impression, not always favourable. He persisted in making entrances from unusual or unexpected places which resulted in making life difficult for the stage-manager and unnerving the other actors. His erratic behaviour seemed to take no account of any other presence on stage, and he did not hesitate to let the rest of the cast know how *his* performance was affected by *their* actions. In time, the singularity of his style and the stature of his performances were usually recognized by his colleagues for what they were, and they treated him with wary respect.

During that first year, Elspeth Cochrane tried to persuade Macrae that he would be foolish to refuse offers to work elsewhere, but, rather naively, he constantly asserted that he belonged to the Citizens' and he would stay there. It was to be some time before that advice seemed to him to be realistic. In 1943, the weekly wage of a non-graduate teacher in Glasgow was on average, £7 10s. This compared very favourably with Macrae's Citizens' contract for £5 per week during rehearsals and £10 for the run of the production. The Citizens' Company was in fact a generous employer. £10 for a small-part player was in excess of the average English repertory company wage. It was on a par with what the Scottish actress Molly Weir was earning at that time in *The Happiest Days of your Life* with Margaret Rutherford at the Apollo Theatre at the very hub of London's commercial theatre. In the short term his security was assured.

Now confident that he could earn a living as an actor, Macrae and Peggy Scott decided that there was little point in delaying their wedding. They were a practical couple and as there was no question of a church wedding with a flurry of bridesmaids and flowers, they had none of the usual dilemmas that accompany arranging all the panoply of the traditional white wedding. Their overwhelming problem was finding a mutually convenient date and hour. Not many professions require a bridegroom to go to work on his wedding day. Macrae's contract with the Citizens' committed him to a full schedule which left no prospect of any evening available for celebration in the foreseeable future. Honeymoons were not even discussed. The Christmas school vacation was the first opportunity for many months that Peggy would have of being free during the day and so Monday 27 December was chosen. As *Noah* was due to open at the Athenaeum that night, they booked the registry office for a morning ceremony.

Like so much of their lives together, the wedding was quiet and private. They were married in a brief civil ceremony witnessed only by Macrae's brother Kenneth, his wife, Jenny, and Peggy's sister, Jean Scott. The bride was dressed simply in a light-coloured wool crepe dress, a short double row of pearls the only adornment and the groom was dapper in a dark double-breasted, checked tweed suit. Then, in what might have appeared to have been an uncharacteristic extravagance, the little party lunched at the Malmaison, one of Glasgow's most elegant restaurants. But considering the wartime price restrictions and the availability of food in 1943, it was perhaps not such a reckless expense after all. In the evening, Macrae reported to the Athenaeum for the opening performance of the play. The family, however, did not allow the occasion to pass unmarked and the newly-weds returned home after the show to find that a surprise party had been organized. Rationing forbade elaborate or expensive presents but amongst those most treasured was a painting of sailing ships, gifted by Macrae's friend, the painter William Crosbie.

Macrae described his partnership with Peggy in his inimitable way: 'We're like an iceberg — I'm the visible tip.' He also used to say, 'The thing I like about you Peggy is that you do things.' For Macrae, his wife's faculty for action was always one of her most attractive features. She was possessed of bustling, organizing energy and if Peggy Macrae said she was going to do something, it was done.

At first, many of their acquaintances doubted the wisdom of the marriage. Many people in Macrae's circle found the new Mrs Macrae to be abrasive, even domineering. As for *her* friends, they were wary too, for Macrae's directness had antagonized them on many occasions. The sceptics were proved wrong. Peggy worshipped the ground her husband walked on and defended his every move with fierce pride and he, for his part, knew he could depend on her. Their personalities and commonly held beliefs were sufficiently complementary to make the marriage work and survive the strain of the vagaries and demands that theatre inevitably imposed on conventional family life.

In appearance, the new Mrs Macrae was as crisp and business-like as her nature. Slightly built, she was only 4'11" tall, every inch exuded confidence and efficiency. She dressed discreetly wearing her light brown hair caught neatly back at her neck, a deep wave over her forehead. Her one occasional extravagance was hats.

In 1955, Peggy Macrae wrote an open letter to the *Glasgow Herald* expressing her views on how to recapture audiences. Tom Honeyman wrote to congratulate her and in her private reply, she revealed her 'credentials' for entering into the fringes of the theatre world with such lively enthusiasm:

> Since schooldays I have loved the theatre. My Mother used to board 'pros' and as a student I thought J.D.G. Macrae could act. My life story is not interesting but the views I expressed are based on 30 years of being 'in the wings'.

Never reticent, her opinions were welcomed and her informed contributions to many a late-night discussion were highly valued. She was, on the whole, liked and respected by her husband's colleagues although there were times when her sharpness made for her a few silent opponents who treated her with caution. Those closest to her knew of her understated generosity and many charitable efforts.

After the wedding there was some feeling amongst a number of her friends that she had become rather aloof, even affected. But as is often the case, such observations are not always entirely objective. In many eyes, Peggy Scott had 'done well' and was perhaps envied. There were those who resented her marriage as Macrae had become the favourite bachelor in his own circle and it came as quite a shock to have him thus appropriated. As for his sisters, it was some time before they became reconciled to the idea of his being married, for by then, typically of their generation, they had come to look on him as 'the man of the house'. Over the years, their relationship with Peggy remained affectionately cordial, if somewhat distant.

The Macraes rented their first home in the upper flat of a converted terrace house at the corner of Southbrae Drive and Crow Road in the west-side suburb of Jordanhill. For a time they shared this house with his brother Kenny, and his wife. Like everyone else in wartime they had the familiar struggle to put a home together, coping with rationing, shortages and coupons. For a while sharing made good economic sense. Peggy's precious baby-grand piano was given pride of place in a living-room which boasted little else. An invitation to supper at the Macraes invariably meant sitting on the floor. Peggy's new lifestyle made quite an impression on her friends, who dubbed it, 'quite daringly Bohemian'.

Within a few months, Peggy was pregnant. She continued to teach and the routine of Macrae going off to the theatre every evening suited her. Everything seemed to be going so well for the couple when her father took ill. Peggy insisted on travelling across the city every day to help nurse him. It is impossible to tell whether or not this extra burden affected her health. The months passed and she was delivered of a baby girl — stillborn. The Macraes' distress was acute, but in time the sadness passed and they recovered from the disappointment. Never one to wear her heart on her sleeve, Peggy soon returned to work and as for Macrae himself, the show, as ever, had to go on.

At the beginning of January 1944, he took the significant step from supporting actor to leading player in the Lennox Robinson comedy, *Is Life Worth Living?*, which portrays the trials and tribulations of a touring company playing an Irish seaside town. The actor-manager, Hector de la Mare, is a character very much in the tradition of the Donald Wolfits of the touring circuits. De la Mare believes he has a mission to reform and instruct his audiences and presents a series of 'plays with a message' which have a profoundly depressing effect on the impressionable locals. Macrae was in his element as the 'ham' actor, rising to the challenge of portraying the ridiculous man in a skilful display of stylish burlesque. The critics were unstinting in their chorus of approval. *The Bulletin* claimed Macrae's performance was 'easily the best thing he has done'. A Macrae performance was now beginning to carry with it certain expectations and, in the next production, a Shaw double bill, *Man of Destiny* and *The Shewing Up of Blanco Posnet*, his interpretation of the supporting role of Elder Daniels in the latter was hailed as making the production 'well worth seeing'.

The last production in the repertory season was scheduled for the week beginning 13 March. During rehearsals, Priestley's *Bull Market* had caused some difficulties with the cast who thought the play very mediocre. After some re-casting, Macrae doubled as Lord Fleetfinger and Garnett. Set in a spa hotel, the plot hinges on the discovery by a chambermaid (played by Molly Urquhart on a guest appearance from Rutherglen) that she has inherited both the hotel and a quantity of valuable shares. The chambermaid was a gem of a part and the critics, gratefully latching on to something worthwhile in the production, devoted their reviews to praising Miss Urquhart's performance.

Macrae did not play many leading roles in that first season, yet he showed a distinct affinity with clerical and revolutionary parts and a marked penchant for comedy. Every sign of his maturing as a gifted character actor invariably singled him out for praise. The next opportunity to expand his range and popularity came at the end of the season when the company took Bridie's *Mr Bolfry* on a C.E.M.A. sponsored tour of thirty-five towns and villages throughout the Scottish Lowlands. Macrae was the natural choice for Reverend McCrimmon, the role he had understudied for Alastair Sim at the Westminster Theatre in London only eight months before. Playing McCrimmon was a great personal satisfaction to him for it was being said that Sim would have to look to his laurels. But the very idea of the tour was an even greater achievement in Macrae's eyes. This was exactly the proper function of theatre in Scotland as he had envisaged it. Scottish drama for the people of Scotland at large — at last.

The company toured from mid-April till July. Travelling in two buses with all the props, scenery and costumes, they played in anything from small village community centres to grand town halls, working very hard but having a great deal of fun too. Mishaps occur in the best of all well-regulated theatres. No company returns from touring without some tale to tell of

scenery too wide for doorways, missed trains and lost props —
and the Citizens' Company was no exception. Macrae relished
the occasion when a costume hamper failed to turn up. A startled
minister's wife opened the manse door to the tall, gangling actor
who, with infinite charm, persuaded her to lend her husband's
black jacket and hat for the evening performance.

Artistically, the tour was an unqualified success. There were
problems however on the business and administration side as the
company was unfamiliar with the logistics of touring. The
management found, to its cost, that lack of forward planning
hampered the smooth commercial operation of the tour. Unlike
normal dealings with conventional theatre managements, it was
essential to foster, in advance, good relations with the hosts, the
local dignitaries and committees who managed the village hall or
community centre. At one town on the itinerary, the Lord
Provost lodged a formal complaint to the Citizens' Board of
Directors on behalf of his harassed and indignant Town Clerk.
Because the company had failed to take account of the routine
preliminary tasks of publicity, arranging temporary seating or
advance ticket sales, the good gentleman with the aid of his wife
had to post the playbills round the village, put up the temporary
seating in the village hall and sell tickets at the door. All this
coupled with the fact that the company's two buses parked in the
lane outside the hall, limiting easy access for the audience,
resulted in less than full houses. These experiences were to stand
Macrae in good stead when he eventually formed his own
touring company.

The new season began in August. It was company policy to
conform to a specific programme framework which should
include an Irish play, a Scottish play, a Christmas show, an
Elizabethan play and an 'international comedy'. The repertoire
for the 1944-5 season was made up of nine plays, with Macrae
taking on roles of varying importance. In the opening play, Paul
Vincent Carroll's *The Wise Have Not Spoken*, Macrae acquitted
himself creditably in the leading role of Francis McElroy, an
embittered victim of the Spanish Civil War. It was one of the few
outstanding 'straight' parts Macrae was given during this period.
This success was followed by a string of successful

characterizations: Scraggy Evans the Post in *A Comedy of Good and Evil*, by Hughes, the cunning grocer McLaren in John Brandane's *The Treasure Ship*, Justice Greedy in Massinger's *A New Way to Pay Old Debts*, Sir Charles Farwaters in Shaw's *The Simpleton of the Unexpected Isles* and the trade unionist, Andrew Craigie, in Joe Corrie's *A Master of Men*.

The company still retained many of the original members who, by the end of 1944, were becoming welded into an efficient ensemble, familiar with each other's way of working. Molly Urquhart had joined as a more permanent member of the company when it had become financially impossible to continue running her own theatre at Rutherglen. During their years at the Citizens' she was frequently teamed with Macrae, continuing the partnership that had been so popular at Rutherglen. Their off-stage relationship was respectful of each other, cordial, even affectionate, but often explosive. James Cairncross was also engaged for Corrie's play. Travelling to Glasgow on the overnight London train he went immediately to rehearsals at the Athenaeum where he walked straight into the middle of a flaming row between Molly Urquhart and Macrae which had brought the rehearsal to a complete standstill. He recalled that, to his surprise, the company seemed to be handling the situation as if it were a common occurrence, each responding in his own way to the passing crisis.

In December, after five months of playing routine parts, Macrae was given the chance to develop his singular style in the Christmas production. The title page of *The Forrigan Reel* script declares itself 'Farce Comedy'. Less formally, Bridie described his latest piece as 'The daftest thing I've ever written'. His intention was simply to provide the company with a bit of good fun for the Christmas season. It was of greater consequence for Macrae.

Set in the MacAlpin bothy on Speyside in 1740, the anarchic comedy springs from the exploitation of the hilarious healing gift of Donald MacAlpin, a true 'natural' who can 'dance' away ills as diverse as chronic melancholy and the bizarre affliction of ticking like a clock. Macrae played Donald. Not just inspired casting, it is almost certain that Bridie wrote the part with him in mind. The stage direction for Donald's first entrance reads:

> Donald is a tall man of about 40 dressed in the most
> extraordinary collection of variegated rags. He wears a long
> pigtail, a kilt and slashed brogues

Bridie had created a character which depended for its comic
effect not only on the idiotic situation, but also on the crucial
element of the true grotesque which was integral with, and
sympathetic to, Macrae's idiosyncratic style. With few
reservations, the local press notices were quick to spot the
strengths and weaknesses that were to become typical of
Macrae's comic creation. A tendency to overplay was noted in
passing, but the 'devastating display' of his capacity for
portraying the comic grotesque was identified for the first time.
Audiences were whirled into the very spirit of *The Forrigan Reel*.
It played to packed houses for a full month, with extra matinées
testifying to its runaway success.

Despite Bridie's modest claims to frivolity, a more serious
analysis in the *Glasgow Observer and Scottish Catholic Herald* came
nearer to the essentials of the piece:

> *The Forrigan Reel* is not to be judged by the conventions of
> modern drama, for it is not modern drama. It is a calculated
> and extreme grotesque, an appeal to a wild and almost
> mad spirit of violent fantasy, to the old goliard spirit of
> lawless hilarity that once was the peculiar mark of Scottish
> literature, but was smothered by Calvinism.

The play and Macrae — and the rest of the cast for that matter, in
particular James Gibson as Old MacAlpin and Molly Urquhart as
Mrs Grant of Forrigan — served each other very well. In
February 1945, the company presented Bridie with a silver cup in
appreciation of 'the grand Christmas present' he had given them.

The excitement over, the company settled into the closing
weeks of the season with Macrae playing John Duffy in Lennox
Robinson's light-hearted comedy, *The Whiteheaded Boy*, and the
waiter in Gogol's *The Government Inspector*. Then, encouraged by
the success of the earlier *Mr Bolfry* tour, the company set off on
the road again with the production of *Hedda Gabler* which was
already in their repertoire. Macrae played Lovborg.

Drama, however, was not confined to the stage. By Christmas it had become common knowledge that the Citizens' Company would be moving house. Confounding the sceptics and weathering the normal storms faced by any new project, they had proved during their brief existence that there was an appreciable popular demand for a repertory company in the city. Although the choice of plays was not always to the taste of the audiences, it became clear that a larger house would be not only desirable but also a necessary condition for continuing expansion and development.

At this point, luck took a hand in the person of Harry McKelvie who owned the Royal Princess's Theatre in the Gorbals, on the south side of the city. The theatre had first opened as Her Majesty's in December 1878, with a pantomime, *Ali Baba and the Forty Thieves*. It closed in July the following year but reopened as the Royal Princess's under the management of Harcourt Beryl. Over the years it became home to one of the city's best-loved traditional, annual, family pantomimes. Famous for appearances by generations of the finest Scots comedians, including Tommy Lorne, it established its unique tradition of having thirteen letters in the pantomime title. It was there that the Macrae brothers and sisters first saw live theatre.

Nearly sixty years later, in 1945, the fortunes of the theatre were to change when, on retiring, Harry McKelvie decided to offer to lease the theatre to the Citizens' Company at a very economical rent, if a certain sum could be guaranteed. This could have been a stumbling block, but with a timely gift of £10,000 from Sir Frederick Stewart, the Board was able to meet McKelvie's conditions and the offer was accepted. On the Citizens' part it was a courageous step for the Royal Princess's was virtually double the size of the Athenaeum. Many sceptics doubted the wisdom of siting the company in the heart of the Gorbals, a district to which the notorious reputation of the 1920s still clung. Crossing the Clyde to the south side of the city was believed by the self-styled intellectuals of the West End to be tantamount to an expedition to a cultural waste land! The reasonable fear that their loyal audience would not follow them unquestioningly proved, in the long term, to be unjustified.

The most radical change was the proposed adoption of the repertory system which John Gielgud was operating in London. In theory, there were definite advantages to be gleaned from this method of devising programmes. A number of plays would be played in rotation on different evenings in each week, the idea being that more people would be able to see the plays over an extended period. The actors would reap the benefit of not having to be under the continual pressure of rehearsing new plays and the finished productions would be altogether more polished. Bridie is quoted as saying that 'the Old Vic has achieved the impossible in the Waterloo Road — we shall have a smack at it in the Gorbals'.

In Bridie's absence, Tom Honeyman made the farewell speech at the final curtain in the Athenaeum. In his praise for the actors and staff who had loyally supported the company since its birth, he singled out James Gibson, Molly Urquhart, Elspeth Cochrane, Denis Carey and Duncan Macrae. Then, accompanied by Honeyman's good wishes to Unity, who intended to 'keep the flag flying in this place', the first chapter in Macrae's association with the Citizens' drew to a close.

Air raid sirens, blackouts, bombs — those first two years of the company's life were remarkable. For the few actors, actresses and stage crew who can still recall the pioneering days, the dominant memories are of the cramped back stage with no space in the wings, of the tiny prop room and rat and flea infested dressing rooms, of Lang's tea-room, digs in India Street, arguments and discussions, triumphs and set backs, and of Bridie. Above all they testify to the entirely justified feeling of being involved in something unique and special.

The logistics of the move to the Gorbals were creating tensions. The business manager, Winifred Saville, resigned and was replaced by Colin White who had experience of managing a theatre for E.N.S.A. when he was in the army.

Eric Capon had decided to move back to London and the selection of a new director was the most pressing business the Board had to address. The consensus of opinion was to appoint someone with Scottish connections. The successful applicant,

Matthew Forsyth, despite his name, had no such links north of the Border. Regardless of this, he was favoured by Bridie because he did have relevant experience. Before the war he had produced for Birmingham Repertory at the Malvern Festival under Sir Barry Jackson and had, for a time, run his own repertory companies at Bexhill-on-sea and in London. The repertoire for the coming season was agreed and negotiations to contract players started. But, it was clear that Forsyth was going to meet resistance. Before he even settled in Glasgow, chauvinistic hysteria rumoured that he would favour English actors in preference to Scots already with the company. In the event, when the curtain went up in September at the Royal Princess's the stalwarts Jimmy Gibson and Molly Urquhart were in the casts, but not Duncan Macrae.

As a prelude to a six-week European tour of *The Forrigan Reel* in the summer, the company had taken the production to a festival at Bristol where it had been seen by Alastair Sim. Sim was so impressed by both play and Macrae that he made plans for producing the play in London. He would play the Old MacAlpin role, originally played by Jimmy Gibson and Macrae would again play Donald. But there were countless obstacles to be overcome and no opening date was fixed. In light of the Citizens' imminent move to the new theatre, together with the prospect of a new director, Macrae was understandably anxious to clarify his own position and accordingly wrote to Bridie. He was already in Germany with the tour when he received a diplomatic reply, reassuring him that his Glasgow contract was secure and that there was every expectation that he would be 'a star by the time you come back to us'. Macrae was still concerned about the financial aspect of Sim's contract, but Bridie once again allayed his fears, pointing out that £20 a week was 'very handsome for an actor who had no previous West End experiences/appearances to his credit or discredit'. Perceptively, Bridie pinpointed the dilemma central to Macrae's anxiety, forecasting that he would 'be able to hold the blunderbuss to the head of any management, Citizens' Theatre Ltd included'. All was resolved. Macrae did not take part in the move to the Gorbals because he expected to be working in London. Loyalty to a company is one thing, but Macrae realized it is quite another matter when attractive offers arrive from other sources.

It had been the Company's own idea to entertain troops on active service in Europe, in particular Scottish regiments. Bridie arranged the European tour under the auspices of E.N.S.A. When the run at Bristol was over, the Company travelled to London. Then, after a final rehearsal at the Theatre Royal, Drury Lane, for the approval of the E.N.S.A. director, Basil Dean, the seemingly endless formalities required before departing for the Continent, were concluded. The company assembled in the foyer of the hotel, waiting to be piped out ceremoniously by their own piper, Sandy McNeil. A sudden buzz of excitement swept round with the report that victory in Europe had been announced. Amidst all the cheering and confusion the company began to wonder if the tour would be cancelled. But it was obvious that the army would not be returning overnight and the arrangements went ahead as planned. The company embarked in the Thames Estuary at Harwich where they spent a miserable forty-eight hours on board, in very cramped conditions, before setting sail. Many weary hours later they landed at Ostend, to be hustled forthwith onto the train for Louvain.

One of E.N.S.A.'s strictest rules was that all entertainers should wear army uniform. This posed something of a dilemma for Macrae who had adopted and maintained the stance of conscientious objection from the outbreak of war in 1939. In reality, he had little choice. But whether by accident or by design, it was remarked by several members of the company that he never seemed to wear the uniform quite correctly, as if in silent protest. He could be heard muttering, 'This is not really a uniform — it is just cloth made by workers in a factory', to salve his own conscience. It was over this matter of uniforms that one of the recurring contradictions in Macrae's character was highlighted — that of élitism. Actors working in the war zone were ranked as officers which meant they travelled first-class on railways. Nobody on the tour could fail to notice that it was usually Macrae who pointed out to any unfortunate soldier seeking a seat on a crowded train that their compartment was reserved for officers! He never seemed to need to reconcile such an attitude with his views about the oppression of workers. In much the same way, his disparaging attitude to amateur actors, after he turned professional, was equally hard to reconcile with the fact that his origins were in the bedrock of amateur theatricals.

Quite unlike their Scottish tours when they had been greeted as conquering heroes at every stop, the Citizens' company arrived in Louvain to find that they were not even expected. It was not surprising. There was indeed an army camp, but it was an American base. Needless to say they were exhausted and demoralized. But in the best of tradition of show business, troupers to a man, they rallied and played their first performance to an eager audience who understood barely one word. The American soldiers seemed to enjoy every minute of the show, particularly the piper, and above all the rich comedy of Macrae's Donald, which was essentially visual. The performance turned out to be a roaring success and the tone for the tour was set that evening at Louvain. They were met with warm enthusiasm and instant success at every stop. Ironically, during their six weeks in Europe, they never played to a Scottish regiment!

For many members of the company this was the first time abroad. Macrae had been on a walking tour in Germany in the 30s, but this was a totally different experience. There was no freedom to climb hills or wander through the countryside. The risk of stray snipers meant that wherever they went, even on swimming trips, they were accompanied by an armed guard. It was hard for someone of Macrae's individuality to take kindly to the restrictive aspects of this supervision as, for the most part, the Germans seemed welcoming and friendly. Macrae's apparently endless supply of cigarettes — he was seldom to be seen without one in the corner of his mouth — seemed to attract an 'admiring' following.

It was foolish to believe that the Germans harboured no ambivalent feelings towards their visitors and on more than one occasion this proved to be a problem for Macrae. At the end of one performance, all the Germans present refused to stand up for the British national anthem. This sparked off a furious row between the superior officers and Macrae who was convinced they should be permitted to remain seated if they so chose. Elspeth Cochrane believed that he had misread the situation and the superficial friendliness masked a resentment of the actors who appeared to have so much in the way of material goods. Molly Urquhart too was disillusioned when, under the pretence of friendship, her German dresser attempted to join the company to get out of Germany. Molly Urquhart refused to co-operate and, to her distress, the girl became aggressive. Professionally, however, the German stage crews were impressive and unfailingly helpful. On the one occasion when a hamper of props went missing, the Germans buckled to and faithfully reproduced everything that was required.

During the tour which included stops at Lübeck, Flensburg, Brussels, Hamburg and Paris, the company stayed at the most comfortable hotels not in ruins. At Hamburg where bombing had ceased only two weeks prior to their arrival, their hotel and the railway station were amongst two of the few intact buildings amidst terrifying rubble. But there was always a lighter side. At Hamburg, Macrae met Ian Fleming who was stationed nearby. They spent the day together between the matinée and evening performance — arguing. When the company arrived in Paris, they were booked into the same hotel as the Old Vic company who, also with E.N.S.A., were touring their productions of *Richard III* and *Peer Gynt*. The hotel was beside the Opéra-Comique and on one glorious summer's evening, hundreds of Frenchmen joined the American, Canadians and British soldiers who had gathered with the two acting companies on the square outside the theatre, to watch a Scottish soldier, serving with the British Second Army, take off his boots and give a fine display of the sword dance. The Scottish actors wound up the entertainment, dancing a riotous eightsome to the swirl of the Citizens' piper's bagpipes.

At the end of six memorable weeks the company flew home exhausted but satisfied that to the credit of all concerned they had fulfilled their mission. In spite of the more traumatic experiences the tour was, in theatrical terms, an enriching experience, punctuated by these happy encounters. But on a personal level, the memory of the utter devastation and misery of the people was to remain with Macrae for a very long time.

Although the renewal of his Citizens' contract was guaranteed, by the time Macrae returned from Europe at the beginning of August, the opening date for Sim's London production was still not fixed. His contract with Sim required him to be available at a moment's notice for London rehearsals, which made it impossible for him to undertake any other work. So, untypically, he spent eight weeks 'resting', the theatrical euphemism for 'out of work', with no income apart from the four guineas earned for taking part in a radio production of Robert Kemp's documentary, *The Forty-Five*.

— 4 —

CITIZENS' AT THE ROYAL PRINCESS'S

Into the Gorbals - the film career begins -
a growing reputation

The Company meanwhile moved across the river and on 11
September 1945, it began its tenancy at the Royal Princess's.
In 1995, the Citizens' Theatre enjoys widespread national and
international recognition. The theatre itself is now fronted by a
spacious glass-roofed, high-tech entrance whose circus-like
illuminations by night brassily proclaim its presence in the heart
of Glasgow's once notorious and ever changing Gorbals. Inside
the foyer the statues from the original façade of the Royal
Princess's stand guard to the richly refurbished auditorium. It is
a far cry from the Company's salad days in the old Athenaeum
theatre. In 1945, Alan Dent's column in *The Sunday Times*
described the new home as 'the excellent little house with a great
tradition of rough and ready melodrama and pantomime'. He
was relieved to find that, 'redecoration in primrose and chocolate
has done nothing to frighten away the playhouse's atmosphere; it
retains the right reek of orange peel'.

Macrae, meanwhile, was making his London debut in Sim's
production of *The Forrigan Reel*. It was not an unqualified success.
To begin with, there was the problem of the language barrier. It
remained quite impenetrable to the majority of the audiences in
spite of the Anglicization of much of the dialogue. Added to this,
Bridie's brand of esoteric Scottish absurd comedy was totally
alien to the English sense of humour. The addition of Cedric
Thorpe Davie's musical score did little to enhance the play and
certainly did not compensate for the struggle the company had in
communicating with the baffled audiences. According to some
critics part of the problem was that the theatre, Sadler's Wells,

was too large for the intimate and homespun nature of the comedy, and the company was hampered by 'lurid scenery' and 'over elaborate costume'. Poor box office closed the show after only three weeks. Macrae, however, made a good impression. Eric Crozier gave a considered retrospective review in December in *Our Time*, which was too late to be of any influence:

> Duncan Macrae is a comedian of remarkable parts — long-boned, loose-jointed, with a serious look, strong features that are infinitely mobile, a pleasant voice, and a talent for step-dancing.

He noted the similarity of Macrae's movements to those of the *commedia dell'arte* actors, depicted in Callot's engravings, whose physical skills had impressed Macrae since his earliest days in the amateur theatre. Crozier also noted the underlying pathos essential to good comedians declaring, 'it will be our loss if he is not tempted south again in a more favourable enterprise'.

In the reasonable supposition that he would be in London for an extended period, Macrae had not been cast in any of the Citizens' productions running up to Christmas. So with time on his hands during November, he worked in three BBC radio plays, *Kidnapped, Julius Caesar,* and *The Master of Ballantrae*. The fee for each of these radio plays was six guineas — quite a drop from the giddy heights of the £20 he had earned for each of the three weeks in London.

Although coming home to Glasgow fell short of the ceremonial return Bridie had predicted, it did not matter much to the Macraes as Peggy was pregnant again and, given the vagaries of the acting profession, the long term prospects seemed as happy and secure as they could be. Stardom would have to wait. Their happiness, however, was tempered by the death of Macrae's father, James, in September. The Jordanhill flat was too small to supply the needs of a growing family so they moved nearer to the centre of town. The new flat, at 282 Woodlands Road, had spacious rooms with an open outlook up the tree-lined avenues which lead to the terraces overlooking the east side of Kelvingrove Park. Its only drawback was that it was up one flight of stairs which eventually proved to be very inconvenient for small children. Nevertheless, for several years 282 Woodlands Road became the focus for lively discussion and the occasional party with the 'Citizens' crowd'.

Macrae rejoined the company inconspicuously as the member of a pirate gang in *The Pyrates Den*. A swashbuckling tale derived from *Peter Pan* and *Treasure Island*, Bridie's latest Christmas show appeared under one of his favourite pseudonyms, A.P. Kellock. Then, cast only in minor roles in the next three productions, Robert Kemp's *Victory Square*, Shaw's *Fanny's First Play* and Louise Romoff's *Babble of Green Fields*, Macrae attracted the most modest of notices.

The first overt signs of serious stormy waters for the Board were beginning to surface. The true repertory system was abandoned at the end of January. This in itself was not a failure. Such a system puts huge pressure on a company's resources, both financially and in terms of manpower, to say nothing of the logistics of making and storing scenery. Even though the audiences continued their loyal support, the Committee began publicly to air the growing conflicts over policy and personality in singularly acid and blunt terms which might well have prejudiced the future of the Citizens' venture. Bridie's alleged dictatorship was challenged but in the end Tom Honeyman succeeded in reversing the impression of discord and defeat. In a letter to the *Glasgow Herald*, he concluded that it would be 'a terrible thing for Scotland if this theatre was allowed to die out'.

The public skirmish died down. The company, restoring the pioneering image, enhanced its reputation by inaugurating its first out of town season with a three week visit to the Empire Theatre, Inverness. The welcome innovation was a great success and they played three productions, *Mr Bolfry*, *Fanny's First Play* and *The White Steed* to highly appreciative audiences. Macrae went on the tour.

On their return to Glasgow the company opened with *Mr Bolfry*. Macrae, back in his own element, displayed his comic gift to advantage as the Reverend McCrimmon, the role originally created by Alastair Sim. The press did not fail to notice this. On 2 April, *The Bulletin* critic confessed:

With due respect to Alastair Sim I like Duncan Macrae's McCrimmon better. For a very simple reason too. Both can handle the argument but Macrae has quite a bit more of the Free Kirk in him...

The *Evening Citizen* confirmed that Macrae 'provided serious competition for Alastair Sim'.

In May, still under contract to the Citizens', Macrae was 'loaned' for two weeks to play Pastor Manders in Unity's production of *Ghosts*. At this point, John Casson, the son of Lewis Casson and Sybil Thorndike, joined the company as an actor. Macrae returned to play a lawyer in Robins Millar's *Day in Day Out* and the Bishop of St Andrews in Gordon Bottomley's *Kate Kennedy*. During the run of the latter play, Ann, the Macraes' first child, was born in Redlands Maternity Hospital on 9 June. There was at last real joy and fulfilment in their private life.

It was quite another matter at the theatre. The hints, rumours and whispers of discord, briefly and faintly heard in March, had been quietly simmering away. While the previous management disquiet did not affect Macrae directly, the controversies were symptomatic of the growing uneasiness about the area of Macrae's own declared concern, namely the diffusion of the Scottish slant in the Board's policies. But whatever the essentials of the altercations amongst the Board were, Macrae now became involved personally in friction over Matthew Forsyth. Expressing his unhappiness and resentment over Forsyth's directorial manner, Macrae had apparently made up his mind to leave the company and he approached Bridie for advice. Bridie told him that as an artist, he should be free to do as he pleased, provided the undertaking was in a spirit of adventure and not one of 'Christian martyrdom'. Bridie was reluctant to back Macrae openly against Forsyth, who had after all been engaged for another year, yet he advised the actor to go all out for a London reputation and then come back to Scotland and dictate his own terms.

Five days after his communications with Bridie, Macrae resigned from the Citizens' and two days later his film career began with a contract to play John in *The Brothers* for Sidney Box Productions Ltd, on location at Broadford in Skye.

Whether or not Macrae was unhappy working with Forsyth, he did in fact have a film contract in his pocket. The negotiations for this had not exactly been shrouded in secrecy. In May, when he was working with Unity in *Ghosts*, he had gone to London for a film test at Riverside Studios. Indeed, the local press ran the story of how he missed the last plane back to Glasgow because the day's filming had overrun. Unity had gone so far as to delay the curtain-up to accommodate him should there be any hitches. But as he did not even reach Glasgow that night, the director, Robert Mitchell, went on instead. In light of such publicity there could have been no question of underhand operations, or of his conducting his affairs without the knowledge of the Citizens' Board. What is surprising is that the film contract does not appear to have figured specifically in any discussions with Bridie, at least not in the slim written evidence that still exists. But perhaps 'all out for a London reputation' encompassed the idea that film would bring him wider recognition in a more significant way. On the other hand, the chance of a film contract may simply have been a happy coincidence which permitted Macrae to register his discontent from a position of strength. The prospect of lucrative employment over a period of weeks at a salary far in excess of anything live theatre was offering could not be dismissed lightly. It would almost certainly enhance his reputation. He now worked through an agent, Chris Mann in Park Lane in London, who incidentally handled many of Bridie's contracts. A fee of £664 was negotiated for nine weeks on location and two weeks in studio.

The Sidney Box production of the film adaptation of L.A.G. Strong's novel of jealousy and passion in the Hebrides, *The Brothers*, was originally conceived with Michael Redgrave and Eric Porter in the title roles. But when shooting began in July, it was Maxwell Reed and Duncan Macrae who went over the sea to Skye to wrangle over the affections of Patricia Roc.

It was Macrae's first film and he had to learn to comply with the precise requirements of the camera — a novel experience for the actor who wantonly improvised his way around the stage in live theatre. Going on location was another novelty. When the company disembarked from the short ferry ride from Kyle of Lochalsh to Kyleakin, to their surprise — and to the glee of the fascinated islanders who gathered to watch the high jinks of the film crew — they were met by the ample bearded figure of the location manager — none other than James Robertson Justice, dressed for the occasion in full Highland regalia, looking for all the world like the local laird. The Misty Isle lived up to its name. For two days the crew and actors sat around in Broadford waiting for a break in the overcast skies. Eventually the director, David McDonald, decided that because of time schedules he had no alternative but to shoot in cloud, which turned out to be the right decision for the film's brooding atmosphere. The croft interiors however, were not filmed on Skye but in the London studios.

The islanders had a fine time. Many were hired as extras and one man hired his horse to the film-makers for £4. When the day's filming was over, the cast was inundated with traditional Highland hospitality which entailed a great deal of drinking, eating and dancing at the rowdy ceilidhs organized in their honour. It was a memorable interlude.

While Macrae was filming on Skye, matters at the Citizens' came to a head in May, when it was announced publicly that Forsyth intended to leave at the end of the following season. It was presumed that John Casson would be offered the succession. There is no doubt that Forsyth had done creditable work with the company, but the problems they were experiencing were perhaps in excess of his competency to solve. Nevertheless, as the director, he was central to many policy decisions that had been taken, or were to be taken in the near future. He could legitimately be held responsible for failure as well as credited with success. That Honeyman and Bridie were now in agreement is corroborated in correspondence and memos passed between them during that June and July.

The problems they addressed were wide ranging: programme planning, the repertory system and declining audiences, salaries and expenses, employment of local artists, and above all the composition of the Board. Most of this agenda would have required the director's co-operation on both artistic and financial policies. George Singleton tendered his resignation. In Honeyman's opinion, Singleton resigned partly because Bridie supported Forsyth, but chiefly on account of the extravagances in employment both on and off the stage, for which he, Singleton, held Forsyth responsible. Honeyman questioned Bridie on two points: he wanted to know if the rumours about the strained atmospheres backstage were well-founded, if the popular image of the company as a happy family was accurate, and if not, why not.

The discord rumbled on until a 'stormy and full-blooded' extraordinary meeting was held in November. There was open confrontation with Forsyth. When Macrae heard this, he was reassured that he was not alone in his misgivings and he was prepared to let his difference with the director rest.

The contrast of earning approximately £60 each week on *The Brothers* with the average weekly repertory wage must have been quite intoxicating. But the bright lights and high living were never Macrae's style — besides, he was not exactly overwhelmed with offers to make more films. In October he came down to earth in Glasgow where he earned seven guineas for each of four radio plays broadcast during November and played in Unity's production of *Torwatletie* for two weeks at the Queen's Theatre. He returned to familiar surroundings at the Citizens' as a regular member of the company. Picking up where he had left off to go to Skye, he was cast in every production from December until the end of the season in July 1946, with the exception of *Gaslight*, which was produced in Glasgow while the Citizens' Christmas show, *Lady Precious Stream*, went to the Gateway in Edinburgh. By January, Casson was given sole charge of the production of *Gaslight* as a trial run.

In January 1947, Macrae had his first taste of the more innocuous variety of publicity that can do no harm to any actor. Nothing more than an appetizer to the media exposure that was to become routine meat and drink to him, it was noteworthy as the first occasion he had taken part in a 'celebrity' performance. It was incidentally the kind of exposure that was also beneficial to the Citizens'. The *Scottish Daily Mail* had organized a series of concerts for 1947 which aimed to provide a radio link for Scots living abroad. The first concert was presented in the afternoon of Sunday 5 January in the Odeon Cinema in Glasgow. Macrae joined a programme which featured Will Fyffe, Patricia Roc, Gordon Jackson, Robert Wilson, The Orpheus Choir, Joe Loss's Orchestra and the pipe and drums of the Highland Infantry Training Corps from Edinburgh. It is difficult to imagine what the Joe Loss Orchestra's claim to appear under the banner of Scottish nostalgia might be, but Patricia Roc, Fyffe and Macrae quickened the heart, to say nothing of whetting the appetite with excerpts from *The Brothers* which was not yet on release. It was recorded and broadcast as *Scotland Calling*. The progress of the publicity machine is relentless and for many months after filming was over, photographs of Macrae making personal appearances at cinemas or peering into the model of the island croft appeared in the popular press.

Ironically, during the last six months of Forsyth's tenure, Macrae played three of his most interesting roles, John Hannah, Michael Geraty and Jamie the Saxt and to Forsyth's credit when Bridie's *A Sleeping Clergyman* opened on 28 January 1947, after a lean period, the Citizens' had a real box-office winner on its hands at last. Macrae's contribution to this was significant by any standards. In a cast that included Lewis Casson, James Gibson, Lennox Milne and Jane Aird, Macrae's performance attracted the best of the notices in the supporting role of John Hannah, the medical student who is poisoned at the end of the first act. The *Evening Citizen* hailed his 'stolid, dour and ruthless' John Hannah as a 'masterpiece of acting' and the *Glasgow Herald* critic thought his was the 'best piece of acting in the play'. The *Evening Times* review declared Macrae was 'outstanding' and commended the skill of his dying. His performance struck one critic in its similarity to Jean-Louis Barrault's in the film *Les Enfants du paradis*. This affinity with the French style was to find subsequent expression in translations and adaptations of Molière's comedies. Comparison with Barrault, the doyen of mimes, became a feature of many appraisals of his acting. Quite inadvertently, while offering the audiences a morsel of harmless backstage gossip of the kind that claims to disclose the tricks of the acting trade, the *Evening Citizen* columnist revealed the practice of 'milking' the audience, a practice at which Macrae became singularly adept — not always to the liking of his fellow actors:

> Every evening at the Citizens' Duncan Macrae is given a dose of prussic acid and dies on stage during 'A Sleeping Clergyman'. Being a stickler for detail, Duncan has looked up reference books and found that this quick and painful death takes only 40 seconds.
> But the other evening there was a particularly responsive audience, and Duncan, putting on a most spectacular death for them, found when he came off that he had taken too long to die — nearly 80 seconds.

Bridie himself paid him handsome tribute in a letter of appreciation he wrote after the opening night:

> I hope you weren't born to play John Hannah, but that was the impression you gave last night. I don't think you have done anything very much better. Very many thanks indeed.

Lewis Casson so enjoyed playing with the Citizens' that he stayed on for the next production, Frank Carney's *The Righteous are Bold*, a play that had previously enjoyed an outstanding success at the Abbey Theatre, Dublin. Once again Macrae received the ultimate compliment from the author who, on a visit to Glasgow, praised his interpretation of Michael Geraty. The *Daily Mail* agreed that 'the play might have been written for him'. The character of a raw-boned Irishman, 'carrying with him the feeling of the soil that yields him his meagre sustenance', was in the mould of the courageous, underdog rebels that suited Macrae so well. The play ran for five weeks.

The season continued as something of a personal triumph for Macrae. The next play was the first professional production of McLellan's *Jamie the Saxt*. Ten years before, as an amateur, Macrae had created the title role. The play opened on 24 March in Perth as an exchange production with Perth Repertory Theatre who took their production of *A Winter's Tale* to Glasgow. When *Jamie* came to Glasgow it played for three weeks to mixed reviews. Almost unanimously taking precedence over the usual criticism of the production and acting, the columnists debated the question of the delay in bringing this play to the professional stage. They were puzzled in light of the Citizens' avowed policy to present good Scottish drama. There had clearly been two camps on the Board. *The Scotsman* revealed that for years 'a small but determined coterie' had agitated for the production of McLellan's play, while the 'exasperated' opposition complained that *Jamie the Saxt* 'must be the only play they had ever heard of'. Underlying the discussion in the press, there was an immense sense of relief that Scotland could produce a world-class playwright, capable of making the distinction between sentimental nostalgia and historical truth.

The spotlight, in the end, was on Macrae, playing Jamie in a blond wig. Apart from the discerning observation in the *Evening News* — at least three years before the spectacular change to pantomime — that Macrae failed 'to check a tendency to get laughs with clowning that is out of character', he was cheered to the echo. Notices dappled with phrases like 'perfect', 'first class', 'remarkable performance', 'unlikely that we shall ever see a better performance of this part', were the order of the day. What the reviews had in common, although the thought was not articulated in so many words, was the recognition of Macrae's instinctiveness in a role that was so perfectly suited to the quirkiness of his physical attributes and the facility with which the music in his voice breathed life into the Scots tongue. And yet there was nostalgia for the freshness of his original creation in 1937.

The next production, Robert Kemp's comedy, *Polonaise*, centred on a troop of Polish soldiers stationed in the Fife village of 'Haufstarvit', was acknowledged to be 'ice thin'. It was another of those occasions on which the critics said the script was only saved by Macrae's presence. A closer look at how Macrae handled the minor role in this insignificant play is rewarding as it sheds light on the way he was developing at this period of his career. The part of the Bellman, a choric figure who intermittently steps out of the action to address the audience, owed as much of its success to the actor as to the author. It was a gem of a vehicle for Macrae's capacity to communicate directly to an audience and he exploited it for all it was worth. This was typical of how many a mediocre play was graced by Macrae and the reputation of many a mediocre production was enhanced.

The play is set in the second world war, but the Bellman, armed with a large handbell, is dressed in the traditional eighteenth-century costume of the town crier, with cocked hat, gold braid, blue coat and breeches, cotton stockings and silver buckled shoes. The action is played out against a backcloth of the village street, painted in the stylized and fantastical style reminiscent of pantomime scenery. Macrae's interpretation and performance prefigured the pawky comedy characters he made his own, and gave clear notice of the future pantomime star.

The season finished with productions of O'Neill's *Anna Christie*, Shaw's *You Never Can Tell* and a new piece by Katherine Kennedy and Marcel Wallenstein, *Scuddievaigs*. John Casson directed O'Neill's play prior to his definitive appointment. Forsyth bowed out with *Scuddievaigs*. Billed as a 'world première prior to production in New York' — *Scuddievaigs* had been bought by the Broadway impresario, Lee Shubert — it was an improbable tale, set in the Highlands, about paternity claims when an illegitimate child inherits £10,000. One critic commented that neither cast nor audience believed in it and that New York's reaction to 'the bottle party frolics after the funeral tea' would hardly be favourable. But the combination of Macrae and James Gibson was a 'triumph' as the bald-headed Holy Willie undertaker/postman and the foxy provost/lawyer, very much in the vein of the characters they were soon to play in *Bunty Pulls the Strings*.

It was speculated that Macrae might be going to America to appear in the Broadway production. There were also rumours that he was to have a part in *Bonnie Prince Charlie*, a prestigious production with David Niven in the title role and Margaret Leighton as Flora McDonald. The Scots in the cast were to include Rona Anderson, Will Fyffe and Finlay Currie. Jack Hawkins, Franklyn Dyall and Macrae were to play clan chieftains. As it turned out, Macrae was not in the film because his commitments clashed with the shooting schedules, which had been already rearranged to accommodate Niven's prior engagements. Even though nothing came of either the film or the Broadway project, the press attention now being paid to Macrae's fortunes was the measure of his growing fame.

The season in Glasgow was over. Macrae went for two weeks to Inverness with the company in *You Never Can Tell* and *The Righteous are Bold*. It was time to rest and reflect. The Board analysed the season, dividing the fifteen plays into three groups which were categorized as 'Outstandingly Successful', 'Moderately Successful' and 'Least Successful'. Seven of the fifteen were Scottish — three of these were in the first group and Macrae had been a major contributor to the success of three of the five plays in the outstanding group. As for the company, it had weathered the threatening storms, confounded its critics and consolidated its reputation. That at least was the cosy picture for public consumption, an image which did indeed match the company's popular success. But backstage, personalities and policies once again became caught up in arguments which threatened the Citizens' enterprise.

A barely concealed argument between Bridie and Tom Honeyman, which escalated into a total reassessment of policy, was triggered by Bridie's newest play *John Knox*. When Honeyman read it in April 1947, he did not like it and forcefully expressed his views on it to Bridie. As far as the administration of the Citizens' was concerned, in Honeyman's opinion the major issue was the apparent separation of financial and artistic policies. He believed that declining audiences were the result of the Board's failure in its choice of plays and actors. He agreed with Bridie about the need for the company to have an actor with charismatic personality. They were proved correct when, over the next three years, Macrae developed a following that made a significant contribution to the company's resilient survival.

As for *John Knox*, the Old Vic had taken an option on it, intending to present it as the companion piece to *Richard II* at the Edinburgh Festival. The Citizens' hoped to open its 1947-8 season with a play by Bridie. *John Knox* was naturally not then available. But in June, the Old Vic changed its mind on the grounds that it would be too costly to hire Scottish actors to cope with the language and so, with Honeyman and Bridie having buried the hatchet, a Citizens' production of the play became a viable proposition. Then, contrary to the traditional September opening of the repertory season, the Citizens' Society announced that *John Knox* would launch the season in August, 'to be timed simultaneously with the opening of the Edinburgh International Festival of Music and Drama'. The advance publicity attracted by this announcement was unprecedented for the Citizens'.

Macrae hoped for the title role, but Bridie, conscious of the focus now on the production, was adamant that Knox would be played by John Laurie, a Scottish actor with a growing reputation in film.

The publicity machine slipped into gear. John Casson's first production as the new director was given the full show-business treatment. Information about the lavishness of the sets and costumes was released to titillate interest. Much was made of the gift of a precious, pearl-encrusted, white and gold silk gown which was being refashioned in Elizabethan style. To the delight of an eager press, Macrae, getting over his disappointment, grew his own drooping sixteenth century moustache for his part as Lord James Stuart, laughingly claiming it was the perfect foil to the more undesirable kind of attention and recognition he was receiving after the release of *The Brothers*.

Newspapers, doubtless alive to the competitive edge the production had acquired, twittered with anticipation, but the event failed to live up to its promise. Reviews ranged from the defensively apologetic to the downright dismissive. The critical focus was concentrated on the play itself, but the production and the acting were given due credit. Laurie's Knox was excellent and, in his few brief lines, Macrae stole the stage with 'a beautifully smooth performance'. Hugh MacDiarmid claimed that the play, 'a miserable fiasco' had 'very properly' received bad notices. He believed that the Old Vic had rejected it on grounds other than language.

Not a promising beginning for the new regime at the Citizens', but under Casson's direction, the company settled down well and was soon winning a permanent place in the cultural life of the city. It is impossible to decipher the extent of the influence exerted by the financially circumspect Board, but the programme for the months that followed revealed a healthy mixture of experiment, caution and popular appeal.

The company's growing reputation over the next four seasons was partly attributable to John Casson's patient, tactful and creative direction. His directorship marked the beginning of a period of relative harmony between artistic and administrative management as Bridie and Casson were in accord on various aspects of both practical policy and ideology. Both men conceived a Scottish National Theatre as an entity with horizons much wider than a parochial operation. This encompassed the notion that such a theatre would function, not only nationally but internationally, by bringing the best of international drama to Scottish audiences. In this respect they were being wholly realistic. There was still insufficient good native drama to justify or sustain the existence of a Scottish National Theatre purveying a wholly Scottish diet. It was also virtually impossible, to maintain a national pool of actors. There were not many prepared to sacrifice wider career prospects to the nebulous concept of such a theatre by remaining in the North. Although there had been constant striving by means of a variety of ingenious schemes — many of which were initiated by the Citizens' — to foster native playwrights, it was not until the period 1947-51 that the Citizens' became a recognized breeding ground for promising Scottish actors. Macrae, Molly Urquhart and James Gibson were joined by fellow Scots actors, who cut their professional teeth in the Gorbals, such as Stanley Baxter, Fulton Mackay, Andrew Keir, Archie Duncan and Robert Urquhart. Fulton Mackay and James Gilbert were discovered at RADA on one of Casson's 'scouting' expeditions. The company began to forge a special identity which was the basis for true ensemble playing.

With *John Knox* behind them, the company returned to Priestley and mounted the first Scottish production of *An Inspector Calls*. As Inspector Goole, the role created in London by Ralph Richardson a short time before, Macrae played to notices ringing with superlatives. But the struggle for the company was still uphill and the next production, the première of St John

Ervine's *The Christies*, a pedestrian piece about the rehabilitation of a financier after ten years in prison, received little approval although it was agreed that Macrae, as Christie, made the best of a poor part.

The beginning of October opened a new chapter in the company's history with the 'Ayr experiment'. Matthew Forsyth had been so successful with the two plays he had taken to the Gaiety Theatre the previous year that, in 1947, the Popplewell management invited Casson to consider a much longer season. Initially, the logistics of keeping the theatre open when half the company was out of town, was ingeniously solved by inviting the Abbey Theatre from Dublin to play in Glasgow for the month. When Ayr subsequently became a regular date in the company calendar, it was a great tribute to their strength that Casson contrived to have two plays running simultaneously with the most frugal of resources. Five plays, *Wild Horses, While the Sun Shines, Jamie the Saxt, The Righteous are Bold,* and *Mr Bolfry,* were taken to Ayr that season. Macrae played in the last three while in Glasgow, Kenneth McIntosh took over his role in *An Inspector Calls*. For a brief period, Ayr had the pleasure of a resident repertory company and Macrae became a firm favourite with the audiences.

In contrast to the tour's achievements, the next production turned out to be a less than happy experience. Paul Vincent Carroll had asked Bridie to produce his latest play. Casson was not impressed by the script of *Weep for Tomorrow* which examined the drift away from rural communities to the cities. The Board, however, especially Bridie, had a loyalty to Carroll, one which incidentally was not always reciprocated. Against Casson's better judgement, the play was produced.

Carroll was confident. There was a distinct tone of patronage in his curtain speech on the opening night when he revealed that he had offered the play to the Citizens' for two reasons. The first was purely sentimental, but the second was that he saw the production as a prelude to one on Broadway. He urged young Scottish playwrights to concentrate on interpreting contemporary Scotland. In a pithy rebuke, *The Scotsman*'s critic feared that 'Carroll had not shown the way'. When the notices came out, the backstage pressure on Carroll was such that, by the second night, he had made several changes in the script. Most reviews agreed that the play was only worth seeing for Macrae's performance as Angus Skinner, a part 'made to measure'. For Macrae at least, Carroll had created another ideal role.

Casson wisely handed the direction of the next production over to Jimmy Gibson. In response to continual requests to produce Graham Moffat's *Bunty Pulls the Strings*, it was decided to revive the long-time favourite for Christmas. The volume of advance booking assured success. Moffat sent his good wishes for the opening and in his curtain speech, Macrae confessed 'a dreadful sense of responsibility putting on a Christmas show at the Princess's with its long pantomime tradition'. There was no need for modesty. Gibson had the perfect eye and ear to interpret the couthy pawkiness of the homespun Scots humour. Macrae headed a fine cast which included James Stuart, Rona Anderson, Lennox Milne and Andrew Keir. *Bunty* was a riot of good wholesome entertainment and critics and audiences loved it. The *Evening Times* admitted that at the risk of becoming monotonous, it had to report, 'once again that Duncan Macrae has a role that might have been made for him'. The *Glasgow Herald* raved about his 'star performance' as Tammas Biggar, the kirk elder with a past:

> Macrae almost turned the comedy into drama; and in every movement and expression he belongs perfectly to the world of Paisley shawls, pandrops and the Shorter Catechism.

Amidst all the praise and pleasure, one doubting voice bravely raised the spectre of the dilemma that continually bedevils theatre management, namely the extent of compliance with the tastes of the audience. In Scotland, this particular dilemma assumed a much deeper significance in the context of the struggle to establish a corpus of national drama. Commenting on *Bunty*'s perennial popularity in the sobering light of Boxing Day, the theatre correspondent of the *Evening Times* thoughtfully mused on the problems of play selectors in terms of 'Kailyard comedy':

> Do we really want to see the higher drama? Are we keen to
> be educated in appreciation of the finer points of theatre as a
> cultural focus? Or are we merely reactionaries who go to the
> playhouse in order to cry a little, laugh a lot, and agitate our
> brains as little as possible?

Thinly veiled inferences about casting pearls before swine were
frequently uttered by a cynical Bridie in private and, on occasion,
in public. The opposition of 'higher culture' to popular taste is a
standard debate in the arts world. In theatre it poses questions of
choice for playwrights, managements and performers alike,
giving rise to the bitterest of ironies when circumstances force
any change of direction or policy.

1948 marked the beginning of a period when, seemingly
unable to put a foot wrong, Macrae turned in a series of
matchless performances which finally bestowed on him the
elusive mantle of fame. And yet, at the peak of his success, there
were many who felt he betrayed his long-held ideals and vision
of a theatre for Scotland by taking advantage of the opportunities
afforded by the wider appeal of the variety stage.

THE CAMELOT YEARS

The Three Estates - Whisky Galore - Gog and Magog

With more than hint of nostalgia, Stanley Baxter labelled the years between 1948 and 1952 at the Citizens', the 'Camelot Years'. It was certainly a golden time when a company of the finest Scottish actors and actresses — Lennox Milne, James Gibson, Andrew Keir, Gudrun Ure, Rona Anderson, Robert Urquhart, Fulton Mackay, Paul Curran, Molly Urquhart, Madeleine Christie, James Cairncross, Roddy McMillan, Laurence Hardy, Baxter himself and Macrae — came nearest to fulfilling the dream of a truly Scottish national theatre. All the ingredients that seemed necessary to make it happen were in place; the committed company, a nucleus of good Scottish dramatists whose example could have established and nurtured a solid school of native dramatic writing, a reasonably co-operative management, directors willing to encourage and produce such drama and there was an audience eager for it. Macrae was entitled to a proportion of the credit for this magic, for magic indeed it was. Macrae was by now undeniably 'box office', and the public loved him.

Macrae's way to the stars, a gradual but steady ascent to the position of one of the Citizens' leading actors, was signposted by gems of keenly observed character and comic acting. During his first five years with the company, Macrae seldom had bad press. His career was not unique inasmuch as it can be charted in a series of peaks and troughs. The notion of troughs, however, is relative, for Macrae was seldom out of work and rarely, after 1948, received anything but glowing reviews either in leading or supporting roles on stage. The most remarkable feature is that concentrated in only eighteen months between August 1948 and Christmas 1949 he played in three productions which, partly due to his singular performances, passed into Scottish theatre mythology. It was in Tyrone Guthrie's production of *The Three Estates* at the Edinburgh International Festival in 1948, that Macrae first came to the notice of the serious critics in the national press. Then in October 1949, his portrayal of the ragged philosopher-poet, Harry Magog, in Bridie's bizarre play, *Gog and Magog*, earned him praise and kept him in the focus of critical opinion beyond the local Glasgow press. This was followed at Christmas in 1949 by the phenomenon of *The Tintock Cup*, and the wayward comic genius was finally captured by the variety stage the following year. It was then that Macrae achieved stardom.

The Citizens' programme for the second half of the 1948 season, which began in January, was an attractive blend of well-tried favourites, the classics and the experimental which meant that Macrae was cast in the usual repertory range of leading and supporting roles. But the attention of the Scottish theatre world in January was focused on reports that Bridie, Tyrone Guthrie and Rudolf Bing, the current director of the Edinburgh International Festival, had met to discuss the feasibility of a joint Scottish repertory venture to produce a truly Scottish production at the Edinburgh Festival that summer. The Festival would be an ideal occasion to display the wealth of Scotland's gifted performers to a wider audience.

Macrae progressed in style into the new year. *Bunty* could have been a hard act to follow but Robert Kemp provided the company with another winner in his 'idiomatic Scottish prose' version of Molière's *L'École des femmes*, entitled *Let Wives Tak Tent*. The production opened at the Gateway Theatre, Edinburgh, where as Mr Oliphant (Arnolphe) Macrae demonstrated once again how the synthesis of a role perfectly tailored to his particular talents and his performance could be totally spellbinding. After the Edinburgh run finished he fulfilled a long standing promise to direct a play, *A Hundred Years Old*, for Rutherglen Repertory Theatre. He rejoined the Citizens' to play a supporting role in the psychological thriller, *Double Door*.

Heralded by copious advance publicity, the next production was a modern-dress version of *A Midsummer Night's Dream*. The experiment was a success although there were reservations about transporting the mechanicals to a forest glade in Scotland 'fur wir stage'. The *Evening News* review nevertheless found that 'Duncan (Quince) Macrae and his mummers prove that Shakespearian wit in Lallans has an extra sparkle'. At the interval on the first night Bridie was heard to say, 'I don't know about anyone else, but I'm enjoying it.' The season finished with Macrae giving another superlative performance in *Let Wives Tak Tent* and winning praise for a sympathetic Gaev in *The Cherry Orchard*.

One of the more interesting developments in Macrae's work during this period was his increased exposure on radio. He took part in magazine programmes such as *Chapbook*, arts symposia, poetry and story readings and in the ever popular radio parlour games. Month by month he was acquiring the status of 'the personality', making personal appearances at charity events and social gatherings, often accompanied by the actress, Rona Anderson, who was now carving out a successful film career in her own right.

The Macraes' second daughter, Christine, was born on April 14 1948 and the family was complete. But there was not much time for family life that summer as The Citizens' schedule and a film contract meant that Macrae was effectively away from home until he went into rehearsal for the revival of *Tak Tent* in mid-October.

The first departure was on a four-week Irish tour, playing two weeks each in Dublin and Belfast. Astutely balancing budget with popular appeal, it was decided to take *Bunty* and *Forrigan*. As the casts were interchangeable, neither production would incur fresh costs and both were proven home successes. It was not unreasonable to hope that Glasgow's evident appetite for Irish drama would be reciprocated by a taste for Scottish fare. The small company included James Stuart, Gudrun Ure, Peter MacDonnell, Lennox Milne, James Gibson, Moira Robertson, Norman Tyrell, Dorothy Primrose and of course Macrae. Walter Roy, one of the old school of Scottish actors who should have gone with them, died aged seventy-six and thus another of the few remaining links with the early days of the Scottish National Players was severed.

The visit by the Scottish company was eagerly awaited in Ireland. Expectations were high as their 'big reputation', according to the *Irish Express,* had gone before them. When they opened in Dublin the majority of the press paid tribute to their achievements with favourable notices. The *Dublin Standard* affirmed that 'Glasgow possesses a company of players whose work bids fair to rival our Abbey quality at its best'. Macrae's clowning qualities, in particular in *The Forrigan Reel,* were described as 'standing forth in a remarkable feat'. There was however, one dissenting voice. Informed perhaps by misplaced chauvinism, the *Irish Independent* was less euphoric and, contrasting the Citizens' with the long established Dublin Abbey company, its critic belittled the Glasgow actors, accusing them of pandering to popular appeal. Conceding that the only good moments, 'for which the credit goes to Duncan Macrae', he confessed that he had been 'bored to tears'.

This acid notice perhaps lay behind the revelation of a side to Macrae that was altogether blacker than the one familiar to anyone who had hitherto worked him. Nobody ever claimed that modesty was one of his strongest features, but blatant self-centred arrogance, capable of undermining the company's spirit, had never before been in evidence. They were playing to very good notices in Belfast when, after one evening performance, to everyone's surprise, they were summoned by Macrae to attend a meeting on stage the next morning. There, he proceeded to inform his fellow actors that all the success they were enjoying was due to him and that any contributions from other members of the cast were purely coincidental. The older troupers in the company shrugged this off as just another of Macrae's eccentricities. But Gudrun Ure, a young actress who had only recently joined the company was so shattered that when, at the next performance, she had to make an entrance to Macrae, she dried up completely, unable to move or recall lines. She recovered, but the experience remained with her for a very long time. By the middle of August, most of the company was in

Edinburgh rehearsing for the Festival production of *The Three Estates*.

When the Edinburgh Festival Committee announced early in 1948 that the major drama production that year was to be the first revival since the sixteenth century of the Scottish morality play by Sir David Lindsay, *Ane Satire of the Thrie Estaitis*, to say that most people were sceptical would be an understatement. Nevertheless there were some who believed that it was appropriate to produce the archaic Scottish masterpiece at a Scottish-based festival, however limited the appeal.

The idea began to take shape in January when Bridie, Tyrone Guthrie and Rudolf Bing met in Edinburgh to discuss the drama programme for the coming August. Bridie, passionate as ever about furthering the cause of native drama and possibly fired by the Old Vic Company's rejection of his *John Knox* the previous year, pressed for the production of a Scottish piece. His suggestion that the main theatrical presentation might be a joint venture between the Citizens', Unity, Dundee and Perth repertories was welcomed. Reaching agreement on the principles, they next addressed the question of an appropriate play. Guthrie favoured *Ane Satire of the Thrie Estaitis* in spite of seemingly insurmountable difficulties — the play was originally played in the round in the open air. The language and the length of the original text added to the problems. But the others were convinced and Bridie undertook to commission the playwright, Robert Kemp, to tailor the text to modern needs. Kemp described his meeting with Bridie in the introduction to the published text:

> My own share in the adventure began one afternoon in a Glasgow club [the Arts Club] at the dead of winter when at the tail end of a conversation about something completely different, Mr James Bridie told me that I ought to read 'The Three Estates' It was evidently for my own good that I should peruse the Satire.

The first objective was to find a hall large enough to encompass the complex staging requirements. One very wet afternoon, armed with a tot of rum, Guthrie, Bridie and Kemp and a representative from the Festival, set out in 'a venerable Daimler' to make a tour of Edinburgh halls. Guthrie described how, after visiting several unsuitable venues, he was increasingly conscious of having started a wild goose chase: 'Then spake Kemp in the tone of one who hates to admit something unpleasant: "There is the Assembly Hall."'

And so it was in the gloomy twilight of a wet and drab Edinburgh afternoon that the 'venerable Daimler' chugged up the hill of The Mound. Guthrie knew he was home as soon as the gaunt silhouette of the twin-towered Church of Scotland Assembly Hall loomed into view in the shadow of the historic Castle, high above and far removed from the bustle of Princes Street.

The Assembly Hall had never before been used for any kind of theatrical purpose. There was a nice irony in this innovative choice as the entrance to the hall is dominated by the formidable statue of the reformer John Knox. As a result of his searing condemnation of all manner of entertainments, it was Knox who was largely instrumental in suffocating native drama and inhibiting its development.

By April, Guthrie was reconnoitring amongst the Scottish repertory companies for promising actors and a production team. Molly MacEwan from the Citizens' was commissioned to design sets and costumes and Cedric Thorpe Davie to compose music. Guthrie gradually assembled a cast that read like the 'Who's Who in Contemporary Scottish Theatre'. Impressed by Macrae's Peter Quince at the Citizens', Guthrie cast him in the dual roles of Flatterie and the Pardoner. The other main characters were played by: Bryden Murdoch as King Humanitie; James Stuart as Solace; Molly Urquhart as Dame Sensualitie; Lennox Milne and Jean Taylor-Smith played the two virtues, Veritie and Chastitie; Jean Carrol, Hamliness; Audrey Moncrieff, Danger; Dudley Stuart-White, Fund Jonnet; Ian Stewart, Divine Correction; Stanley Baxter, Correction's Varlet; Archie Duncan, John the Commonweal and Edith Ruddick, The Prioress. Macrae was joined by James Gibson and James Sutherland as the other two Vices, Falsett and Deceit. In all there were thirty-two speaking parts plus forty-eight supernumeraries playing the members of the estates, townsfolk and soldiers. Added to this number were singers and musicians making it a vast undertaking. The production was presented by the Edinburgh International Festival of Music & Drama, in association with the Arts Council of Great Britain and the Corporation of Edinburgh.

A concentrated publicity campaign released all sorts of information — the costumes were being made in an empty shop in the Gorbals and twenty yards of slipper satin were being sewn into Molly Urquhart's 'Dame Sensualitie' dress. Interest at the box office was good but not remarkable. By June, advance bookings were £85,000 out of a possible £110,000. When it was announced that the other major drama at the festival that year was to be John Gielgud's production of *Medea* — hardly a play with popular appeal, even with Scottish Eileen Herlie in the title role — the competition for audiences was frankly thought to be equal. The production gradually took shape and by mid-August the cast was in rehearsal.

On Tuesday 24 August, under Guthrie's direction, the long-dormant play sprang to renewed life on the specially constructed apron stage in the Assembly Hall. No one could have predicted the phenomenal success. The press unstintingly acknowledged the credit due to Guthrie, but accorded almost equal weight to the brilliance of the performances. *The Weekly Scotsman* declared:

> The whole cast was obviously in love with what it is doing, and there is such uniform excellence of playing that it seems almost ungrateful to mention individual actors. But Duncan Macrae's wonderful clowning in the dual roles of Flatterie and the Pardoner was a masterpiece of a flavour as Scottish as whisky. But the real triumph was in the wonderful direction It is nothing less than a landmark in the history of the European theatre.

Bridie was justifiably proud of his Citizens' people who had not only played the leading roles but had also supplied both management and production teams. Characteristically impish, he indulged in a little exaggeration in a lecture to the Royal Philosophical Society of Glasgow, claiming that the play was now the talk of the civilized world. There is no doubt that the resounding success brought in its wake a much wider recognition for the actors, nationally and internationally, for such was the spectacle that even non-English speakers could enjoy and understand the significance of the gestures and pick up the nuances in tone. Macrae was frequently singled out in reviews as a clown of genius. Robert Kemp explained the apparent flowering of a truly Scottish acting style as an inborn affinity with the French traditions of stylized mime and identified Macrae as a master exponent of the form. With insight, he declared that Macrae's genius required the nourishment of his native soil to fertilize his talent, something that would not have happened if he had succumbed to the blandishments of English commercial theatre.

The production became the 'smash-hit' of the Festival. Bookings soared. Four fifths of the requests for tickets at the long box-office queues were for the Assembly Hall. At matinées 'House Full' notices were displayed. For the first time in many years, there was pride in the Scottish theatre, something that has rarely been recaptured on such a scale.

That first modern reconstruction of *The Three Estates* led to its subsequent revival at intervals over the next thirty-five years, adding to the play's brief but already colourful early history. The Lord Provost of Glasgow wanted the play to come to the city's St Andrew's Halls and advocated that it should then tour to Aberdeen, Dundee and Perth. Edinburgh, however, would not release the production for exhibition elsewhere, wishing to retain as much exclusivity for their patronage of the production as possible. Encouraged by the euphoria of success, there was excited discussion and speculation about the possibility of the production becoming an annual Festival event. Although this ambition was not to be wholly realized, the production was revived in 1949, with most of the original cast recreating their roles. That year some 27,000 people saw the play and, in terms of both critical and popular opinion, it was every bit as successful.

The play was again revived in 1951. This time Moultrie Kelsall co-directed with Guthrie and the production was enhanced by new costumes and additional music by Thorpe Davie. It was much tighter with greater emphasis on the morality form than on the comedy. There were changes in at least 75% of the original cast, most notable amongst them being the replacement of Bryden Murdoch by Fulton Mackay, Molly Urquhart by Madeleine Christie, Dudley Stuart-White by Paul Curran, Graham Squire by Leonard Maguire. James Cairncross now played Divine Correction, Roddy McMillan joined the company to play the Poor Man and Andrew Keir took over from Archie Duncan as John the Commonweal. The three Vices were still played by Sutherland, Gibson and Macrae who added fresh laurels to his now glowing reputation.

Perhaps it was the occasion of the Festival, with the inevitably heightened atmosphere, perhaps it was the unexpected continuing success and popularity of the production, but whatever the reason, the opportunity was gleefully seized by the press who launched into lengthy debates about the merits of Bryden Murdoch's Humanitie over Fulton Mackay's or Molly Urquhart's Dame Sensualitie over Madeleine Christie's. Not to be outdone, pedantic intellectuals and academics joined in the minute dissection of almost every aspect of the production, some even went to the length of reading the text during performances, audibly rustling pages, sometimes to the distraction of the cast who, allegedly, were 'listening for the obvious signs from the audience that denotes the end of another page of the published text'. Even the spelling of the title came under the magnifying glass. When the Lord Provost of Glasgow proudly announced that, after successful negotiations with the Edinburgh Festival Committee, the play was going to be shown in Glasgow, it was not without a certain air of superiority, redolent of the traditional rivalry between Edinburgh and Glasgow, it was to be advertised in the original sixteenth-century spelling.

Ane Satire of the Thrie Estaites finally came to Glasgow in September. In a way, the production was playing to home audiences as the majority of the players were Citizens' actors. Preceded by a vigorous sales campaign, they played to 80% house capacity. The critics, rapturous as ever, reported that the impact was tremendous and *The Scotsman* forecast that Glasgow would take the play to its heart. The *Glasgow Herald* constructively discussed the loss of intimacy with the pageant due to the length of St Andrew's Halls, although the specially constructed apron stage had been brought from Edinburgh. Again Macrae was singled out. Whether or not the observation that he borrowed the part 'straight from pantomime' was intended as praise or criticism, it is significant that critics were now, however subconsciously, beginning to associate Macrae with the music hall stage after his first success with the Alhambra pantomime earlier that year.

Eight years passed before the Edinburgh Festival Society, in conjunction with Wharton Productions Ltd, revived the play in 1959. Guthrie, assisted by John Gibson, again directed. James Gibson and Macrae recreated their original roles, only this time they were aided and abetted by a new Deceit, Walter Carr. Other major changes in casting were John Cairney as King Humanitie, Tom Fleming as Divine Correction and Roddy McMillan was elevated from The Poor Man to Spiritualitie. The play was not revived again during Macrae's lifetime.

It was revived in 1973 by Bill Bryden for the Royal Lyceum Company and in 1984, 85 and 86 by the Scottish Theatre Company. But in the annals of Scottish theatre, it is Guthrie's first sparkling production that remains the definitive one, mainly because it was an adventure into new territory. The pioneering spirit was conspicuously alive in everyone who took part in *The Three Estates* during those three historic weeks in August 1948. Duncan Macrae's name was now on everyone's lips and the reticent Scottish public took him to its heart, gratified that at last Scotland had produced a 'star' worthy of international recognition.

Macrae was now recognized as a leading player in the theatre if not yet achieving that status in film. He was nevertheless beginning to establish a sure, if small, foothold in that medium, gradually becoming known as a reliable character actor who was regularly sought by agents and directors, usually to play a Scot. His stage reputation, in turn, was enhanced by appearances in films. In 1948, when the Festival was over and the return to the working routine of repertory might have been something of an anti-climax, the contrast was diffused for Macrae by a film contract.

In September he joined the Ealing company filming on the Hebridean island of Barra, to play Angus MacCormac, a small part in Michael Balcon's production of *Whisky Galore*. The film still appears on television with engaging regularity.

With a cast that included Basil Radford, Joan Greenwood, John Gregson and Gordon Jackson, *Whisky Galore* was Alexander McKendrick's first full-length film. It was an adaptation of Compton McKenzie's novel, based on an actual incident when the SS Politician, bound for New York, was wrecked off the Island of Eriskay in the Outer Hebrides. Describing his novel as 'a fairy story' and the characters in it as 'creatures of fancy', McKenzie relaunched the Politician as the SS Cabinet Minister and transformed Eriskay into the whimsical island of Toddy. For twelve weeks in the summer of 1948, the island of Barra became Toddy.

The making of *Whisky Galore* was an experiment which turned out to be resoundingly successful. The Ealing Studios devised The Mobile Studio Unit to forestall the hazards of filming on location in the unpredictable Scottish climate. Instead of installing expensive portable constructions, cowsheds, barns and church hall served as canteen, projection room and wardrobe. Local interiors, such as the bar or the schoolroom, were used, but most of the crofts, shops or houses were reconstructed in Ealing and shipped to the makeshift studio in Barra. The shooting schedule was flexibly arranged to accommodate the vagaries of the Highland weather. It was a very wet summer but not one day was lost during all the weeks the crew were on the island. They were finally defeated by gale-force winds which actually broke up the reconstructed ship before the shipwreck scenes could be completed. Unable to tolerate the horrendous weather any longer, the unit escaped south to finish these scenes in the studios.

The islanders, in contrast to their weather, were extremely hospitable, entering into the spirit of the enterprise with great enthusiasm, advising and even appearing in crowd scenes. The headmaster of Castlebay School and the Northbay postmaster were given small parts to play at the betrothal ceremony, the local Homeguard was pressed into service and May McNeil, the mother of the island's tailor, made a tiny bid for fame in her first ever acting role at eighty years of age, as Duncan Macrae's screen mother.

Macrae thoroughly enjoyed his stay on Barra. The routine of the simple life, the wholesome food, the friendliness and charm of the islanders were the perfect antidotes to the exhausting Festival schedule and the daily journey to and from Glasgow and Edinburgh. Feeling fit and strong, he was prepared for the Citizens' strenuous autumn programme, beginning with *Let Wives Tak Tent* and then the season at Ayr which included *The Linden Tree*, *The Story of Madeleine Smith*, *Bunty Pulls the Strings* and *The Forrigan Reel*. While the company was in Ayr, the Dublin Gate Theatre were guests at the Citizens' with *The Mountains Look Different* (MacLíammóir) and *The Vigil* (Ladislas Fodor). There followed a brief interlude at Ealing Studios for 'post-synching' the soundtrack on *Whisky Galore* and then it was time to begin rehearsals for the Christmas show which was to be a revival of the 1944 production of *The Forrigan Reel*, 'tricked up a bit' by Bridie and the addition of music by Cedric Thorpe Davie. The show ran until the third week in January 1949 with critics slipping into the phrases that had become commonplace in the vocabulary of Macrae criticism: he was 'more comically brilliant than ever'.

The programme for the next few months promised to be interesting and varied. In direct contrast to the gaiety of Bridie's play, *Macbeth* was to follow the Christmas show. Amidst controversy and misgivings in certain quarters, Macrae was cast in the leading role. Margaretta Scott, who had been invited to play Lady Macbeth, was impressed. She came up to Scotland to begin rehearsals and went to see a performance of *The Forrigan Reel* to gauge the calibre of 'my Macbeth'. She told her husband that if Macrae was as good a Macbeth as he was as a clown he would be a genius.

Fate, as so often happens with 'the Scottish play', took a hand. Despite being one of the few actors of genuine Scottish origin ever to tackle the part, Macrae was not destined to become one of the great Macbeths of all time after all. With only three

performances of *The Reel* left to run, he tripped over a set of
bagpipes in the wings, and broke his foot. The pain was so great
that he was unable to finish the last two performances and his
understudy, James Stuart, took over the part.

Yet Macrae went into the *Macbeth* rehearsals. The show duly
opened and he went on, leg still encased in clumping plaster
which, according to Margaretta Scott, was a sinister sound effect
in the murder scene! After the second performance, it was
obvious to all that Macrae could not continue and Casson took
over the role. Replying to Tom Honeyman's telegram of
sympathy, Macrae admitted that it would be unfair to the rest of
the cast to carry on. He was unfortunately unable to prove
whether or not he was equal to one of the mightier acting
challenges. But a tragic hero limping noisily to his destiny was
surely inimical to tragedy in its highest form.

Tyrone Guthrie testified that Macrae did, nonetheless, show
promise, in a radio programme, *Arts Review*, broadcast on 28
January:

> And now finally to Duncan Macrae's Macbeth? The actor
> had broken a bone in his foot and was hobbling in a plaster
> cast. It was impossible therefore to judge his performance.
> To an actor who relies immensely upon rhythm and
> plasticity of movement it was crushing to be deprived of all
> freedom of movement — not merely a technical handicap
> but maddeningly inhibiting to his imagination. For the
> critic it is impossible not to be either too much swayed by
> sympathy, or alternatively to make too much allowance for
> the handicap.
>
> Taking all this into consideration, let me say that I was
> very much impressed. One was shown a real progression of
> character — not merely degeneration but also growth. This
> Macbeth grew steadily in grandeur and humanity as he
> became engulfed in the torrent of blood. I admired
> immensely the style with which the verse was spoken and
> was confirmed in my belief that Shakespearian rhetoric
> need not — and MUST not be ranted. Meaning must come
> first and music second. The fact that music is subordinated
> to meaning does not, with a really good artist, means loss
> of music — there are places where the music *is* the
> meaning. There is a pernicious tendency, fostered by

dramatic critics, to think that the Voice Beautiful can be pulled out like an organ stop, that 'beauty' can be added to speech like jam to a slice of bread. Mr Macrae knows better than this. And his verse speaking was an object lesson in good sense, good taste and good workmanship

One other point: this was the first Macbeth I have ever seen who gave a witty performance.

I am still not sure if Mr Macrae is really able to play Macbeth. To decide, one would have to see him sound in limb. This hirpling about was often clumsy and absurd — poor man — and, while there's no doubt that Macrae is a comedian of the very first rank, one would need reassurance that the faintest aroma of the satiric, even of the ridiculous, did not pervade his performance, in places where it was not intended.

But of this I am positive: it was a performance of a very highly sensitive, thoughtful and thrilling actor. It is a thousand pities that the thing was disintegrated by this tiresome accident.

Significantly, Macrae never played any other major roles in tragedy. As time passed, while his skills might have developed in that direction, for better or for worse he employed his gifts in comedy as often as the opportunities presented.

The 1948-9 season continued with *The Devil Was An Irishman*, a modern morality in which Macrae gave 'an excellent performance as the leering serpent-tongued Irishman'. He followed this by playing Peter Stockman in a Scottish setting of Ibsen's *An Enemy of the People* and Lieutenant MacFee in a highly acclaimed production of Kenneth Woolard's *Morning Departure*, a play about the reactions of a trapped submarine crew. It had originally been produced in London by Nigel Patrick and was later filmed with John Mills. Casson had gone to great lengths to achieve a realistic claustrophobic atmosphere, spending time studying conditions on a submarine anchored at Rothesay. The majority of the reviews were devoted to praising the play and the production. The chief acting laurels were reserved for Robert Urquhart's submarine commander. The playwright, Alexander Reid, commenting on the masterpiece of intelligent mime incorporated in Macrae's portrayal of the engineer, Macfee, said that as long as Macrae was an influence on young actors 'our acting will never be in danger of becoming muscle bound'.

The last play of the season, *The Face at the Window*, had been produced at the Royal Princess's in 1913 in the days when melodrama was all the rage. Some of the 1949 audience even remembered a production at the Theatre Royal nearly fifty years before. It was clearly an attempt by the Citizens' to reconstruct all the terror and exaggerated acting style of the original form, with Macrae 'at his elegant best as the moustachioed villain', and the audiences loved it.

In June, the company was to take part in a summer repertory season at the Embassy Theatre in London which included The Peter Cotes Players from Manchester in *The Rising Wind*, the Nottingham Theatre Trust in *Othello*, and the Bristol Old Vic in *Wilderness of Monkeys*. The Citizens' chose to revive its production of *Let Wives Tak Tent*. Critics who saw the week's run at the Royal Princess's prior to the London performance reported that Macrae had refined the Oliphant role with greater subtleties, casting 'a spell through the whole theatre'. Bridie was confident that the company would arrive in London 'preceded by a reputation second to none'.

The company did not let him down. The London performances were well reviewed. W.A. Darlington of the *Daily Telegraph* expressed surprise to find that the Citizens' play was none other than a Scots version of Molière's *L'École des femmes*, and relief to find a glossary in the programme. On a more serious note, verifying that Macrae had an established reputation amongst the London critics, Darlington stated that proof of his excellence as a comedian in *The Three Estates* was now being confirmed. Beverley Baxter in the *Evening Standard* urged his readers 'to hasten to Swiss Cottage and crowd the Embassy till its ribs creak' for an evening of 'rare delight'. *The New Statesman*, however, regretted that Casson's production had a strong romantic tendency which prevented Macrae, 'delightful as a comedian' from showing 'the deeper side of Mr Oliphant (Arnolphe) in that dignified pathos his Glasgow audience knows'. The London visit coincided with the first trade showing of *Whisky Galore* which was in itself excellent publicity for the Scottish players.

On returning to Glasgow, Macrae agreed in an interview with the *Evening News* that the experience had been stimulating. The company had found that many Londoners apparently took an interest in the Citizens' work and that their reputation had indeed gone before them.

The company returned to Glasgow to prepare for the gala opening of the new season in a lavish production of Terence Rattigan's *Adventure Story*. It was reported that £12,000 worth of costumes and props had been hired from London. Macrae played a supporting role to Robert Urquhart's lead. The next production, George Munro's *Vineyard Street*, stirred up a minor furore over its theme of religious hypocrisy which was, mistakenly, interpreted as blasphemous. The performances given by James Gibson, John Young and Macrae as the over-fervent brethren managed to surface and be recognized above the clamour of objections.

If *Vineyard Street* enjoyed passing notorious publicity, the production that followed basked in the glow of unreserved and more lasting recognition. The unique inspiration that matched Duncan Macrae with Bridie's creation of the ragged philosopher poet Harry Magog, in *Gog and Magog* — a play that defies critical definition — stands out vividly in the memory of anyone who saw the first performances at the Citizens'. It was a landmark not only in Macrae's career but also in the history of Scottish drama.

Bridie first titled his 'farcical new comedy' *Gog and Macgog*. He quickly dropped the 'c' and the title flowed more easily. Based on an incident in the life of the poet McGonnegal — 'I have the words if only I could put them in the right order' — the play has never been published. Amongst the attempts to label it appropriately the critics struggled with phrases like 'unashamed nonsense', 'a curious piece', 'the jigsaw of its message', 'concoction', 'hardly to be considered a major contribution by Scotland's leading dramatist' and 'as delicious piece of sense-in-nonsense as anyone in search of a holiday from austerity could ask for'.

The play is deceptively simple and unstructured, falling into the category of those plays of Bridie's which are commonly charged with lacking a strong third act. The plot is sparse, centring on an evening's entertainment for the customers in a tavern, purchased at the expense of the humiliation of the central figure, a bizarre, tattered poet. In Harry Magog, Bridie created a monumentally towering character whose unbridled half-crazed ranting is underpinned by a deeply moving appreciation of the human condition which reaches its climax in the scene where he realizes he has been mocked. Apart from the Citizens' production and Macrae's own production in 1954, there has never been any attempt to revive the play since its original production at the Arts Theatre Club in London in December 1948, with Alec Clunes in the title role. Macrae made it his own. Alexander Reid wrote in the *Scottish Daily Mail*, 6 October:

> Macrae's achievement in this play is, in fact, not that he made the audience laugh but that by his superb acting (based on most affecting lines) he forces the audience to stop laughing and see the pathos of the situation of the poet whose means of expression makes a mockery of his genuine inspiration.

Bridie met Winifred Bannister at the second interval on the opening night and paid Macrae the finest of compliments. Almost in tears, he told her that he had been deeply moved by Macrae's performance. But the depth of pathos achieved by Macrae's playing in the humiliation scene was most eloquently described by John Grierson when he wrote simply that 'it takes your breath away'.

November took the company back to another highly successful Ayr season which was sold out in advance. The repertoire included *Love in Albania, Gog and Magog, The Devil was an Irishman, The Rivals, The Glass Menagerie* and *Laburnum Grove*. Macrae was now a public personality, sought after to perform the unlikeliest public relations exercises. At Ayr he was invited to judge a 'Macrae and Rona Anderson look-alike' competition — such was the price of fame. It was at this point in his career that the speeches and talks for which he was constantly in demand, began to receive much wider press coverage, especially as they were rapidly becoming more controversial.

On his return to Glasgow, he was the guest speaker at the Glasgow Publicity Club on 16 December, when he launched an attack on the integrity of some actors' approach to publicity, linking it with an appeal to the public to resist being 'gulled'. Acknowledging that while the profession was servant to 'our august master, the public' and that legitimate exploitation of good publicity is valuable, he criticized the more dubious methods by which certain reputations had been created. He conceded that if the public wanted 'the tawdry', they should have it, but he admitted that on occasion, he felt a certain envy of the reputations falsely gained by such means. Finally, he challenged the audience, the actors and the publicity men to 'justify their connivance in this sordid business'. He maintained that actors should sell their skills rather than themselves, declaring that he had no intention of permitting any invasion of his privacy in the interests of publicity. He did confess, however, that he had 'a guid conceit o' mysel'.

Macrae seemed to thrive on such provocative outburts which never failed to attract publicity. He was now about to go into rehearsals for the production that proved to be the major turning point in his career.

— 6 —

THE REAL TREASURE OF TINTO

The Tintock Cup - Edinburgh Festival again -
films - the first moves towards variety

The 1949 Christmas show was to be *The Tintock Cup,* an original pantomime by Bridie. His notion of using pantomime traditions as the framework for a more sophisticated subversion of the form was essentially sound. The rhyme about the lost treasure of Tinto Hill served as a loosely connecting theme for a series of sketches interspersed with music. An army of characters, as diverse as Six King Jamies and a modern baby-sitter, whisked through hilarious adventures and misadventures, travelling from the bloody battlefield at Bannockburn to the sedate chambers of Kelvingrove Art Gallery. Billed as a 'Christmas Extravaganza', the new style pantomime derived its humour from a disrespectful view of Scottish history similar to the treatment of English history in *1066 and All That.*

'Our Christmas answer to our highbrow accusers', the management announced with a certain defiance. But when rehearsals began, everything seemed to be wrong. The basic difficulty was that the sketches simply did not 'work'. Struggling to bring some cohesion to the enterprise, Casson made feverish cuts, entertained any suggestions and gratefully accepted contributions of any kind.

In November, before rehearsals had actually begun, the Macraes were introduced to Alex Mitchell, a crime reporter, at a press reception. Mitchell's fictitious court cases were a popular feature in the *Sunday Post.* Peggy Macrae jokingly suggested that Mitchell might be interested in writing something for her husband who was looking at material for the Christmas show. Mitchell told her that he was already writing comedy sketches

100

under various pseudonyms such as Robert Simpson, Sandy Reid and Kelso Robertson as his newspaper contract prohibited him from taking freelance commissions. The idea appealed to him, but the suggestion was not, at that stage, pursued.

Several days later, Mitchell casually called at the theatre during rehearsals to see Macrae who presented him with the problem of sketches which had sparse dialogue and no laugh lines. Mitchell agreed to look at the script and use the framework of the sketches to try to 'get some cracks into it'. Only a few days passed before Macrae received a letter with suggestions for the 'Polly at the Palais' sketch and the promise of material for other sketches, 'The Widow', 'The Schoolgirl' and 'The Hing'.

Macrae then introduced Mitchell to Stanley Baxter, a young actor who was equally frustrated by the leaden nature of Bridie's script. Baxter joined in the collaboration to streamline much of the material and add some sketches of his own. The most successful of these turned out to be 'Tatty Bacchante', which he wrote expressly for Molly Urquhart. Baxter's meeting with Mitchell marked the beginning of a long association between scriptwriter and comedian and launched Mitchell on a very successful independent comedy writing career.

When Macrae received the dance hall queen scene, he edited it and reordered the material, making only one cut. The much celebrated sketch began with Macrae's show-stopping entrance, exuding pure glamour in a long, black, sequinned evening gown, hair piled high with blond curls, singing:

I'm Polly from the Palais
You'll see me doon oor alley
Trying out my steps and doin' the Shimmy
Barrowland's ma palace of dreams

Not content with the meticulously observed Glasgow vernacular, the Macraes are said to have spent some time seeking further inspiration at the Barrowland Ballroom, watching and listening to the dancing throng. A typically Glasgow witticism, 'Champ dancer - dampt chancer' or couthy riposte, 'Here lay go Mac. The dance is feenished' were added to the script. The gown took on extra glitter and became a fraction slinkier, the hairdo was piled

101

even higher with swirling curls. The caricature was built in exaggeration of voice, mannerism and costume until it was honed to perfection.

The sketch most fondly remembered amongst so many sparkling creations, was 'The Hing', a riotous scene with Macrae and James Gibson playing two local Gorbals women who, leaning, or 'hanging' out of facing tenement windows, carry on a garrulous gossip in the broadest Glasgow vernacular. It brought the house down.

Mitchell continued to write for Macrae. Over the years, he provided him with many of the sketches he used in pantomime and other variety appearances. Ironically, because of his newspaper contract, Mitchell's considerable contribution to *The Tintock Cup* was only acknowledged relatively recently. He never met Bridie and, much to Macrae's annoyance, was not included in the backstage celebrations when the show closed. In an article entitled 'Random Ideas About How to Compose a Pantomime', published in the Citizens' magazine, *The Prompter*, Bridie confessed to his own misgivings:

> At last, impelled not by inspiration but by my sense of honour I began to churn out some turgid stuff on my typewriter. I called in George Munro to help and at last faced the company with a script neither John Casson nor I dared to read to them. I told my clowns that they must by no means consider what was set down for them. They must go for their own laughs. They took me at my word.

By opening night on 20 December 1949, the team effort had fashioned the unwieldy text into the semblance of a show. A.P. Kellock, one of Bridie's favourite pseudonyms, was advertised as the author. The company waited apprehensively backstage for the call, 'house lights, curtain, go'. A stroke of sheer inspiration took Stanley Baxter and Douglas Campbell, playing the Broker's Men, into the auditorium before the lights went down to 'warm up' the staid Citizens' audience. Their improvisations sparkled. The mood was set for a memorable evening.

The legendary production exploded joyously on to the Gorbals stage, rocketing Macrae into an entirely new orbit. The reviews were ecstatic. Much of the pleasure derived from watching actors the Citizens' audiences were accustomed to see in Sheridan, Priestley or Carroll, take to playing burlesque so brilliantly. Their experience as a dramatic ensemble company brought a genuine abandon to the show that no ordinary company might contrive. The 'outlandish nonsense' of the script did not hide the literary and cultural background which lay behind the wit. Although the *Glasgow Herald* singled out Stanley Baxter's impression of a Glasgow boxer, giving a radio interview in America, as 'the best single turn', by the end of the first week it was Macrae's dame who had 'the whole town talking'. His cameo character gems all but defy description. But float names like 'Polly at the Palais' or the 'Queen of Crossmyloof' before anyone privileged, for privileged indeed they were to have witnessed their creation, and they will become misty eyed in the gleeful recollection of the sheer genius of Macrae's unique comic style. Gordon Irving wrote in the *Daily Record*:

> Something new happened in Scottish theatre last night in the old Princess's Theatre, in the Glasgow Gorbals, where pantomime under the late Harry McKelvie, flourished for so many years... Biggest hit is the lanky actor-droll Duncan Macrae. He's cast as Dame, has all the mannerisms and gawky humour of the late Tommy Lorne.
>
> You should see him as a winsome Flora McDonald, you should see him as a gawky schoolgirl, mixing the baby up with the dumpling... He's uproarious. I suggest that all present-day Scots comics should spare an afternoon from their music-hall pantomimes and study the Macrae technique.

That would have been an interesting exercise indeed, as it is almost certain that observers would not have described anything that was consistent in any two of his performances. Several notices rightly identified the sources of Macrae's hilarious characterizations as his ability to be as 'Glesca as Gallowgate' and build 'his rich comedy on a sure Glasgow foundation'. On the credit side, while that natural empathy with the vernacular and the dry couthy wit unique to Glaswegians was the mainspring of much of his comedy, Macrae was not confined by it, thanks to his innate comic sense. But on the debit side, he retained a tendency to resort to that type of parochial humour which must have fallen on deaf ears any time he worked outside Scotland.

Irving continued his article prophesying, 'If he cared to desert the legitimate stage for vaudeville, Duncan Macrae would be at the top within three months.' The theme was picked up and discussed at length in the press, but it was tempered by the belief that Macrae was too much the idealist to abandon his dreams of a Scottish National Theatre by going into music hall. Many reviews continued to compare him to Tommy Lorne. Jack House stood out alone, maintaining that Macrae was a new comic in his own right.

The celebratory mood at the Citizens' Christmas Eve party was dampened when Bridie suddenly took ill and was admitted to hospital on Boxing Day. He was soon restored to full health and his familiar ebullience.

The Tintock Cup was a box-office 'smash-hit'. Newspapers published photographs of long queues of people, booking for the unprecedented eleventh and twelfth weeks. By 10 January, it was reported that the run would be extended until 25 February. And still the show was playing to packed houses. Casson, with an eye to the company's philosophy and future commitments, was cautious about forecasting a closing date. He need not have worried. Public demand, bordering on indignation that anyone might be deprived of this singular treat was such that the Citizens' directors threw a party to announce that the show would run until 1 April. By this time, *The Tintock Cup* had assumed all the characteristics of a cult production. Such was the phenomenon that the Board, motivated no doubt by a mixture of pride and astonishment, untypically issued a series of statistics. The show ran for fifteen weeks, giving 116 performances, some of which were extra matinées. A total of 138,200 people saw it, including 415 large party-bookings. 17,400 spectators happily occupied 'standing room only', 20,000 watched from the unreserved gallery and 9,280 were turned away by 'House Full' notices. On a more frivolous note, the public was confidentially informed that John Humphrey, who played 'The Spider' in the Bannockburn scene, was raised and lowered from the flies a total of 5,800 feet, there were 585 curtain calls and the 'call girl' walked more than 100 miles. But for the Board, the financial statistics were the most attractive of all. With weekly takings of £1,500 and a total of approximately £22,000, they could breathe more easily and the budget deficit, that existed before the production, was cleared.

While Macrae was the star of the show, it would not be fair to claim that the success of *The Tintock Cup* was due only to him, for the show was the result of a corporate effort. The cast boasted the most gifted players in contemporary Scottish theatre, many of whom were to became nationally recognized through the medium of television. Amongst them were Fulton Mackay, Stanley Baxter, Molly Urquhart and Gudrun Ure. Also in the cast were Laurence Hardy, John Young, Lea Ashton, James Gilbert, Moira Robertson and Casson's children, Penelope and Jane.

The Tintock Cup had been running for only a very short time when it was obvious to everyone that Macrae was possessed of something special. The momentum of success was continued in the press by reports and articles fuelling rumours that Macrae was about to sign a contract with impresario, Tom Arnold. The *Daily Record* and the *Daily Mail* reported that Macrae had received the offer of a 'very lucrative contract to play in a top Scottish show next Christmas'.

No one claimed to know who had made the offer, but Ramsden Gray, the theatre correspondent for the *Evening Citizen*, revealed that Macrae had confided in him, but he was sworn to secrecy until the contract was signed. In an interview, Macrae assured his public, 'If I leave the Citizens' it will only be for the pantomime season.' He added that his aim was 'to recapture the spirit of the dames I knew when I was a boy'. Gray restated the well worn adage that there were few real comedians who lacked the burning ambition to play Macbeth, but here was a man who had played Macbeth and had a burning ambition to be a comedian. Such an assertion was never made by Macrae. Before he had even confirmed he would cross the river to the beckoning city lights, the press, fickle as ever in its loyalties and hungry for sensation, lost no time in 'king making'. The *Evening Citizen* prophetically announced that Baxter, 'a young man of outstanding ability' was the most promising candidate for Macrae's high heels, beehive hairdos and slinky gowns.

Macrae signed the pantomime contract with Arnold in March, to play one of the Ugly Sisters in the 1950-1 *Cinderella*, for sixteen weeks at a fee of £80 per week — four times as much as he was earning in *The Tintock Cup*. Arnold announced that all the principal parts would be taken by Scottish performers, — Donald Layne-Smith from the Wilson Barrett Company was to play the other sister — and for the first time in Scottish pantomime, the principal boy would be a man, the singer Robert Wilson. Macrae could allay any misgivings he might have had about selling his soul to English commercialism.

The announcement was accompanied by a flurry of press attention that was now an integral part of Macrae's life. He was becoming more at ease with the interview and the pert quote, telling Logan Gourlay in the *Scottish Sunday Express*:

> I feel that a really adaptable actor can play the clown and be a first-class dramatic actor as well. Alastair Sim is an example. Besides I have never played what you might call 'straight' parts. I have been either funny, or sinister — or mad.

This was an uncanny flash of self-awareness and insight, for quintessential to Macrae's art was a sense of danger, arguably the most elusive and desirable of all dramatic actors' attributes.

There was no ambiguity about the contract. Macrae would simply be leaving the Citizens' for the duration of the pantomime run. Bridie could hardly have felt that the company was in any way threatened by this sudden diversion of attention from the company to a single member. But the announcement, albeit coincidental, that the Citizens' would be staging three-quarters of the forthcoming Edinburgh Festival dramatic productions was well-timed to take advantage of the current concentrated focus on the company's activities.

The Tintock Cup finally closed in April and the company took two weeks holiday with pay. The image of the lanky, leggy comedian had gripped the public's imagination. Macrae, sharp as always, turned this to advantage when he was invited to address the Radio Manufacturers' Association on 15 April. Replying to the vote of thanks which described him as having the most expressive legs in Britain, Macrae, referring to his accident before *Macbeth*, quipped that demons had given him a broken leg saying, 'Thou shalt not play Macbeth. Thou shall be a comic.' With a hint of resignation, tempered by apology, he confessed he was becoming accustomed to being a comic.

Macrae still adhered to the political affiliations that motivated most of his life; he devoted as much time as he could spare to supporting a friend, Dr Robert McIntyre, who was standing as the Scottish National Party candidate for Motherwell in the forthcoming general election campaign. The prospect of hearing Duncan Macrae speak was always the guarantee of a good attendance at any kind of meeting. He rarely disappointed and seldom failed to shock with either an unconventional view or blunt language. On the final afternoon of that particular campaign, his colourful vocabulary stunned the assembly at a women's rally into shocked silence. But in reality there was little time to indulge in such exercises as his career was now developing in a direction that would increasingly take him away from the Citizens' and away from Glasgow. What might appear to be a desertion of the company that had fostered and nourished him was a logical progression up the career ladder. It would have been professionally stultifying to remain with the same company, year after year, regardless of whatever stature he might have achieved within that company.

Initially, the outside work was in film which meant he would have to be temporarily released from the Citizens' contract. The company learned to recognize the pattern. Macrae would receive a film offer. Casson would resist — not very forcefully, because he was not a man to stand in the way of his actors — there would be raised voices in the office and Macrae would eventually emerge, satisfied with permission to take up the offer.

In May, he set off for London to play in J. Arthur Rank's thriller, *The Woman in Question*, destined to be consigned to obscurity. Dirk Bogarde and Jean Kent were given star billing while Macrae shared the credits below the title with the other supporting actors including Hermione Baddeley. Bogarde and

Kent were undeniably household names. But as Police Superintendent Lodge, Macrae's part was central to the film's narrative. In a finely controlled performance, Macrae captured the essential characteristics of the genre of quiet, well-spoken, well-groomed, intelligent sleuths fashionable in the 1940s. Macrae was transferring to screen the kind of character he had been playing to good effect since the days at the Curtain some twenty years before. When the film went on general release in October, Gordon Irving wrote in the *Daily Record*:

> A new type of film detective has arrived on the British screen — a quiet, brisk-spoken inspector with eagle eyes, sharp features, a knowing smile, a gangling gait, a shrewd, far-seeing mind and large expressive eyes... The new personality is Scotland's own Duncan Macrae.

Filming was completed by the middle of August and when Macrae returned to Scotland, the family went for a brief holiday to the island of Millport.

The Citizens' took over the Lyceum Theatre for the three-week duration of the Edinburgh Festival that year. Tyrone Guthrie was to direct their three productions: *The Queen's Comedy*, Bridie's comic view of the relationship between gods and men in time of war; Linklater's *The Atom Doctor*, an updated version of Jonson's *The Alchemist*; and the eighteenth-century Scottish piece by John Home, *Douglas*. The Old Vic was at the Assembly Hall, with Ben Jonson's *Bartholomew Fair*, directed by George Devine and costumed by Motley. The opposition — on paper at least — was formidable.

Confident that their Scottish fare would attract good audiences, the Citizens' opened on 21 August in *The Queen's Comedy*, amidst a blaze of publicity for the guest artists, Walter Fitzgerald and Sonia Dresdel who were playing Jupiter and Juno. The revues were disparate, ranging from 'Bridie at his most serious and his most entertaining' and 'A cup of nectar for those with that kind of palate' to 'It is a good enough joke within its limits' and 'slow moving'. The critics were however unanimous about the quality of the acting, praising 'the silky allure' of Sonia

Dresdel's Juno and the 'quiet strength' of Walter Fitzgerald's Jupiter. But it was Macrae, making only two brief appearances as Vulcan, the gods' armourer, who stole the show in 'a gorgeous ten minutes or so of broad comedy'.

Three days later *The Atom Doctor* opened with Macrae in the lead as Dr Mortimer. The reviews again diverged, some liking the production, some the acting, some the play itself, while others placed the undertaking in the 'fiasco' category. Not even Guthrie was spared the lash. Macrae fared rather better, but some critics felt that his ten minutes as Vulcan were worth his entire Dr Mortimer. He was not cast in *Douglas*. The Citizens' played to packed houses for the duration of the Festival. In the event, the Old Vic had not proved to be damaging competition. When the plays returned to the Glasgow repertoire, *The Scotsman's* critic subtly damned Linklater's play by commending Macrae's performance in the most glowing terms, asserting that he was capable of transforming into comical dumb show even the most banal of material. Macrae had abandoned the quirkiest of his angular mannerisms and had become 'a comedian of ripe authority'.

Macrae now took advantage of his own high profile, and of the Citizens' popular success, to make one of his renowned impassioned pleas for the cause of native drama in a speech he delivered at Edinburgh College of Art on 4 September. He was widely quoted. Reminding his audience of the thrill of listening to the Scots tongue in *The Three Estates*, he declared:

> Now that we have achieved the distinction of presenting two new plays at one festival, both by Scots and one partially in the common tongue, I quite shamelessly advocate the performance next year of a new play in Scots. Such an occasion would allow the greater part of the Scottish people to judge a play in their own language, as none of the plays this year claims to do.

The actor, Esmond Knight, who was with the Old Vic in *Bartholomew Fair*, retorted that if the programme committee had accepted plays from Bridie and Linklater, 'two of our brightest playwrights', they had fulfilled their duty adequately. He believed that the question of a special festival play could become too serious and that it should suffice to have a play by a reputable author.

Naturally enough this exchange provoked correspondence in the press, with an assortment of ingenious suggestions flooding in, ranging from Lallans play writing competitions to casting Macrae as Bailie Nicol Jarvie in a production of *Rob Roy*, directed by Tyrone Guthrie.

The *Daily Record* critic had the last word with the light-hearted suggestion that the ideal Scottish play should include amongst its characters, Mary Queen of Scots, Bonnie Prince Charlie, Rabbie Burns, the Deil, the Minister's Man, a razor slasher, a fitba' fan, an assortment of dominies, medicos and the Washin' Hoose Key. The settings should include a picture gallery at Holyrood House, a cave in Skye, Gorbals at Midnight, Hampden Park, the auld clay biggin' at Alloway, a steamie and the Hunterian Museum. The play should move to a powerful musical climax with the cast joining the audience in singing 'We're no awa tae bide awa', or perhaps 'The Wells o' Wearie'. Tongue in cheek, he concluded by proposing that willing playwrights should contact the Arts Council.

In a few brief words, he had encapsulated years of indictment against the sentimental tendency in Scottish culture which militated against valid native creativity. This was the very heart of the problem that continually vexed so many critics of Scottish drama. It was a problem addressed by Macrae throughout his life, at least in principle. In practice, however, the need to earn a living is paramount and, in the theatre, audience taste repeatedly dictates the choice of material. That particular artistic dilemma is universal.

One aspect of the question of how Scotland was to achieve its own brand of theatre was solved on 14 September when Dame Sybil Thorndike formally inaugurated the first Scottish College of Drama. The principal, Colin Chandler, had portrait photographs prepared to hang in the main foyer of the four significant people who were most helpful in setting up the college, namely, James Bridie, Lewis Casson, Sybil Thorndike and Duncan Macrae. From that date the well-trained graduates — amongst whom we find

Hannah Gordon, John Cairney, Andy Stewart, Bill Paterson, Ian Richardson, Tom Conti, Phyllis Logan, Gregor Fisher and Ruby Wax — were ready to take part in anything the Scottish stage had to offer.

Macrae remained in the spotlight when he was immortalized as Harry Magog, in bronze, by the Queen's sculptor in Scotland, Benno Schotz. The statuette was first seen at the Royal Institute of Fine Arts Exhibition where it was displayed with a companion piece, a bust of the poet Hugh MacDiarmid entitled 'The Bard'.

The run of *The Atom Doctor* at the Citizens' finished at the end of October. The shortening autumn days gradually turning to bleak November darkness, Macrae now prepared to add his own brand of sparkle to the long winter nights. The contract with the Citizens' was formally suspended on 4 November. The Alhambra show was to open on 9 December. It was curtain up on panto time. There were new horizons to be explored. But before Macrae could make the move, the prospect of the sudden dramatic rise in salary brought about a major change in family life.

The flat at Woodlands Road had become increasingly difficult to live in. Ann was now four and Christine two. It was the last straw when a burst pipe brought the ceiling down. So in November, immediately after the contract was agreed, the Macraes purchased a flat on the south side of the city at 9 Queens Park Avenue. Peggy had always preferred the south side of the city and Queens Park was much more convenient to the Royal Princess's. The flat on the ground floor of a red sandstone tenement building, tucked away in a quiet cul-de-sac, was in an ideal situation, especially for Macrae himself who still took great pleasure in walking everywhere. It was adjacent to the playing fields and recreation ground extension to Queen's Park. Here, Ann and Christine learned what it was to be taken on one of their father's notorious all weather 'marches'. Many a visitor was dragged willingly or otherwise for 'a turn round the park' while Peggy made tea. Peggy, efficient as ever, soon tailored the three rooms to their needs, converting a large 'walk-in' cupboard in the sitting room to an 'office' for her husband. It was duly equipped with desk, chair and shelves and Macrae worked there on scripts and the speeches and articles which were fast becoming an indispensable feature of the Macrae persona. Peggy was very contented, with her piano in pride of place.

From the time of the move, the Queens Park flat became firmly established, both in private and in the eye of the public, as a family home. Even though he had vowed in the past that he would permit no intrusion into his privacy, Macrae was astute enough to allow selective interviews with his family, all grist to the publicity mill. There were articles and photographs of Peggy and the girls at home, in a group round the piano, walking in the park or cooking — all supplying the endless curiosity of the fans. She had adapted very swiftly to the role of the 'star's' wife and readily gave the kind of interview beloved of the gossip columnists, recounting her day, how she adjusted the family routine to reconcile the unsociable hours of her husband with the demands of two small children, how she managed to juggle her priorities to support her husband's needs, whether it be preparing late night suppers or learning lines. This apparent acquiescence to the insatiable inquisitiveness of the public did not contradict Macrae's views about the manipulation of reputations. He considered this kind of co-operation to be a necessary and harmless concession which he owed to himself and the profession. Unlike many show business personalities, there were never any personal scandals in his life that could be used against him for cheap publicity. For his part, he gave lectures, delivered talks, opened fêtes, judged competitions, wrote articles and, on the surface at least, seemed to jump heart and soul on the public relations merry-go-round.

The regular traffic of visitors to the Macrae home was assured of the warmest hospitality. To Sybil Thorndike, Lewis Casson, Roddy McMillan, Fulton Mackay and countless others, not always in the profession, it became the focal point for numerous momentous occasions, and a gathering place where they could reminisce, celebrate, relax or argue away the hours.

For the Macraes, the real treasure of *The Tintock Cup* was the promise of security they gained following the resounding success of that sparkling show. But the calm stability of the routine of family life was about to be disrupted by the unexpected vehemence of the reaction provoked by the pantomime contract.

A DAME FOR ALL SEASONS

The consequences of pantomime -
Bridie's death - changes

The Alhambra pantomime was a Glasgow institution. Over many years, Harry Lauder, Will Fyffe and Harry Gordon were amongst the most illustrious and beloved Scottish comedians who had steadfastly maintained the purest of pantomime form in their Christmas shows. Generations of enchanted children and their parents, collaborating in the suspension of disbelief, cheered to the echo the daring of the principal boy, adore the languishing heroine, hissed the cruel oppressing villain, sang with gusto, wondered at the glory of the costume and spectacle and took to their hearts the sheer exuberance of the grotesqueries and extravagances of the dame. Stanley Baxter, Rikki Fulton, Jimmy Logan and, for a brief period, Macrae, were only a few of the many household names who, joining the ranks of the famous comics, followed and upheld the age-old traditions.

The signing of the pantomime contract in 1950 unleashed an unprecedented storm of comment and criticism. It proved to be the most controversial career decision Macrae was ever to make. Many of his colleagues held him in such esteem as an actor on the legitimate stage that they interpreted the move to variety as nothing short of betrayal of the craft. He was accused of being seduced not only by the popularity of variety, but also by the lucrative rewards to be reaped from theatre that operated its finances on a level entirely removed from the modest economics of a provincial repertory company.

The move to variety dogged Macrae for the rest of his life. Some critics were blunter and more direct than others. John

Cairney expressed regret over what he considered a loss of integrity. Cairney, fresh from drama college and imbued with the most genuine of ideals, had been an extra in *The Three Estates* at the 1950 Edinburgh Festival. Every morning he had joined Macrae on the walk from their theatrical digs to the Assembly Hall, listening eagerly to all the wisdom Macrae was happy to impart. Watching him work night after night for three weeks, his admiration and respect deepened. It came as a shock to find that, in Cairney's opinion, Macrae was turning his back on the avowed principles of his art. With quiet simplicity, the young man's reproach was answered by an invitation to supper. When he arrived, Macrae welcomed him in front of the children: 'Here's the man who doesn't want you to eat', he announced. Then he gently explained that he was resolved to earn the best possible living for his family.

But it was also alleged that popular success fed Macrae's vanity to intolerable proportions and that, in consequence, he became quite impossible to work with, more temperamental and wayward on stage than ever. Actors who worked with him after the first season in pantomime alleged that he became even more guilty of consciously playing 'out front' to the audience, outrageously upstaging other members of the cast. Criticism of this nature can, however, be suspect as it might well have been informed by envy of his phenomenal success and popularity. There was many a 'victim' of Macrae's seemingly innocent ploys to attract the spotlight. In spite of this, the bonus was that he had created a new personal following for himself amongst pantomime audiences, a following which was prepared to support him not only in pantomime but also on the legitimate stage. Admirable and desirable though this might have been, this two-way traffic produced its own problems. The pantomime audience brought to the legitimate theatre certain expectations of Macrae and his every entrance tended to be greeted by gales of laughter. The uninitiated seemed to find comedy in the most unexpected places. While nobody was deluded that the average music hall devotee was about to undergo instant conversion to a taste for Ibsen or Shakespeare, the subtler forms of comedy were in danger of being submerged when Macrae was in the cast of a 'straight' play.

There were six shows in Glasgow in the 1950-1 festive season. Only three of these were traditional pantomimes: *Babes in the Wood* at the Pavilion, *Red Riding Hood* at the Citizens', and *Cinderella* at the Alhambra. The King's was running the American musical, *Brigadoon*, the Empire and the Royal had chosen the more sophisticated revue form with *Fine and Dandy* and *Queen of Hearts.* Macrae was competing in a field of well established and highly successful performers. Dubbed the 'refugee from the Citizens' by Harry Gordon, would he be equal to the challenge?

The excitement in the first night audience at the Alhambra on 9 December was almost palpable. One report claimed that the entire Glasgow Citizens' Theatre Society was there to cheer on their man. W.J.W. in *The Bulletin*, 11 December, likened Macrae and Layne-Smith to 'a giant whippet and a French poodle masquerading as a pair of coy faded flappers'. From his first entrance, the adoring fans gleefully cheered their lanky favourite's every appearance with bursts of laughter and applause.

Macrae showed signs of being the novice in the 'big time'. Some critics quibbled over details: 'need [Macrae's] make-up be quite so grotesque?' complained the *Glasgow Herald* on 11 December. But the general opinion was that the two newcomers matched Harry Gordon's experience and virtuosity, step by step. Gordon Irving, in the *Daily Record,* 11 December, asserted that Macrae had not disappointed those like himself who had forecast a great future for him after the recent triumph in the Gorbals. Irving commented on the importance of good writers to the comedian and particularly admired Alex Mitchell's bird watcher sketch. Mitchell had not let Macrae down. He continued to enhance the treasures of *The Tintock Cup.*

There was so much more to be learned in this new magical world. Macrae was a product of the repertory system in the days when an actor only relied on the theatre wardrobe for period costume or specialities. An actor was expected to travel with his own costume hamper, containing the formal suit, the sports clothes, the dinner jacket, shirts, hats and shoes — everything that might be called for in a contemporary dressed production. The lavish budgets, trips to London for costume fittings, the art of make-up for the pantomime dame were amongst the many practices that were quite unfamiliar to an actor used to the restrictions imposed by the relatively modest budget of a repertory company. On an individual basis, there were traditions of which Macrae was quite unaware. Throughout their careers, most pantomime dames build up a personal collection of sparkling costume jewellery to embellish their costumes. The curtain call is the moment when, resplendent in her most spectacular outfit, the dame gilds the lily with show-stopping, breath-taking panache. On opening night Macrae was caught unprepared. His dresser, Mrs McGuiness, took him under her wing and cobbled together an impromptu collection of baubles and bangles hastily purloined from the dressing rooms. The lesson was quickly learned and before long Macrae sparkled and glinted with the best.

There was one noticeably dissenting voice amongst all the approbation. Alan Dent in the *News Chronicle*, 6 January, was not impressed. His disappointment over the performance of 'that beautiful actor' found expression in suggesting that Macrae might cross the river and watch Stanley Baxter's developing mastery of the comedian's craft. It seemed that the pattern was going to be repeated for it was widely rumoured that Baxter was also going into prestige pantomime. Baxter had indeed been offered a contract by Howard & Wyndham in April to play the Dame in their next pantomime at the King's, Edinburgh. He declined as he felt he must honour his Citizens' contract. Shortly afterwards, he received another offer, this time to play the Dame opposite Jack Anthony at the Glasgow Pavilion. Casson resolved Baxter's growing dilemma by convincing him that, if he stayed with the Citizens', they would produce another traditional pantomime and that he would be doing the company a service by appearing in it. Baxter stayed but before long he too succumbed to the blandishments of the big time show where he swiftly climbed to his now familiar prominent position on the variety stage.

The Macrae Family, 1910. Five-year old John, front row.

Emergency Call

A New Play by
ROBINS MILLAR

Characters
(in order of appearance)

Mrs. McGinney - -	Jean Faulds
John McGinney - -	John Morton
Helen Cowan - - -	Mary H. Ross
Peter Cowan - - -	J. D. G. Macrae
Peggy Allison - -	Jessie C. Morton
Mrs. Robertson -	Nora C. Ewing
Eleanor Robertson -	Janie Stevenson
Professor George Teddings	Guy Mitchell
Edward Teddings - -	Ian Dow
Mary Plover - -	Pearl Colquhoun
Robert Plover - - -	James Keddie
Allison - - -	Robert C. Gaston
John Fraser - - -	W. S. Smith

Cast list, *The Curtain*, 1938.

Publicity. The Curtain Theatre, 1930s.

Wedding photograph. John and Peggy Macrae, 1943.

Alastair Sim as 'Old MacAlpin', Molly Urquhart as 'Mrs Grant', Macrae as 'Donald MacAlpin' in *The Forrigan Reel*, Sadler's Wells, 1945.

he Citizens' Theatre Company's first laybill, 1943.

Duncan Macrae as 'Mr Oliphant'; Gudrun Ure as 'Agnes' in *Let Wives Tak Tent*, The Citizens' Theatre, 1945.

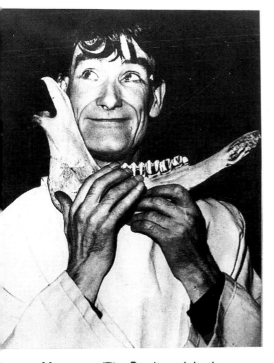

uncan Macrae as 'The Pardoner', in the dinburgh Festival production of *The Three states*, 1948.

Macrae's personal income record showing the 'Pantomime Contract'.

Cinderella at the Alhambra, 1950–51. Alec Finlay ('Buttons'), Harry Gordon ('The Dame'), Duncan Macrae and Donald Layne-Smith ('The Ugly Sisters').

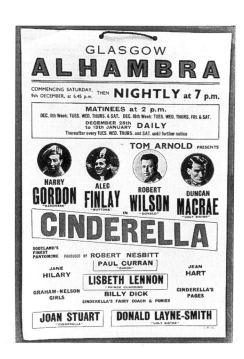

Poster for *Cinderella*, 1950.

Duncan Macrae as 'Tartuffe'; Yvonne Coulette as 'Elmire' in *Tartuffe*, Citizens' Theatre, 1951.

Robert Cartland (left) as 'Briskett', Duncan Macrae (right) as 'Harry Magog', in *Gog and Magog*, Citizens' Theatre, 1951.

Duncan Macrae as 'Grandaddy' in *The Kidnappers*, with Vincent Winter and Jon Whiteley.

Peggy, Ann, John and Christine at 'Dundonald', Millport.

Just Daft at the Empire, Glasgow 1956. Macrae (centre) with Robert Wilson, Jack Anthony, Dave Willis, Chic Murray and Maidie.

Party on the set of *Rockets Galore*, 1957. Standing (left to right) Jameson Clark, Duncan Macrae, Donald Sinden, a piper, Jeannie Carson, Ronnie Corbett, Noel Purcell, John Laurie; seated, Gordon Jackson.

The crew of 'The Vital Spark' in the 1959–60 TV series, *Para Handy*. Angus Lennie, Duncan Macrae, Roddy McMillan and John Grieve.

Duncan Macrae, Laurence Olivier and Orson Welles rehearsing *Rhinoceros* at the Royal Court Theatre, 1960.

Duncan Macrae as 'The Hoopoe' with Joyce Bell as 'The Nightingale' in the Royal Lyceum Theatre Company's *The Burdies*, Edinburgh Festival, 1965.

Although there was such a fuss about the decision to sign the pantomime contract in 1950, Macrae appeared in only seven traditional pantos. While after that time there was certainly a bias towards playing comedy, even on the legitimate stage, that need not imply inferior engagements or loss of integrity. But the financial attraction of working in commercial theatre was undeniable. By 1961 he could command a weekly sum of £300 in pantomime in contrast to the meagre £35 for his last appearance at the Citizens' 1962 Christmas show.

Off-stage, the pantomime world opened up a whole new experience in personal relationships for there was a warm camaraderie that was rather foreign to Macrae's private and reserved nature. He was frequently thought to be stand-offish and was perceived, perhaps unjustly, to assume an air of superiority. This made him vulnerable to the kind of spoof that Alec Finlay played on him during the run of *Cinderella* in 1951. Finlay drove Macrae home every night after the show. One night, he commented on the recent theft of the Stone of Destiny from the throne of Edward the Confessor in Westminster Abbey — allegedly the work of a Scottish Nationalist group. Macrae voiced his hearty approval of the action. Nothing more was said. Several nights later, the phone rang in Macrae's dressing room. A low, husky, barely audible voice muttered something about the Stone of Destiny. Immediately on the alert, Macrae thought he was being approached as a known sympathizer to the Scottish National cause. Macrae listened to the whispered suggestion that he might hide the Stone in his garden. Convinced that this was a *bona fide* overture, he agreed to keep silent. A few nights later Finlay remarked that the Stone had not yet been found. When the car stopped and Macrae got out, Finlay wound down the car window and, calling out in an instantly recognizable throaty voice that 'they' would soon be coming to Macrae's garden, drove off leaving Macrae shaking his fist in the middle of the road.

Cinderella closed at the end of March 1951 with the understanding that Macrae would return to the Alhambra for the show next Christmas. Such security meant that he could confidently plan some way into the future — a rare luxury for an actor.

Nevertheless, in February, obviously nursing ambivalent feelings about the fierce reaction to his pantomime stint, he still felt obliged to make statements justifying his past actions and to cover his future options. He wrote in *The Prompter*:

> I find myself between the upper and nether millstones of art and artifice. The former gladdens the soul and the latter the purse. If the rigours of the 'legit' represent bread and butter, the glamour of pantomime promises a little jam too. Killing two birds with one stone is always rare and exciting. If one bird is fatter, the other is perhaps more succulent. What matter? Variety is the spice of life, and who would not sicken of caviar daily?

A week later, the *Sunday Express* reported that he had turned down the comic lead in *London Melody* which was planned as a prestigious Festival of Britain show at the Empress Hall in London. He also turned down a part in a 'Robin Hood' film. It was claimed that he preferred to appear at 'a modest salary' in the Citizens' forthcoming production of *Mary Stuart* which was to be Glasgow's contribution to the Festival of Britain. That he was remaining faithful to his avowed loyalty to Scotland and his promise that variety engagements would be confined to the pantomime season could not at this stage be challenged. He returned to the Gorbals in April.

1951 was the year of changes. James Bridie died on 29 January. People gathered at the Macraes' home when they heard the news, as if tacitly acknowledging Macrae's place in the fortunes of Bridie's brain-child, the Citizens' Theatre Company. Norman Duthie was appointed to succeed Bridie as the Company chairman. Capable though Duthie was, Bridie's confrontational thrust would be missed by everyone. John Baxter summed up popular sentiment in the *Daily Express*: 'I shall miss his eloquent hatred of all dramatic critics.' Neither the board room nor the theatre would be same again. But Bridie's legacy to Scottish theatre was a thriving company, committed to advance the reputation of Scottish theatre. In May, Casson gave notice of his intended departure at the end of the season to take up a post in Australia.

Welcomed back from the kingdom of make-believe, Macrae went straight into rehearsals for a production that could not have been more contrasting to pantomime in its spirit of stark realism. Set in 1938, *Spindrift*, jointly written by Naomi Mitchison and Denis Macintosh, is a tale of the trials and triumphs of a Scottish fishing community. Encouraged by Bridie, they had worked on the play for over four years. When it finally went into production, Macintosh's own boat, 'Maid Morven', sailed from Carradale on the Mull of Kintyre to the Clyde and its gear was used as props on John Russell's ingenious set. Macrae played the trawler skipper, Alec MacMillan, 'a dark man, with a thin face and blazing blue eyes'. In Naomi Mitchison's opinion Macrae was 'exactly what was needed'. She was most impressed by his insistence on creating an accurate image of the seaman, down to the last detail of his rolling gait. During rehearsals he sought constant reassurance that everything they were doing looked authentic and, according to the reviews, it did. The impressive cast included Roddy McMillan, Fulton Mackay, Madeleine Christie and Andrew Keir. Casting the skipper's wife, Jennie, however was more difficult. Casson wanted Lennox Milne for the part but she was not available. He took a gamble with the young and inexperienced assistant stage-manager, Marillyn Gray, who had been hired on a temporary basis for the 1950 season in Ayr and the Christmas show. She had stayed on with the company because in the heyday of the repertory system, the traditional way of learning all aspects of the theatre business was taking on the job of assistant stage-manager. This meant that while waiting for the 'big break', a young hopeful, with little or no stage experience, could sweep floors, help build sets, make costumes and props, learn about lighting, take walk-on parts or even have a line or two. Marillyn Gray was terrified to play opposite 'the great Macrae'. Her fears were groundless for Macrae was kindness itself, coming to the theatre an hour before rehearsal call to go through the lines with her. His gift for teaching came again to the fore. Working with Macrae was a tough school for a youngster to cut her teeth in. She learned to 'act on her feet', dealing with his notorious *ad libs* and his cutting across her best lines. The reward lay in the unanimous accolade that she was outstanding. The play was a great popular success and ran for an extra week. Naomi Mitchison subsequently tried to have another play, with a part specially written for Macrae, accepted by the Citizens', but it found no favour with the Board.

Strained relationships arose over another Scottish play. The journalist, Tim Watson, had written a new play about the antics and mishaps centred on a parochial Scottish undertaker's parlour. *Bachelors Are Bold* was due to come in to the Citizens' after *Spindrift*. But as *Spindrift* ran for an extra week, Watson's play was squeezed out of the Glasgow season. It was to be directed by James Gibson at Ayr in May, with Macrae as the undertaker Gilbert Dalgleish. Watson wrote to Tom Honeyman saying that, as far as the public was concerned, it looked as if the Ayr date was a consolation prize. Honeyman replied soothingly, dismissing such a suggestion and revealed that the executive were 'in the throes of some difficult transition problems' which he could not disclose. He assured Watson that nothing would please him more than to see his play included in the regular repertoire and the matter was closed. The *Bachelors Are Bold* affair strengthened the long-standing friendship between Watson and Macrae which had begun in the days of The Curtain Theatre. It confirmed their common determination to bring Scottish drama to the Scottish people.

At the end of May, the company contributed to the Perth Festival season with a new production of Alexander Reid's *The Lass wi' the Muckle Mou*. Macrae took over the role of Thomas the Rhymer which had been created by Roddy McMillan in the first production at Ayr in 1950. He was 'excellent... making every point in his comedy without overplaying'. Thus far pantomime was not charged with exerting a detrimental influence on his sense of comedy.

In June, Casson embarked upon his last production with the company, Robert McLellan's *Mary Stuart*. Great things were expected of this play which was advertised as a 'Festival of Britain Special Production under the Patronage of the Lord Provost and Magistrates of the City of Glasgow'. McLellan had proved with *Jamie the Saxt* that he was very comfortable with Scottish history. Mary Stuart had long since exercised the minds and imaginations of the literary world, but on the stage, she continued to defy all efforts to do her justice. The Citizens' production was no exception. The *Glasgow Herald* critic labelled the play more of a 'historical discussion' than a drama. Whilst McLellan's deft handling of the Scots tongue was unstintingly lauded, the real enthusiasm was reserved for the production and the acting. Lennox Milne's powerful performance in the title role gained all round admiration. This was the play that Macrae had declared he particularly wanted to do, as he was attracted by the minor but important role of Maitland. According to *The Scotsman*, Macrae 'imbued him with all the suavity and ruthlessness the author had in mind'. But he was criticized in the *Glasgow Herald* for a tendency to overdo the 'sliminess', and the *Evening News* confessed expectations of a character 'more subtle and sinister'.

There is no doubt that Casson's tenure at the Royal Princess's had been a creative and largely harmonious one. He proved himself not only as a director of some vision but also as a tactful and thoughtful link between actors and management, an indispensable prerequisite, especially for an Englishman working in Scotland. During his time in Glasgow, he had evolved a method of working with Macrae. To ensure that his own ideas would be included in Macrae's work, Casson would casually insinuate his notion into conversation, taking care never to make it a subject for formal discussion. Macrae usually picked up the idea and introduced it into the role. This resulted in a very harmonious actor/director relationship. In his farewell speech to the Citizens' Theatre Society, Casson claimed that it was not a bad thing for an essentially Scottish company to have a Sassenach producer. He hoped that the company would not become just another British rep and that word would spread that the Citizens' was the Scottish theatre. It did not work out quite like that.

As soon as Casson's intention to quit Glasgow had circulated around the enclosed theatre community, there was a rash of suggestions, and even volunteers, for his replacement. There was a circuit of repertory theatres in Britain all working to a pattern similar to the Citizens' and directors moved readily from company to company as the opportunities arose. The Board canvassed suggestions for the post. Amongst the proposals they received were Michael Langham from Birmingham Rep, Peter Potter from Salisbury Playhouse and André van Gysegham who had been working at Nottingham. Peter Potter was appointed. Significantly, at no time was there any suggestion that a Scottish director might be found, although amateur Scottish directors, including Michael Finlay and Avrom Greenbaum of the Glasgow Jewish Institute Players, offered their services. An opportunity to develop Scottish directorial skills was missed.

Bridie or no Bridie, the show had to go on. Before Potter took up his appointment, there was interesting work scheduled for some of the company during the summer months, not least of which was the prospect of making a television film. Although the film industry recognized Macrae as a reliable character actor, he had not yet ventured into the infant television world. The BBC had planned to film a production, directed by Matthew Forsyth, of Bridie's *The Baikie Charivari*. It was to be broadcast in August with the Citizens' actors Macrae, Lennox Milne and Fulton Mackay in the cast. Advance arrangements had even been made, at the beginning of August, for the Scottish players rehearsing *The Three Estates* to fly to London for filming. But long before it could reach that stage, on 20 June, Gordon Irving reported in the *Daily Record*, the sudden cancellation of the broadcast. One of the reasons offered was that the Scottish dialogue might prove to be incomprehensible to audiences on the national network. Disappointment was natural, but there was nothing to be done.

That year, in recognition of their contribution to the Edinburgh Festival, Macrae and Lennox Milne were accorded the honour of being invited to deliver Robert Kemp's farewell oration at the Festival's closing ceremony. It was a grand occasion, backed by the Hallé Orchestra conducted by Sir John Barbirolli. *The Three Estates* company then went to Glasgow for the long awaited production of the play in St Andrew's Halls, which the BBC recorded and broadcast on radio in September.

Potter's first winter season began with Miles Malleson's version of Molière's *Tartuffe*. Macrae yet again proved his affinity with the French comedy style. Ironically, he would have been unable to have the pleasure of seeing the Comédie-Française's production, which came to Edinburgh and Glasgow in July 1945, as he was then on the Continent with the E.N.S.A. tour of *The Forrigan Reel*. The reviews were very favourable, praising Macrae for bringing to the role of the arch hypocrite exactly the right degree of sanctimonious humbug. But the more discerning eye spotted an inclination to play for easy laughs. There is no doubt that part of the problem was that the audience now greeted his every entrance with merriment. Macrae sometimes found it impossible to resist playing up to their expectations. This must have made it difficult for the rest of the cast to maintain an even balance. But an actor of James Cairncross's calibre was more than up to this kind of challenge, providing the perfect foil as the readily deluded Orgon. Yvonne Coulette returned to Glasgow to play Elmire and Madeleine Christie played Madame Pernelle, backed by Molly Urquhart as Dorine, Stanley Baxter as Damis, Andrew Keir as Cléante and Marillyn Gray as Flipote. The company then revived *Bachelors* with Cairncross playing the undertaker and Andrew Keir the Bailie. Macrae was not available to take the part as he was about to go on one of his 'temporary leaves of absence' to make a film.

You're Only Young Twice, a screen version of Bridie's play, *What Say They?* was described by Bridie as a 'university frolic'. The play, which had been previously produced at the Malvern Festival in 1939 by H.K. Ayliff with Yvonne Arnaud and Alastair Sim, recounts the tale of a university janitor who is chosen as rector by the students. Macrae was cast as the janitor. The film was produced by a company called Group 3, headed by John Grierson. Group 3 was London-based but the film crew spent two weeks shooting in and around Glasgow University with a cast which included Roddy McMillan, Molly Urquhart, Patrick Barr and Robert Urquhart. Five hundred students were recruited to take part in a rectorial procession along Kelvin Way, while notable Scots were hired to play members of the senate. An amusing feature of the Kelvin Way parade was a huge life-like plaster cast of Macrae's head, carried shoulder high by the students. Filming was completed in the Southall studio, but the rushes were screened every night at the Cosmo Cinema in Glasgow. Macrae's fee was £1,000.

By the beginning of December, Macrae was back in the Alhambra rehearsing the comic villain role of M'Abanazar, an out-of-work local magician. *Aladdin* opened to good notices. Still not quite top-billing, Macrae was blending perfectly with the well-seasoned Harry Gordon-Alec Finlay comedy team. Material was nevertheless being specially written to suit his particular brand of comic gift. The *Glasgow Herald* of 10 December pointed out that, 'There are many Glasgow and district allusions, a song about Sauchiehall Street and Duncan Macrae adding a salty local flavour as M'Abanazar.'

At the handsome salary of £100 a week, Macrae settled into the comfort of the sixteen-week run. Working in pantomime is not an easy option. The demands of the performance schedule, with matinées and sometimes extra charity shows, is exacting in the extreme. The sheer physical effort involved in timing exits and entrances, the frantic costume changes and the acrobatic moves would tax even the fittest of athletes. It was not a problem for Macrae whose addiction to physical fitness stood him in good stead.

Across the river Stanley Baxter was making the critics sit up and take notice in The Citizens' Christmas show, *The Happy Ha'penny*, confirming him as the worthy successor to Macrae.

The 1950-1 season turned out to be the last season in which the Citizens' could claim Macrae as one of their regular company members. The only 'outside' contract was the Alhambra one. But with the pantomime season taking up fully four months, he was available for only half of their repertoire which included works by Goldsmith, Christopher Fry, Shakespeare, James Thurber and a Scottish writer, Murray McClymont. For Macrae, the Citizens' as a platform for furthering Scottish theatrical horizons now seemed to have outlived its usefulness, in particular as Casson's successor was yet another Englishman. Yet Potter and the Board still pursued a policy of including a fair proportion of old and

A Dame for all Seasons

new Scottish plays. During his two seasons in Glasgow, Potter produced no fewer than nine new works by Scottish authors. Macrae fared well under his direction, turning in sterling performances in *Tartuffe*, *Our Town* and a revival of *Gog and Magog*.

But despite Potter's artistic achievements, the fact that he was English and that, when he saw fit, he invited English actors to join the company, was enough to alienate certain members of the company. A discernible schism appeared which included on one side such Scots as Andrew Keir, Roddy McMillan, Stanley Baxter and Macrae and the English 'imports' on the other. George Coulouris, for example, was invited to join the company to play Lear, and the local actors with the skills to play the major leading roles resented being passed over. It seemed to them that the essential Scottishness which was so lovingly, if sometimes stormily, fostered by Bridie and the old guard was being whittled away. The fact that Bridie was no longer about casting a benevolent eye on all the proceedings left many feeling exposed and vulnerable. Elspeth Cochrane, the company's first stage-manager at the Athenaeum, was now married to Peter Potter. When she arrived with him in Glasgow in the autumn, she was asked to write an article for *The Prompter*, describing her feelings on returning to Glasgow. She summed up the feelings of many people:

> There is only one thing to make me sad. It is a little like coming home and finding the Master of the House away. I cannot reconcile myself to the fact that Doctor Mavor [Bridie] is no longer here. It is a gap that no one else could ever fill.

With Bridie and Casson gone, something of the 'Camelot' spirit had irretrievably slipped away from the Citizens'.

125

— 8 —

BARNSTORMING ROUND SCOTLAND

The Scottishows experiment

The time now seemed ripe for Macrae to launch into the realization of *his* version of the cherished national theatre dream. What better way to prove his faith in the viability a Scottish theatre than to form his own company where he would have total artistic control? To this end, he had been making plans with his friend, Tim Watson, for some time and when *Aladdin*'s run at the Alhambra finished at the end of March, Macrae announced their intention to form a new company, Scottishows. The gradual 'Anglicizing' of the Citizens' was not the only reason for Macrae's belief in the need for a different kind of theatre for Scotland. But the evident encroachment of English influence, confirmed for him that this was the most opportune moment to strike out again in the name of the cause. At the heart of this belief were two fundamentals: first, to champion native playwrights and, second, to take plays to those people who had no access to mainstream professional theatre, by travelling the country from the far north to the Borders. The concept was to form a company of Scottish actors who would go on the road with one Scottish play for an extended season. This had two significant consequences. The first was that Scottishows would provide employment for actors during the closed season in repertory. The second was that any actor in Macrae's company, himself included, was effectively ruled out of being part of the official Festival programme as the season for the new company was planned to begin in late summer and run into the autumn. As early as January 1952, Mamie Crichton, one of Scotland's leading theatre critics, discussing the possible Scottish content of

126

that year's Festival, pointed out that actors like Macrae 'could not afford to mark time' on the chance they would be invited to be part of the official programme. As it turned out, when the Festival Society eventually invited Macrae to play in their Assembly Hall production of *The Highland Fair*, it was too late.

Messrs Scottishows Productions was formed with £1,000 capital, invested by Watson and Macrae from their personal savings. The first contracts were signed on 22 March, between the artists/employees and T.M. Watson, manager. These were standard Esher contracts which stated the weekly salary and included the clause, 'Travel provided'. The small company included Macrae himself, Jean Taylor Smith and Nell Ballantyne who were the highest paid members at £25 and £20 respectively, James Stuart, Jack Maguire, Norah Irvine and Frances Slaven at salaries between £10 and £12, two stage-managers, Russell Hunter and Anthony McFadyen, and two assistants stage-managers, Hugh Evans and Ethel Philpotts. They were to go into rehearsal in July and open at Paisley in August. Earlier, quite by chance, Macrae met Nicholas Parsons in the Piccadilly Club in Glasgow. They had not seen each other since the very first Citizens' production in 1943. Macrae invited him to join the new company. Parsons was tempted. But after serious consideration he decided to remain in London.

In the meantime, there were still seven months between the end of *Aladdin*'s run and the Scottishows' opening. Macrae returned to fulfil his commitment to the Citizens' to play in *Our Town* in April and in a revival of *Gog and Magog* in May. He was then free to take up Geoffrey Edwards's invitation to play Harry Magog with Dundee Repertory. Edwards had issued the invitation in 1951, but it was not until 1952 that Macrae was available to accept. When Macrae confirmed that he could go to Dundee in June, Geoffrey Edwards said that he hoped that it would be the forerunner of many exchanges between the leading Scottish repertory theatres. It was an attractive notion. Macrae was in Dundee for *Gog and Magog* during June. He then went into hospital to have a sinus operation for a condition that had been troubling him for some time. Fully restored to fitness, he was ready for the challenge of his latest role as actor-manager, that most romantic of theatrical figures who had risen to prominence during the nineteenth century: Macrae was about to join an illustrious line of actor-managers which runs from Irving, Kean, Macready and Beerbohm Tree down to Wolfit and Wilson Barrett.

There was never much doubt that the first Scottishows production would be a success. Astutely, Macrae and Watson had chosen Watson's *Bachelors Are Bold* for the inaugural production, for it had already proved hugely popular with Scottish audiences. Premièred at the Citizens' in November 1951 while Macrae was engaged in filming *You're Only Young Twice*, it had played to packed houses. That it was an established and firm favourite with amateur companies around the country was further guarantee of a good following. Nevertheless, leaving nothing to chance, Scottishows embarked on a highly sophisticated advance publicity programme. It was announced with pride that the entire production was 100% authentically Scottish. Not only was the cast Scottish, but the furniture was designed and made in Scotland, the set was built by a Scottish joiner and painted by a Scottish artist. Carpets and curtains were similarly home produced — every detail, down to cigarettes and stockings bore the label 'Made in Scotland'. (A fine large mushroom coloured carpet eventually found its way from the set into the Macraes' home at Queens Park Avenue.) The single exception, regretfully admitted, was that for obvious reasons Scotland's national drink had to be substituted by coloured water. All the human interest stories that could be teased out to whet the public's appetite were exploited in full. Amongst the company recruits was an eighteen-year old Glasgow University student, Frances Slaven, whom Macrae had discovered at Rutherglen Repertory Theatre. Permission was granted for leave of absence from classes and she posed for press photographs with 'former schoolmaster Duncan Macrae', supposedly acting as her temporary tutor. Likewise, the public was informed that James Copeland, who was originally booked for the tour, had been offered a film part in Paris and that the Unity actor, Russell Hunter, had given up an opportunity to act and stage-manage in television to replace him in the *Bachelors* company.

That first tour was a triumphal progress. With the exception of Edinburgh, where they played for the three-week duration of the Festival, they played one week at each stop on the itinerary. Excited anticipation was generated with such consummate skill that by the opening night of the tour on 4 August, the theatre in Paisley, hitherto hardly a mainstream attraction, was the focus of attention for anyone in Scotland with any interest at all in drama. Paisley box-office records were smashed and they played to rapturous reviews. With Macrae heading the cast, the people of Paisley were assured of 'comedy at its best'. It was a proud start to the enterprise.

Macrae was now a celebrity. Taking advantage of the readily available platform for lectures and speeches expected of a 'star', he proceeded to air his unorthodox views on everything from films to the policies of the Edinburgh Festival directors. He launched a vociferous campaign on behalf of an authentic Scottish voice for Scottish culture. Nothing was sacred. With the confidence born of success, he won new friends but doubtless made new enemies, endearing and alienating, entertaining and shocking by turn. Most of his friends and associates never doubted the sincerity of his opinions. But the cynics preferred to interpret some of the more outrageous challenges to mainstream policy as clever publicity. During the run of *Bachelors* at Perth, in a brief ten minute personal appearance at the Alhambra Cinema to promote the film *You're Only Young Twice*, he attacked the attempts of London-based companies to produce a truly Scottish film, asserting, 'I am always wanting to see, and I am still demanding to see, a film unit established in Scotland capable of making feature pictures.'

His goal was a film in which all the credits would be Scottish and the essentials of the Scottish character would not be 'unnaturally expressed'. He cited the difficulties the Scottish-born film director, Alexander McKendrick, had in wheedling, from English managers and executives, the means to achieve the effects he wanted when he was making *Whisky Galore*. He held up, as example, the small Edinburgh unit that made *Auld Tam Maguire*, which in his opinion was far funnier in twenty minutes than *Whisky Galore* in seventy. This small budget film in the Mack Sennet style had been made for the Edinburgh optical company of Campbell Harper while Macrae was working in the Dundee production of *Gog and Magog*. All the *Gog* cast was hired to work for a very small fee on location in the enormous houses built by the Dundee jute barons. They filmed either in the morning, or from lunch-time until half-past four in the afternoon, so that the actors would be back in the theatre in time for curtain-up. The rushes were viewed late at night and if there were problems, the actors were simply called back for re-takes and earned another £5.

After the week in Perth they moved on to three glorious weeks at the Palladium during the Edinburgh Festival. The *Sunday Mail* reported that once again all box-office records had been smashed and that, for the third successive week, attendance figures in different parts of the country had been beaten.

There is little doubt that certain branches of theatre felt threatened by the popular success of Macrae's formula. The closed summer season in the legitimate theatre was filled traditionally by popular variety shows. Macrae was quite conscious of this and he was reported in the *Perthshire Advertiser*, on 13 August, as telling the first-house audience at Perth that his company offered no excuses for challenging these variety shows: 'We think we can beat them.' Whether or not Macrae initially set out to go into competition with such shows, or with the Edinburgh Festival, can never be known. What is evident is that, over the four years of its existence, in box-office terms, Scottishows did consciously rival the official Festival attractions. On several occasions, Macrae joined battle publicly with the Festival administration over planning policies.

Playing in Edinburgh during Festival time was a masterly stroke as all the reputable critics, who would not normally have covered Scottish productions throughout the year, were there. Scottishows' *Bachelors* was booked as a Fringe production. In the 1950s the Fringe programme at the Festival was tiny in comparison to the way it has since mushroomed. Consequently, the best of the Fringe received a fair proportion of national press coverage. Watson's play was praised as a fine example of 'popular art' and Macrae was the focus of mainstream critical attention. *The Spectator* described him as 'the great comedian', *The Observer* reported that Macrae 'triumphantly rides the storm of small-town comedy' and the *Manchester Guardian* urged anyone who had previously been impressed by his 'Pardoner' in *The Three Estates* to see the production and savour this performance too:

> The long-drawn out melancholia glooming from his countenance, the attenuated limbs which might jerk like a puppet's into postures impossible to an ordinarily articulated man, the sorrowful crane call of his voice, his natural attributes are married to rare skill in projection and timing. But to describe the audience's reaction to his mere appearance, one falls back on such vague phrases as 'animal magnetism'. He is a noble clown.

Some of the Scottish press was more carping in its approach, inferring a competitive undertone to the Scottishows enterprise. An article in the *Evening Dispatch*, 16 August, lavished praise on Macrae and Watson for their efforts to put Scottish dramatists on the 'theatrical map', but made critical observation on Macrae's personal decision to play the undertaker at the Palladium instead of appearing at the Assembly Hall — which still echoed to his Pardoner and Flatterie in *The Three Estates*.

The ambiguity of this comment tended to imply that to play in the Palladium was an engagement inferior to appearing at the Assembly Hall and that Macrae was working in a trivial role. Macrae was not insensible to these implications for the *Glasgow Herald* reported that, in his curtain speech at the last show in the Palladium, he countered:

> Although most of our cast have been previously associated with the 'ace show' of the Festival [*The Three Estates*], we have no such pretensions, and we are quite happy to be regarded as the 'joker'.

Macrae's curtain speeches were fast becoming a feature of the Festival. Never twice the same and rarely 'thank you and goodnight', he frequently used the intimate moment between stage and auditorium to reveal, in witty innuendoes, his true feelings about a current topic. His cynical perspective on the 'culture' ethos of the Festival was demonstrated after one show when, calling on all his mastery of the deadpan delivery, he gave the solemn assurance that he would return to next year's Festival with another novelty — a version of Shaw's *Man and Superman*, including the famous Hell scene — on ice. The satire was not lost on the startled but delighted audience.

Firmly established in the public mind as an authoritative arbiter of culture, Macrae continued to be sought after to deliver lectures to establishment societies and institutions. Under the auspices of the British Film Institute and the Scottish Film Council, a series of lectures entitled, 'The Art of the Film', was delivered at the 1952 Festival by a series of prestigious film makers. Macrae was accorded the singular honour of giving the final lecture which he chose to devote to film, the Festival and the Scotch comic. Needless to say he attracted the most colourful press, with banner headlines quoting his assertions about his 'rotten films'. His comment was doubtless calculated to be provocative. Macrae charged weak directors, lack of money and courage with the responsibility of producing poor films, claiming 'most of the films I have been in did not satisfy me'. He concluded his lecture with the hope that he still might 'have the privilege of appearing in a good picture'.

Arrogance or truth, such controversial outbursts neither inhibited him from taking up film offers nor directors from making them. In the same lecture, he dismissed the Festival as 'furtive and ephemeral' and claimed that some people thought of the Scotch comic as the only real theatrical expression of the Scots. *His* objective was to bring the tradition of the Scots comic to the legitimate stage. His constantly reiterated belief that the spoken word from the stage was the most effective way of keeping the Scots language vigorously alive and that in touring *Bachelors* he was creating a market for Scottish playwrights, testified to his single-minded quest for drama for the people of Scotland. But if, on the one hand, he galvanized both the establishment and the public into action by shock and controversy, on the other, he quietly pursued his goals by his own words and deeds. In another lecture, he admitted that in addition to furthering the cause of native drama, the Scottishows company had been formed to subsidize regular returns to the kind of roles which earned less money but had brought him fame. He declared openly that he was prepared to capitalize on the Scottish appetite for pawky Scots comedy. For a time the two reasons Macrae claimed for the existence of Scottishows were not incompatible.·

Edinburgh had been an amazing experience. No one could recall such queues at the box office. Macrae had also proved that he could beat the traditional Scottish summer variety show at its own game. Riding on the crest of the wave of popularity, the little band of players struck the set once again and moved on to Dundee, Hawick, Dunfermline, Falkirk, Greenock and Ayr, criss-crossing up and down the country from north to south and from east to west. They made one cautious move across the Borders to Carlisle, having made some judicious alterations to the more obscure Scotticisms in the script. They were welcomed with warm politeness in contrast to the wilder euphoria they had become accustomed to on home territory. The *Cumberland Evening News* review rather condescendingly admitted it to be 'a modest but refreshing little comedy, a far cry from the hilarious comedies so common nowadays, but just as good in its own way'.

Coming into Glasgow at the beginning of November, Macrae was slightly apprehensive about playing once again to his 'ain folk'. He need not have worried. The week at the King's Theatre was sold out in advance. While the popular appeal was never in question, certain reservations were voiced in the press that Macrae was 'at times too prone to use the grotesque mechanics of pantomime'. This criticism, however, was tempered by praising his generosity in giving the 'meatiest' role to fellow actor, Paul Curran.

The Scottishows Glasgow date gives rise to the question whether or not Macrae saw himself in competition with his old employer. If there ever was any rivalry between Macrae's enterprise and the Citizens', it was never allowed to become overt. But given the ripples and nuances of discontent that were ruffling the smoother surfaces of the relationships of management and artists at the Royal Princess's, it cannot be entirely discounted that such disturbances were a contributory factor to Macrae's decision to break more definitively with the Citizens' than the act of signing the Tom Arnold pantomime contract in 1950 entailed in itself.

In autumn that year, while Macrae was totally engaged in Scottishows, the Citizens' mounted a Bridie Memorial season that opened with Alastair Sim and George Cole in *The Anatomist*, followed by *The Golden Legend of Shults* and *The Baikie Charivari*. It must have seemed strange that Macrae was not on stage to celebrate the memory of his irrepressible sponsor.

At the time, there was a major division between the members of the Citizens' Board over policy. One group was determined to carry the Scottish playwrights' torch ever further aloft by imposing on the audience, plays that the Board believed were dramatically and aesthetically worthy, regardless of the crucial element of potential box-office appeal. The other group was more cautious. No repertory company can afford the luxury of continual experiment. Ironically, when Macrae's bandwagon rolled into home territory, the Citizens' were playing a verse drama by a young unknown playwright, Ian Dallas. Dallas's *A Masque of Summer*, pitched on a cultural plane light-years from the vernacular high jinks of the Scottish funeral parlour, could only be described as a 'flop'. Headlines in the *Daily Mail*, hinting that the two plays could 'divide theatre land', implied the latent sense of competition between slapstick and drama.

Both plays closed on the same night. The critics gave *A Masque of Summer* good notices, the actors thought highly of it, but as Bridie used to say, 'the audiences stayed away in their thousands'. It should have run for another week. The contrast with Macrae's success could hardly have been greater. *Bachelors* played to full houses. The bookings for Glasgow alone recouped the partners' original capital outlay. It was claimed that by the end of the tour the show had played to more than 150,000 people — a record for any similar Scottish tour. Watson believed that their success was due to the public's love of a good laugh. When 'sold out' notices dominated Scottishows entire three weeks at

Edinburgh, Macrae was quoted as saying, 'Don't offer the people art. Don't mention the drama or even the theatre — it frightens them away.'

The Citizens' Board, perturbed by the experience of such a failure felt obliged to make a statement in its own defence. The chairman, Norman Duthie, still affirmed unshaken belief in their professed play policy, while more or less accepting the responsibility for failing to build up sufficient trust in their judgements. He warned that if the Citizens' should collapse as a result of lack of support, it would take at least another twenty-five years before a similar enterprise could be started again in Glasgow. The irony lay in the fact that Macrae and the Citizens' both held the same goal of building a thriving Scottish theatre. The difference was that to win his audience, Macrae was happy to follow the 'custard pie route', as one review described it, and the Citizens' were not prepared to compromise their stated ideals. On his own terms Macrae could be well satisfied with his small victory. His instincts had been correct. In the final analysis, the box office, as always, was his vindicator.

Macrae told the columnist W.T. Foster that after three and a half months of touring, his tired but jubilant company was thoroughly accustomed to playing on any kind of stage. As regular theatres were not always available in the smaller towns, the company learned to play in anything from platforms in town halls to the narrow strips of stage in front of cinema screens. The technical facilities available were as varied as the playing spaces. Some venues had virtually none. The fundamental concept of touring entails fit-ups and get-outs of the scenery and props, all requiring great speed and maximum efficiency. Few companies could afford to travel with a large crew of stage-hands. In those days, everyone, actors included, willingly joined in to help. For the younger members of the company, the touring exercise was very much part of an invaluable process of learning about theatre, absorbing the values of commitment and team work.

The first tour ended in Aberdeen in the second week of November. It had been an unequivocal success. Critics, from the staidest of national broadsheets to the more sensational tabloids, were unanimous and unreserved in their praise. For the actors, the tour had meant financial and personal sacrifices in terms of gaining wider recognition, as they were committed to the tour for so many weeks. Macrae himself had turned down attractive work. The company disbanded with memories of exhausting travel, thwarted attempts to spend weekends at home with families, and of coping with the tensions of awaiting delivery of props, scenery and costume. There were also many lighter moments to be remembered. The classic nightmare of the on-stage mishap occurred at Hawick. A grandfather clock fell down with a great crash. To their credit, and to the delight of an astonished audience, the actors improvised skilfully around the accident. When the company broke up, the exhilaration and enthusiasm was such that, under the direction of Tony McFadyen, some actors regrouped during the winter months, to tour Watson's *The Wee Red Lums* to Invernesshire, Banffshire, Aberdeenshire, Perthshire, Dumfriesshire, and Ross and Cromarty

Macrae had been fêted at every stop. He was inundated with invitations to open anything from factories to charity bazaars; he was the guest of honour at dinners, lunches and teas; he addressed Rotary Clubs and amateur drama societies; he presented prizes, wrote articles, judged beauty contests; received vast quantities of unsolicited gifts of home-made fudge, tablet and jams; he was the authority sought by all and his opinions were cited and quoted daily. What Macrae ate, wore and thought had become the objects of a seemingly insatiable curiosity fostered by the press. He appeared to enjoy it all unashamedly. At the same time, refusing to conform to any particular image, he remained quite uninhibited from expressing himself with all the acid bluntness for which he was now notorious.

Scottishows passed the first hurdle with flying colours. Macrae and Watson shared the profits of £4,259. The company was solvent and it seemed justifiable to contemplate a second season.

Macrae celebrated his return to the extravagant world of pantomime by sharing top billing with Harry Gordon and Alec Finlay in *Jack and the Beanstalk*. His solo spots were now recognized as something special, standing out as they did amidst the traditional music hall humour. That Christmas (1952) his stranded cyclist, calling for his mate Humphrey was hailed as 'a little masterpiece of authentic local comedy'.

Competition came from Stanley Baxter in *Cinderella* at the Royal, *A Glaikit Spell* at the Citizens', *Humpty Dumpty* with Arthur Haynes at the Pavilion and Jack Hylton's production of *Call me Madam* at the King's. The Empire produced *Robinson Crusoe* — on ice. Macrae, earning the princely sum of £150 a week, was set for the run of the show until the end of February. He was then booked to play the 'wisest fool in Christendom' once more, in *Jamie the Saxt* at the Citizens', where Michael Langham — another Englishman — had succeed Peter Potter as director.

Now billed 'guest artist', Macrae was treated to an appreciative and enthusiastic welcome home to the Gorbals by his adoring public. He was supported by a strong cast which included Madeleine Christie, James Gibson, Roddy McMillan, Andrew Keir and Iris Russell. The press, enthusiastic over the merits of his performance, was nevertheless becoming direct in its criticism of what it perceived as 'exaggerated buffoonery' exploited in the service of cheap laughs. The more discerning reviewers summed up what many had feared would happen as a result of the continued exposure to the techniques of the variety stage. *The Scotsman* observed on 30 March:

> When guest artist Duncan Macrae depicted the astute and plot-plagued Scots ruler six years ago, he made him largely a figure of fun — much more so than a reading of Mr McLellan's work would indicate. There is no modification in his latest characterization, and theatregoers unaware of Mr Macrae's recent activities would not be awarded a prize for percipience in guessing that they had been spent on the pantomime stage. No opportunity for laughter is misused.

Some reviews harked back with nostalgia to the Curtain's 1937 production. Had Macrae made a mistake to retrace his steps? Were the criticisms valid? It is impossible to judge if these criticisms had any effect on his subsequent development and professional judgement. It was becoming clear that while his comic gift was as inspired as ever, he seemed to be developing a loss of control which jeopardized the credibility of characterization.

At the end of April, the family finances were healthy enough for Macrae and Peggy to spend a few days in London on one of their rare holidays. May was devoted to planning and arranging the next Scottishows tour. Another play by Watson, *Johnny Jouk the Gibbet*, was the 1953 choice. The previous year a one-act version of the play, *Hangman's Noose*, had been broadcast on radio with Macrae heading the cast. The tour arrangements were completed and Macrae was ready to take up his next film contract in *The Kidnappers* which was to win him an even greater and more permanent audience.

Philip Leacock, the British director noted in Halliwell's film directory as 'having a way with children', first met Macrae in 1952 when in Glasgow, casting for Grierson's Group Three production of *The Brave Don't Cry*, a documentary about a Scottish mining disaster. Leacock was impressed by Macrae who was, however, not available when shooting was scheduled to begin. The following year, when under the banner of J. Arthur Rank Productions, casting for *The Kidnappers* began, Leacock unhesitatingly suggested Macrae for the leading role in the tale of the two small boys — grandsons of a Scottish immigrant family in Nova Scotia — who kidnap a baby.

There was no difficulty in persuading the producers that Macrae was exactly right for the part of the sternly awesome grandfather, despite his forty-eight years and the need for elaborate ageing make-up. The English actress, Jean Anderson, who had played the wife in *The Brave Don't Cry* was a less obvious choice for the grandmother. The executive producers were more dubious about this but Leacock wanted her and he eventually prevailed. If casting Macrae opposite Anderson was well justified, the choice of the two small children was nothing short of inspirational.

Margaret Thomson (now Ashe) was a documentary director and scriptwriter who had previously made a film about children for John Grierson. Discussing this later with Leacock, she realized that she had been mistaken in not coaching the children before filming. On the strength of that conversation, Leacock asked her to work on *The Kidnappers*. The search for two small boys was on. Patiently visiting all the infant schools in Aberdeen, Margaret Thomson finally found two likely lads, John Whitley, aged 6, who had already made a television film, *The Owl and the Pussycat*, and Vincent Winter, aged four — the face of an impish cherub and all the style to go with it. Macrae, no mean exponent of the art of up-staging, was subjected to the rare experience of being up-staged himself by this unselfconsciously artless waif who persistently stole scene after scene. Much of the credit for the children's performance went to Margaret Thomson who worked tirelessly with them, gaining their confidence. Vincent had to learn his lines by repetition because he could not yet read. Both children worked well with their film grandparents, immediately comfortable with Jean Anderson. But Vincent never could quite reconcile the gentle mild-mannered off-screen Macrae with the gruff, forbidding, bearded grandfather figure. Off the set he was not really afraid of Macrae, but he was wary of him and this wariness transmitted itself into his role. On screen, this relationship sparked off an incomparably magical chemistry. Leacock obtained many of his best natural shots of the children by letting the camera run after the scripted scene was finished.

The sheer strength of Macrae's performance however, could not be overshadowed and he delivered one of the finest character studies he ever created. Unfortunately, one of the most memorable scenes in the film between Macrae and Vincent ended on the cutting room floor because it was deemed not to work in the context of the film. The older boy had taken ill and when the relevant scene was shot, it had to be faked without him. The grandfather was trying to explain to the small boy why it was wrong to turn the horses loose. The anguish that he felt when he realized he could not communicate with the child, was brilliantly handled during the dialogue between the tall, gaunt man in black wide-brimmed hat and the wide-eyed, upturned, innocent face of the very small boy. When the cast saw the 'rushes' they could scarcely contain their laughter and tears.

Macrae's reputation as a difficult actor to work with had preceded him. The expectations were well and truly confounded when he was found to take direction easily. His technique derived a great deal of benefit from the discipline imposed by the camera. Playing Macrae's wife, Jean Anderson, who in addition to coping with the ageing process — her forty to the grandmother's sixty —, was extremely nervous of the authenticity of her accent which she based on three Scottish spinster aunts. She was anxious not to falter during the initial script readings with this doyen of the Scottish stage. Her fears were not realized. Macrae was unfailingly patient and courteous to work with, impressing the entire cast and crew as a reticent man who eschewed the glamour and superficial glitter of the film world.

The film interiors were shot at Pinewood Studios. Some location shots were filmed in Scotland at Glen Affric and on the wooded slopes of Glen Morriston. The other exteriors were filmed in Black Park near the studios. Gregory Peck was filming *The Million Pound Note* at Pinewood at the same time as *The Kidnappers* crew were working there. The vast budget film took up most of the studio space and dressing rooms with its huge cast, lavish sets and exquisite period costumes. Its set was filled with the leading theatrical ladies of England, all happily crowding in to play small parts with the Hollywood hero. The contrast between it and Leacock's modest production with Macrae, Anderson, Adrienne Corri, Theodor Bickel and the two children in their humble homespun was unavoidable.

Jean Anderson found Macrae to be a shy man. She noticed that after the first day's filming, when they went into the restaurant where the stars dined, he was taken aback by the superficially exotic atmosphere. Thereafter, he insisted on eating in the canteen with the crew. It was only after some time that he could be persuaded to join his fellow actors for an occasional drink.

The film was a huge box-office success. In North America, re-titled *The Little Kidnappers*, it played to packed houses. For the first time, as he went about his everyday private life, Macrae experienced the price of widespread recognition by his new film-going public as they identified him with the role. He learned to deal comfortably with incidents such as the one when he was challenged bravely and defiantly in the street by a small child demanding to know what he had done to little Davy in the woodshed. But the compensations outweighed the drawbacks. The contract was worth £1,300. When the film was released in America in December 1954, it won an award as 'Best Picture of the Month for the Whole Family' and Macrae was awarded the 'Box Office Blue Ribbon' for his role as the grandfather in *The Little Kidnappers*.

Rehearsals for the second Scottishows play began at the end of July when filming *The Kidnappers* was completed. Tim Watson's *Johnny Jouk the Gibbet* is a macabre joke about the difficulties of filling the post of hangman, based on the Glasgow Corporation Minutes of 1605. The problem is solved by a prisoner volunteering for the job. Macrae was cast as the Town Provost. Once again Macrae wisely chose a play guaranteed to please the world of amateur theatre, from which much of his audiences would be drawn. There was considerable irony and paradox in this choice, considering the frequency of his attacks on the sincerity and integrity of the ranks of amateurs up and down the country — performers and audiences alike. But it seemed that Macrae was so revered that he had licence to say and do as he pleased.

The planned tour route was shorter than the previous year, with only eight stops — Perth, Edinburgh, Hawick, Falkirk, Greenock, Aberdeen, Ayr and Glasgow — compared to the thirteen of the first enterprise. While the tour around the country was very successful most of the publicity again centred on the Scottishows appearance at Edinburgh. There was certainly a great deal of advance speculation about the 1953 tour and many of the predictions were made in the context of the Festival.

A strong company was formed from the first year's nucleus with Eric Woodburn and Doris McLatchie replacing Jean Taylor Smith and Jack Maguire. Jimmy Gibson was to direct despite the persistent rumours that Gibson and Macrae conducted a running feud on stage. It can only be deduced that, in reality, they had a mutual respect for each other's capabilities. The costumes were designed by the Glasgow cartoonist, Coia. Interviewed on the set of *The Kidnappers*, Macrae said he expected Watson's new comedy to be as funny as the previous one. He also revealed that a London West End production was planned by Tom Arnold for *Bachelors* following its success in the previous year, as soon as a date could be fixed to suit his [Macrae's] engagements. That production never happened.

Johnny Jouk the Gibbet opened to enthusiastic reviews at Perth. On the road, actors were treated as celebrities. Macrae, as in the previous year, was eagerly sought to give talks, write articles, open fêtes, visit factories, all of which he did in the best of regal styles. Scottishows took up a three-week residency in the Palladium Theatre.

The 1953 success in Edinburgh was not for want of competition in the official drama programme. Richard Burton was playing in *Hamlet* at the Assembly Hall, Margaret Leighton and Denholm Elliot opened in T.S. Eliot's latest play, *The Confidential Clerk* — one caustic columnist snidely remarking that all the best people would be courteously slitting each other's throats to get good seats for *that* opening night — and Marcel Marceau was playing in *L'Avare* with the Théâtre National Populaire of France. While the audience for these plays might well be attracted to the Palladium, the hard core of Macrae's following was unlikely to want to sample the other, more rarefied, forms of drama. The twice-nightly schedule at the Palladium was tough, even though they played a shorter version than they used for a single performance. The Edinburgh routine was extremely rigorous for Macrae in particular, as he was contracted to make a nightly guest appearance in the London Theatre Group's late night show, *See You Later*.

While the play coasted along on the now familiar tide of delighted approval, Macrae met rather different notices for his début into the more intimate medium of revue. In theory it was a good move to widen his audience, for the late night revue-goer is quite another animal from the average theatregoer who patronizes the twice-nightly commercial show. Unhappily, it became the first demonstration of one of Macrae's major weakness, namely his inherent inability to choose material wisely for solo variety performances. It was a weakness which recurred in the choices of work he made throughout the rest of his career. Some of the material he had himself written, was soon cut. Other sketches, by seasoned script writers like Albert Mackie, were more generously received. But the common thread running through the notices, was that his pantomime material was far superior. Although his sense of timing and clowning were as sharp as ever, he was not as comfortable with the more urbane type of humour demanded by the revue medium.

The critics spotted this instantly. Gordon Irving in the *Daily Record*, 26 August, confirmed that:

> By his odd choice of material for revue in Edinburgh, Duncan Macrae proves that he is suited only for certain roles in light comedy and that he is a better actor than a comic.

Macrae himself was well aware of the shortcomings of his stand-up comedy technique. He ruefully conceded to the critic Mamie Crichton that in Edinburgh, he was 'taking one step forward and two steps back'. Other reviewers were kinder, fixing on Macrae's strengths, his 'bright puckish face and gawky charm' and his immaculate sense of timing. But they still noted that he was ill at ease in sophisticated sketches, such as 'La Belle et la Bête noire'. The tour moved on.

They arrived in Glasgow in the last week of October to be ceremoniously received by the Lord Provost, Thomas Kerr at the City Chambers. The enthusiasm was as fervent as ever. There was, however, one lone voice in the *Daily Mail*, reminiscent of the story of the Emperor's New Clothes. The review seemed intent on puncturing the euphoric bubble, daringly suggesting that Macrae perhaps could no longer conjure up his spark of originality:

> The myth is destroyed... it is the same Macrae we have seen so often, and even the gaily coloured civic robes of the period fail to conceal glimpses of the old beer swilling Harry Magog.

It did not matter: the company again showed a profit and in the estimation of the fans, and of most of the critics, Macrae was still a prince among clowns.

It was time again for the winter pantomime routine. Rehearsals, and the usual trips to London for costume fittings in preparation for the grand Alhambra opening of *Babes in the Woods*, filled the weeks before the beginning of December. Alec Finlay and Macrae were now joined by Jack Anthony to make up a team that was applauded for combining their individual talents in merrymaking. Macrae's skill in portraying outraged dignity was likened to his successful Harry Magog, but it was his dazzling character creation, 'Queen of Crossmyloof', a gangling figure, resplendent in spangled tutu and gleaming white buckskin skating boots that became the proverbial 'show-stopper'. It was still his brilliance as a character actor that singled Macrae out from his co-stars, rather than an aptitude to deliver stand-up comedy lines or to indulge in the more purely physical aspects of slapstick.

The pattern continued. After a short break during April, Macrae returned to the Citizens' in May to make his guest appearance in Michael Langham's production of Alexander Scott's comedy, *Right Royal*. As King Dod III of Fife, Macrae was supported to hilarious effect by a superb cast which included Roddy McMillan, Paul Curran, Iris Russell, John Cairney, Madeleine Christie, Fulton Mackay and Ronald Fraser. John Grieve was making his début with the Citizens' as an extra, making up part of Dod's 'ancient, toothless ragged army' at a weekly rate of £6 10s. Macrae stayed on till the end of the month to play George Triple in Bridie's *Meeting at Night* with Madeleine Christie, Robert Urquhart, Iris Russell and Ronald Fraser. Macrae on the Citizens' stage could be depended on to fill the house.

Planning to produce *Gog and Magog* for the next Scottishows tour began early in February. Macrae wrote to Tom Honeyman at Kelvingrove Art Galleries, seeking permission to reproduce a picture of the bronze 'Harry Magog' sculpture by Benno Schotz, which was displayed in the Gallery. He wanted to use it on the cover of throw-away publicity. Honeyman agreed on condition that Schotz also gave his permission. In his reply to Macrae, Honeyman expressed his delight that the next play was to be Bridie's and his irritation 'beyond measure that it isn't a feature of the official festival'.

The actors, contracted each year on a run of the play basis, were signed up by June. The core of the company from the first two seasons came together again with some additions to form a sound working ensemble of players which included Nell Ballantyne, Frances Slaven, Jack Stewart, Norman Welsh and Joan Scott. After rehearsals at Rutherglen, Macrae took three weeks holiday in July before setting off on the road. The tour was made up of nine stops including the now much advertised visit to the Edinburgh Festival during August.

The welcome to the Scottishows company in the towns on the itinerary was as fresh and hearty as ever, with audiences flocking to see their latest offering. Not many people around the country had had an opportunity to see the play's earlier productions, and although a number of critics considered it to be very obscure and unstructured, the bookings were excellent. Macrae maintained his personal powerful box-office magnetism. The choice of the Bridie play could have laid Macrae open to charges of denying his own policy of fostering new Scottish playwrights. But tried favourites make good financial sense. Macrae had the wisdom to capitalize on his recent success in *The Kidnappers*, for throughout the tour he was billed above the play title as 'Scotland's stage and screen star'. At Perth, he was greeted as 'Macrae the Magnificent'.

By the time Scottishows planned its third season, the geographical organization of these tours was inseparable from the context of the Edinburgh Festival. The Scottish flag was shown in the official drama programme by the local Edinburgh company, the Gateway, with Kemp's *That Other Dear Charmer*. The Old Vic produced *A Midsummer Night's Dream* and *Macbeth* at the Assembly Hall and the Lyceum presented Eileen Herlie in *The Matchmaker*. On the Fringe, where Scottishows was again placed, the drama competition was essentially amateur, with the Oxford University Players offering Marlowe's *Edward II* and

Udall's *Ralph Roister Doister* while the S.C.D.A presented plays by Jack Ronder, Graham Moffat and J. Lee-Thompson.

Regardless of whether or not it was Macrae's deliberate policy to score artistically and compete with the official programme by going into Edinburgh during the Festival, commercially it demonstrated his business acumen. Moreover, the company collectively, and Macrae individually, benefited from the publicity generated by their presence in the capital during the three weeks when the city is the focus of international attention. It suited Macrae's purpose very well to be at the centre of healthy debate and controversy.

As always the Festival engagement attracted the major critics, even though *Gog and Magog* was on the Fringe. Serious reviewers were lukewarm about the quality of the play, but the reservations were compensated by the consensus of approval for Macrae's interpretation of the ragged purveyor of philosophy and doggerel. Newspapers sparkled with superlatives: 'Macrae does such honour to Harry Magog'; 'Macrae, the inimitable, the incomparable, the master'. *Punch* magazine published a glowing appreciation of Macrae's long wildly jumbled recitation of Shakespeare, wishing he could be tempted to come more often to London, 'for he is a wonderful exponent of eccentric character'. The article was illustrated by Ronald Searle's cartoon captioned 'Mr Duncan Macrae' — the full title was surely a measure of his standing and reputation.

But when the tour played its final date at Glasgow, despite the 'House Full' notices, *The Bulletin* reiterated what many people had privately come to suspect:

> Time hasn't improved the play but with the years Macrae's performance has broadened and its edge has been blunted. He is still the queer half-inspired, half-daft poet, but there are too many moments when he seem to have strayed from pantomime.

Isolated although such a comment still was, it was beginning to loom ominously over the euphoria that now coloured all Macrae's reviews. The association with pantomime was made too frequently to be ignored. Paradoxically, although his interpretations and performances of the same roles were still outstanding, the fact that Macrae was not attempting anything new began to look dangerously like stagnation. The decisions Macrae and Watson took in determining their policies for Scottishows were, in reality, governed by audience taste. There was a positive logic in repeating the old favourites. In any case, there was little in the way of alternative plays that would make theatre-going accessible and attractive to the taste of the tour audiences. The burning question however, in terms of Macrae's acting, was invariably directed towards the extent to which the pantomime influence was detracting from genuine characterization.

The tour ended in Glasgow in November when Macrae joined Campbell Godly and other actors who had worked with the Citizens' to make a short film, *Heather on Fire*. The film was produced in Scotland by the Music Corporation of America for Billy Graham whose evangelical crusades were sweeping the country. The supporting actors played without fees. Macrae, who played John Knox, received a reduced fee on a daily basis.

The Scottishows company was still Macrae's chief preoccupation, yet the months between the 1954-5 tours were largely taken up by pantomime. *Goldilocks and the Three Bears* at the Alhambra, with Jimmy Logan and Kenneth McKellar, assumed the importance of a necessary interlude between the two main events. Even though the Macrae-Watson partnership continued to be financially fluid, the buffer of the pantomime income cannot be underestimated.

The switch from actor-manager to 'great pantomime artist' was apparently effortless. The combination of Logan's and Macrae's very different gifts produced comic sketches of the highest order. Their individual styles sparked brilliantly off each other in an uproariously funny trolley bus scene, with Logan as the conductor and Macrae as the passenger. Macrae's first entrance as 'Meg Gemmell, the proprietor of a circus', in a sedan chair complete with telephone, was a masterpiece of comic invention. Progressing in a 'crescendo of mirth' through a series of appearances in a variety of 'grotesque costumes' which culminated in his solo appearance as 'Ingrid the Wren', Macrae was now recognized as a 'great pantomime artist'.

The traditional pantomime competition that year came from the Royal and the Pavilion. The King's and the Empire were appealing to more sophisticated audiences with, respectively, the American musical, *Guys and Dolls*, and a revue featuring the singer, Dickie Valentine, and the actor, Bonar Colleano.

Negotiations for the promised appearance at the Citizens' began in December. Correspondence in February 1955, between Tom Honeyman and Norman Duthie who was in Georgetown, Guyana, hinted that there had been problems involving the director, Richard Mathews, about engaging Macrae to play for two weeks in March. Further correspondence indicated that the Citizens' Board were again facing difficulties and dissent on the management side. Expenditure had gone out of control and the implication was that the director, the stage director and the business manager were equally responsible. The policy of inviting guest directors did not have the Board's unanimous approval and it was argued that the resident director should fulfil his obligation to direct the majority of productions. The tension between management and the artistic side was clearly transmitted to the company, a situation which was not alleviated by the very presence of Mathews, the latest in the unbroken run of English directors. Unlike his predecessors, however, Mathews had spent considerable time working in Glasgow with the Wilson Barrett Company. In spite of this, he was barely more welcome than his predecessors. He too was aware of the schism between the Scots and the English in the company and the antagonism he met was, on occasion, quite overt. When the company planned to produce Robert McLellan's *Toom Byres,* McLellan refused to have any discussions. The Board invited Lea Ashton to direct in Mathews' place.

When Macrae did finally go to the Gorbals in May, he contracted to appear in only one play, *The Sell Out,* by Robins Millar, the theatre critic of the *Scottish Daily Express.* Macrae was caught up, however briefly, in the old Scottish-English divide. Mathews found him to be argumentative and 'intolerable to direct'. Macrae's acting did not impress him, but he acknowledged his popularity with audiences. Macrae, on his part, never missed an opportunity to refer to Mathews' Sassenach origins. There was a guarded mutual antipathy between the two men which, on one infamous occasion, exploded into a blazing row during rehearsals.

Macrae's appearance at the Royal Princess's may have been good publicity for the company, but it did nothing more than provide him with the undemanding part of a portrait painter in a pretentious light-weight comedy. The cast, which included Fulton Mackay, Andrew Keir, Paul Curran and Madeleine Christie were equally unimpressed by the play, but Mathews believed the company should always make an effort to produce plays by local writers. According to John Grieve who was associated with the production, it was only saved by Macrae's presence.

After a period of 'resting' in July, it was Scottishows time again. Reduced to only seven stops, this was to be the final tour. Macrae closed the Scottishows chapter in a blaze of glory as the magician, Michael Scott, in Alexander Reid's charmingly fey comedy, *The World's Wonder.* The play had been premièred at the Citizens' in 1953, during one of Macrae's film breaks, with Andrew Keir in the leading role. Roddy McMillan, Leo Maguire, Ian McNaughton and Laidlaw Dalling formed the basis of Macrae's company. They were joined now by Alex McAvoy who had been 'spotted' as a promising student at the College of Drama by Peggy Macrae.

By 1955, the Scottishows tour dates seemed to be comfortably integrated into the late summer and autumn Scottish theatre calendar. Macrae was accorded the kind of adulation and publicity more familiarly reserved for major film stars. That he had grown a beard for the Michael Scott part, was widely publicized and at Perth, a portrait photograph as Grandaddy in *The Kidnappers*, displayed outside the box office at the theatre, mysteriously 'disappeared', presumably taken by a keen admirer. The photo, which had been a personal gift to Macrae by the film company, was only of sentimental value, but as such he was upset by its removal and he appealed through the columns of the local newspaper for its return.

Scottishows' practice of playing one week out of town before coming into Edinburgh was looked on by many people as a preview for the Festival. The result was that the focus of the public's attention was directed to the three-week run at the Festival at the expense of publicity for the other stops on the itinerary; Perth, Falkirk, Forfar, Inverness, Aberdeen and Glasgow. In some respects this diminished the importance of the purpose of touring. Balancing this, the competitive element that had crept into those short and significant three weeks, promoted and supported Macrae's platform for Scottish drama in terms of excellent exposure in the media.

The show opened at the Palladium to unqualified and uniform reaction from the critics who had, in the previous three years, held reservations about the plays and Macrae's disposition to concentrate on a more superficial level of playing. *The Scotsman* wryly commented on 23 August, 'As the annual quest of Scottishows is not so much the ideal Scots comedy as the ideal Scots vehicle for Duncan Macrae, the 1955 Festival warlock is obviously Mr Duncan Macrae.'

Not only was Macrae's performance unreservedly acclaimed but the play itself won the highest plaudits. The playwright, Alexander Reid, had already been awarded a £500 bursary. Scottishows had arrived at the near perfect formula. Macrae and *The World's Wonder* was one of those rare matches of vehicle and talent which yield theatrical magic.

John Grierson reviewed the play in a radio broadcast. He was enthusiastic about all aspects of the production. He was proud that Alexander Reid's essentially Scottish contribution to the Festival held its own in the face of international competition, maintaining that:

> Macrae's performance effectively debunks all the foreign cultural pretension which is beginning to make Edinburgh seem slightly silly and the cultural poor whites of Europe a sorry sight. Here he has the opportunity of combining all the various dramatic selves he likes to be — the Ugly Sisters, the Pardoner, but also on the great occasion, the most moving actor we have.

The play certainly gave Macrae every opportunity to display the best of his comic gifts as he exploited the playwright's text to best advantage. For once, it seemed that he had contained his inclinations to dominate either script or production.

Lea Ashton had been the stage director for several seasons at the Citizens'. He willingly accepted Macrae's invitation to direct *The Warld's Wonder*. There was mutual respect and affection between the two men who had worked together on many productions. Ashton's version of his experience on the tour that year provides an insight into the way Macrae could subvert a director's intention. It was in direct contradiction to the image of Macrae, held by a public so easily seduced by the sheer bravura of his performances, sometimes to the exclusion of rational appraisal.

Ashton had acted in the earlier production of the play and, knowing it very well, he anticipated several points over which he and his leading actor would surely disagree. To his surprise, Macrae was in accord with all the suggestions except one. They agreed to compromise. Macrae would play the relevant scene his own way at alternate performances. Everyone was satisfied. After the rehearsals at Rutherglen, Ashton went to act in Kemp's *The Conspirators* at the Gateway, reasonably confident and comfortable with the production as he had left it. The first opportunity he had to see the play in performance was at the Palladium in Edinburgh. His immediate reaction was to go backstage and demand that his name be taken off the credits, because he felt that everything he had seen on stage was far removed from the play he had directed in rehearsal. Almost all the moves had vanished, leaving Macrae centre stage with the other actors lined up against the backcloth. Challenged, Macrae was surprised but sympathetic to Ashton's protest. There was nothing malicious in his manoeuvres. It was simply the result of the interaction between himself and the audiences who, by their response to his magnetism, forced him to play directly to them. The review in the *Daily Express* spoke of Macrae as 'casting a spell over the Palladium audience'. This was precisely the nature of a Macrae performance.

The overwhelming reception received by the production triggered off calls to re-examine the Festival's drama policy. Mamie Crichton, an influential voice, who in the past had never hesitated to confront Macrae in her *Evening News* column, joined the ranks of those agitating for representation of native drama in the official programme, with Macrae to grace it. Joining in the exultation over the good press it had received, she complained that Reid's play, and the Macrae-Watson partnership, had been consigned to the Fringe. She suggested, with more than a hint of sarcasm that, in the eyes of the Festival administration, Macrae had not yet sufficiently proved himself to be recognized as a worthy participant in the official programme. Her solution to the Festival planners' reluctance to risk box-office losses, would be to produce *Jamie the Saxt* with Macrae in the title role.

Even if the Festival administration did not have implicit faith in Macrae as a major attraction, 1955 in Edinburgh was indisputably Macrae's year. He had just received an Arts Council Award for outstanding contributions to Scottish Theatre and he was commissioned by the *Daily Record* to write an article each day of the three weeks of the Festival, recording his opinions of the events in the capital. Sometimes Macrae's column consisted simply of the innocuous variety of chatty gossip about chance encounters with the public on Princes Street who might have remarked on the beard he had grown for *The Warld's Wonder*; sometimes it was about the personalities he met at the Festival Club — he took great pride and pleasure in reporting his meetings with people like Jacques Tati and John Grierson. He confided titbits of information about meals and the restaurants he ate them in, on the cups of tea he drank, the walks he had taken, the shows he had managed to see despite his own punishing schedule — he was rushing to and from Glasgow recording *Right Royal* for BBC radio during the day. He told jokes and anecdotes, some of which, with the telling and retelling, became ascribed to Macrae himself in perpetuation of the myth of his eccentricity. A favourite amongst such tales was that he allegedly ordered 'a wee cup of tea and a pheasant' in the grill room of the Savoy in London. In fact, Macrae recounted that particular yarn about someone else, in his 'Macrae at the Festival' column on 29 August:

> Got the 11.15 back to Glasgow Saturday night. The compartment was full of Glasgow folk, everyone of whom had gone to one show or another at the Festival. Some of my fellow travellers were very well up in drama and ballet. One rough diamond remained half asleep until Falkirk. When he was fully awake, he entered into the spirit of the thing. He had called at various places and failed to get in so he consoled himself with supper at a nice restaurant. He told with relish how he had ordered one roast grouse and a cuppa tea.

The tone conveyed in these columns suggested that for Macrae, the Festival was a period of hard work and fun. It was a time for reunions when large numbers of actors, living temporarily away from home, were brought together in a rarefied atmosphere quite different from working in London or touring the provinces. Old acquaintances dropped in to see the show at the Palladium: Margaret Rawlings with whom Macrae had worked as long ago as 1926 and Sonia Dresdel who had more recently played with him *The Queen's Comedy* at the Festival.

The column was not always devoted to such frivolities and when appropriate, Macrae seized the opportunity to give vent to his feelings on the attitudes adopted by the Festival management. He reminded readers that his Scottishows venture was financially independent of the Arts Council and that the Festival Society had said that Scottish plays were not good enough to pay their own way, a charge which he rebuffed as 'null and void' in light of his own achievement over the last four years. In one article, pointedly addressing his remarks to Robert Ponsonby of the Festival Society, he cited the success in earlier years of Linklater's *The Atom Doctor* and Bridie's *The Queen's Comedy*. In answer to Ponsonby's charge that 99% of Scottish plays were historical, he questioned whether that need necessarily condemn them. *Jamie the Saxt* was, in his view, brilliant and he ironically revealed that if he had been willing to play Jamie for the Festival that year, it would have been produced:

> It's not their fault the show is not on now. It's mine. A man in Mr Ponsonby's position should commit himself with the greatest discretion, and with due regard to the facts.

None of this frankness prevented his being in constant demand and the honours and invitations continued to flow. In October, he was made a patron of the London Scottish Drama Guild and appointed as Equity delegate to the German Democratic Republic. He was too busy to accept the latter and Madeleine Christie took his place. Jokingly, he told a reporter that he had promised that he would take 'Peggy and the weans to Millport'.

The final curtain came down on Scottishows after it repeated its *World's Wonder* triumph in Glasgow. For four years, between 1952-5, Macrae steadfastly pursued his Scottish theatre crusade and then, quite suddenly, for no apparent reason, abandoned it. Neither artistic nor financial failure could have been the grounds for relinquishing such a position of strength, for the tours enjoyed popular and critical approval beyond all expectations and at the end of each tour the company showed clear profits.

Looking back at the plays Scottishows had produced, the choices cast a degree of ambiguity over the interpretation of Macrae's and Watson's motives. The first two plays were by Watson himself, *Bachelors Are Bold* and *Johnny Jouk the Gibbet*, the last two, *Gog and Magog* (Bridie) and *The Warld's Wonder* (Alexander Reid) were revivals. On the one hand, Macrae could be credited with the wisdom of playing safe, but on the other, he could be challenged for not breaking new ground. There was just the possibility that with the constantly debated dearth of new Scottish plays worthy of serious attention, the company's basic reasons for existence simply ran out. It would have been artistic suicide to continue playing the same plays year after year, no matter how popular they were. Dominated by the Scottishows tours and the pantomime season, the schedule was rigorous and rewarding but physically exhausting. It could not be maintained indefinitely.

As much as anyone closely involved in the business, Macrae was increasingly aware that the rapidly developing potential of television would pose a threat to ventures such as his and this also perhaps informed the decision to wind up the company after the 1955 tour. There was one other likely reason, according to his daughter, Christine — he did not really enjoy being the actor-manager after all.

The Macraes made their farewells to the Scottishows venture in a mood of celebration, holding a large party at Burlington House to return the extensive hospitality they had received from so many friends. Seven-year-old Christine wrote in her diary: 'My Mummy and Daddy are having a party and my Mummy is wearing an old, gold dress.'

The achievements of Scottishows fashioned the next years for the Macraes in several ways. Not least of these were the changes in their family life. Financially confident, they decided that the time was right to have a holiday home and in 1954 they bought a four-roomed flat at 7 Kelburne Street in Millport for £750. The island of Millport, small enough to cycle around in less than a day, is part of the Cumbrae chain of islands off the west coast of Scotland. It had been a special place for Peggy Macrae since childhood.

In his professional life, the popular and financial success of managing his own company elevated Macrae to an authoritative position in the eyes of the theatre world. It was during the height of his fame as actor-manager that Macrae demonstrated publicly one of his strongest features. In private, many recipients of his kindness had been familiar with his caring and benevolent characteristics for years. While he was earning the family living, his genuine concern for the well-being of his fellow actors, and indeed for everyone who worked in theatre, was to find expression in his association with the actors' union Equity.

— 9 —

SUITING THE ACTION TO THE WORD

Equity - the family man - the first steps in revue -
the Sherek season - Millport - Para Handy -
The Wee Cock Sparra

Macrae was appointed first chairman of Scottish Equity in September 1953. From that date, he championed the cause of actors' rights with the same passion he had hitherto reserved for the cause of Scottish drama. This aspect of Macrae's devotion to theatre received relatively little media exposure.

Even the most rational amongst us are reluctant to separate the on-stage glamour from the off-stage reality. This results in an insatiable curiosity to know as many intimate details about our idols as can be extracted by legitimate or illegitimate means. Actors, for obvious reasons, are prepared to comply with the rules of the publicity game and are willing accomplices to the perpetuation of their own myths. Rarely is anything drab permitted to be revealed, and even the most humdrum of activities is contrived to appear well-lit. Scandal and sensation are headlines — good deeds are boring.

For centuries, the stage — and the actors upon it — has exercised a hypnotic hold on the imagination of the public. The notion of being someone else, with exotic costumes and make-up, has provided an escape route into the world of fantasy where possibilities are limitless. Mundane concerns, such as working conditions behind the scenes, are never permitted to cross the footlights to the unsuspecting front-of-house audiences. Exploitation, cramped, damp, rat-infested dressing rooms and poor salaries are not subjects the average theatre-goer wants to be reminded of on his night out.

Reasonable rights and conditions, assumed nowadays by actors, managers, technicians and the public alike, were not always recognized as a matter of course. Actors made sporadic attempts to assert themselves but, unlike their artisan brothers, they did not think in terms of guilds or movements, for their world was on a very different plane. They were neither militant nor essentially political. At the beginning of the eighteenth century, one group of frustrated actors went so far as to persuade the Lord Chamberlain to tie off Drury Lane with a rope of silk to prevent the management decamping with the actors' benefits and other shares. A genteel protest may have been in order, but striking was beyond their ken.

It was not until the latter end of the nineteenth century that members of the profession began seriously to think of forming associations for their own protection. Gradually two groups emerged: the Actors' Association and the Stage Guild. The British Actors' Equity Association, the trade union of the profession, created by the amalgamation of these movements, was not formally constituted until 1929. Scotland at that time was embraced by this Association and only figured as a separate entity in the sense that from time to time Council meetings were held there.

By 1952, the urge amongst the Scottish profession to run its own affairs seemed to be strong enough to consider the formation of a separate body. The tireless efforts of the actor, Alex McCrindle, recruited a workable membership. The twenty-third Annual Report of the Council, *What Equity is Doing*, described this as 'The Scottish experiment'. The aim of the experiment was to find out if there was sufficient membership potential to justify the appointment of a full-time organizer, north of the Border. McCrindle was to continue acting as organizer. When the position was reviewed the following year, it was decided that the increase in membership and activity did justify the confirmation of his appointment. London had always believed that Scotland should be controlled by a Scot living and working in Scotland. In McCrindle, who had been associated with Equity on an active basis since 1933, they had at last found the right man.

The next step was to form an executive committee. In September 1953, a meeting open to all members of the theatrical profession in Scotland was called in the North British Hotel in Edinburgh. Macrae took the chair for the occasion. The immediate business was to appoint a chairman and two vice-chairmen — one working in the Glasgow area and one in the Edinburgh area. Macrae was then unanimously elected first chairman of the Scottish Committee of British Actors' Equity Association, an honour of which he was understandably proud.

Active participation required total commitment. As meetings were usually held on Sundays , many opportunities to be with the family were relinquished. Macrae was entirely dependable, even turning up for a meeting on the day he returned to Glasgow after a flight from Canada! Of the 160 meetings called during his lifetime, he chaired over half. Most of his recorded absences were due to working out of Glasgow, either on tour or filming on location. In the event of his absence, one of the two vice-chairmen deputized. The first elected vice-chairmen were Lennox Milne and Roddy McMillan and subsequently those succeeding to the posts included Stanley Baxter, Michael Elder, Helena Gloag, Jimmy Logan, Fulton Mackay, Russell Hunter, Clement Ashby, Kenneth McKellar, Rikki Fulton, Iain Cuthbertson and Alex McCrindle.

In much the same way as the Macrae story is inextricably intertwined with the history of the early years of the Citizens' Theatre Company, it is linked with the early years of the first independent Scottish Equity Committee. During the fourteen years of his chairmanship, Macrae was instrumental in instigating and carrying out many major reforms in theatre practices.

It is hard to imagine that Macrae conducted meetings with anything less than the flair, style and individuality he brought to all his endeavours. By all accounts, while competent and efficient in conducting the business of a formal meeting, some of the sessions could become impromptu performances, for he could be briefed for a meeting and then, happily discarding the notes, he would go off at a tangent pursuing a totally different issue. As unpredictable as he was on stage, he could be quite offhand and relaxed one moment and confrontational the next. Although his natural instinct was to be unconventional or dramatic, he never allowed this tendency to interfere with the serious business of representing his colleagues, never at any time descending into being a mere figurehead. His preference, for example, for discussing issues personally with local councils or managements did not arise from an egocentric sense of indispensability but was a demonstration of his genuine personal involvement in resolving the problems of the day. Under his stewardship, the Committee set up a multitude of reforms calculated to raise the overall standards of every aspect of theatre and to rectify the anomalies peculiar to the Scottish theatre system. An excerpt from the 1954-5 Annual Council Report explains succinctly the committee's proposed functions:

> A report of the year's work has been circulated to deputies in Scotland who are immediately concerned with the many problems which have been tackled. These are by no means the same as our problems in England, although many of them, such as conditions in theatres and the fight for decent minimum salaries, have a familiar ring. Then of course the repertory theatres and the No. 1 touring companies use the Standard Esher Contracts. What is peculiar to Scotland is the type of production known as repertory revue where we are seeking to secure the use of a negotiated contract with fair minimum conditions. Scotland is also fighting hard to get its fair share of television programmes originating in Scotland. The first step in this direction is the promise which we have secured from the BBC that a mobile television van will be sent to Scotland in March. The next step must be the building of television studios in Scotland.

A letter of congratulation from Gordon Sandison, the General-Secretary of the parent committee, was read at the first of the monthly meetings held in the Central Halls, in Bath Street, on 29 October 1953. One of the most pressing problems was then addressed — the matter of collection of membership dues. There had been a Scottish committee in the past, but it had failed, largely because subscriptions were only collected on a very haphazard basis. Iris Russell conducted an excellent recruitment campaign at the Citizens' and the members of the seven Scottish repertory companies were following suit. Macrae once proudly announced that the actors in his own *Johnny Jouk the Gibbet* company were all fully paid-up members.

One affair which did achieve some notoriety was the matter of the May Moxon Young Ladies, a chorus troupe working at the Metropole Theatre. The girls were not receiving all their entitlements, such as payments for working away from home. After successful negotiations between Macrae, the secretary and the other involved parties, the girls signed the Esher Standard Contract. Macrae claimed that this was the first step forward in raising the status of the chorus in Scotland. The following year, pantomime and touring contracts were negotiated for a £7 minimum for the chorus, with extra payments for working at New Year. The anomalies of weekly salaries in repertory, which could vary from £4 10s to £15, were attacked and the subject of rehearsal time and payment was constantly reviewed. The vast contrast in pantomime salaries, which ranged from £5 per week for the chorus to £200 for the stars, was examined. Some managements were more generous. Howard & Wyndham, for example, paid £6 10s to the chorus and for the variety revue, *Half past Eight*, the girls received as much as £7.

The conditions operated by the two groups of theatres also came under the microscope. No. 1 theatres, of which there were eight in Scotland, were the larger houses under the management of firms like Howard & Wyndham. Three of these were in Edinburgh, four in Glasgow and one in Aberdeen. They were the King's Theatres, the Royals, the Empires of the circuits. Of the smaller, No. 2 group, there were twelve theatres in smaller buildings like the Theatre at Paisley, the Gaiety at Ayr, the Palace at Dundee and the Metropole and the Pavilion at Glasgow. The No. 1 group was more often than not occupied by touring shows or companies out of London. Such companies were not within the Scottish 'jurisdiction', but local resident shows and pantomimes were. Basically, it was the practices of management that were in question. Conditions for stage-managers and scenic artists were challenged. Above all, the scandalous circumstances in which the more impoverished members of the profession were forced to live, were put under the spotlight. Backstage facilities were often no better. The old theatres were a warren of dark corridors, ill-lit and ill-heated dressing rooms with few creature comforts such as toilets or showers. A more pernicious iniquity that prevailed outside the Wyndham theatres, was the domination of the Scottish profession by one theatrical agent, Galt, who not only functioned as the actors' agent but also controlled the booking circuit. Any artist who incurred his displeasure might not find work. But with Macrae as their eloquent spokesman the underdogs developed an ever strengthening voice.

If there was an element of conservative predictability in Macrae's work until 1955, the next six years found him taking greater risks in the kind of roles he accepted, working in more independent productions on stage, appearing in films and facing an increasing demand in television. With the sense of confidence he derived from the independence of the Scottishows venture, Macrae's career now became more typical of the average actor who, working in the second half of the twentieth century, moved from one medium to another with comparative ease.

His first departure from the familiar niche that had so effectively nurtured his rapid rise to prominence, was to leave traditional pantomime. For Christmas 1955, Tom Arnold decided to experiment on Glasgow audiences with a Scottish equivalent to the 'Crazy Gang' show. Macrae was invited to make up a quintet of Scottish performers, with Dave Willis, Jack Anthony, Chic Murray, and the singer Robert Wilson in *Just Daft*, a revue type medley of sketches, songs and dances. With a script that had been liberally decorated by the censor's blue pencil, it was clearly not a show intended for the usual Christmas audience of children. This conjecture is reinforced by an innovation noted in the *Glasgow Herald* review that nightly, 'only one performance instead of the usual music hall two was played through'.

This time, Macrae had perhaps ventured too far into alien territory. The comedians disparate talents blended well enough and the show was favourably received. On to the scene now stepped Chic Murray, a potential rival to Macrae for the affection of the Scottish audiences. 'Quite quietly and modestly', he stole the show from Macrae and Anthony. Macrae was in danger of being eclipsed, especially as Stanley Baxter had taken over his Alhambra niche, partnering Alec Finlay and Kenneth McKellar with great flair. The Empire show transferred for three weeks to Edinburgh and closed at the end of the first week in March. Nevertheless, the following Christmas, Macrae was prepared to repeat the experiment.

1956 was quite untypical. For the first time in thirteen years there was no Citizens' engagement in Macrae's diary, Scottishows had wound up and the New Year was heralded in, not at the Alhambra, but at the Empire. Sandwiched between the two Christmas shows at the Empire, the year was devoted to only two projects: the 'Sherek Season' and a revival of *Mr Bolfry* with Alastair Sim in London. But there are two sides to every coin. No longer confined by the rigorous demands of the repertory system, the gaps between freelance engagements allowed more time for the private man to be with his family.

Behind the stage mask, the real Macrae presented a picture essentially no different from the image he displayed to his colleagues. Immersed in all things relating to the theatre, his bedside reading was informed by a genuinely academic approach to his craft. Books on Stanislavsky's theories, on Coquelin and Jean-Louis Barrault vied for priority with plays by Ibsen, studies on Shakespeare, Jackson's *History of the Scottish Stage* and contemporary criticism from James Agate to Tyrone Guthrie. His own taste in theatre embraced ballet which he took very seriously, but he had no time for opera which he held to be a bastard form of art. Not a man given to telling jokes, he enjoyed and appreciated the comic performances of his fellow artists, in particular the mimic quality in clowning. As for television, admiring its capacity for vividness and immediacy, he believed its most important function was to report news and current affairs.

Unsociable as the demands of the acting profession may have been, his commitment to stage and screen was never allowed to become so intrusive as to damage the fostering of normal family and social relationships. A circle of friends outside the world of show business, testifying to the loyalty and affection the Macraes inspired in those who knew them best, succeeded in keeping separate the myths from the truths. That the Macraes enjoyed a reputation for warmth, hospitality and generosity is conspicuous in private letters and many tokens of friendship.

In the face of obvious pressure to present the kind of family image usually peddled by the popular press, the Macraes managed to maintain the loving bonds of normal family life. But the children inevitably grew up in an atmosphere dominated by the theatre. Even their games betrayed the theatrical influence of their father's occupation and while other children might play at being doctors, shopkeepers or builders, Ann and Christine Macrae joined school friends, the Frew children, to form their own little acting company which they called 'The MacFrewsers'. In 1953, Macrae sketched a stage in Ann's autograph book with the caption 'The Show Must Go On' and underneath it he wrote, 'I know no other capable of holding my attention so wraptly during a Solo Act of seven years and six months duration — Love from Daddy'.

Bearing in mind that children prefer not to be different from their friends, the fact that their father earned his living as an actor rather than in one of the more conventional professions was never a major problem. It had advantages and drawbacks. At an everyday level the significant difference was that he was rarely at home in the evenings, but this became simply a fact of life, one which the children took in their stride. The best treats were always going to the theatre even though one Christmas Peggy took the children's entire classes to the pantomime and, to their mortification, insisted they wore school uniform for easy identification. Life with a famous father could have been difficult, but in spite of Peggy's warnings that they might be sought after as friends, the children never found that their illustrious father gave them any particular clout with their peers. Nevertheless, as they grew up and other people's awareness of who their father was increased, both girls developed a certain hostility to people who approached them with 'Is your father Duncan Macrae?' Occasionally however, his fame could be a source of embarrassment or discomfort, largely because of his strong streak of eccentricity. It was often difficult to predict how he might react in any given situation. When the girls were very young he took them for walks in the park on Sundays. He would always be recognized and people spoke to him. Depending on his mood, sometimes he would be civil, sometimes he was rude, sometimes he just ignored them.

More traumatic were the long periods of separation when he was on film location abroad and for Ann, the worst times were the White Heather tours in the early 60s which, to a young girl, seemed to last for 'months and months and months'. But although there were several prolonged absences at crucial stages in the girls' development, Macrae always exerted a strong influence on the thinking of his children. The argumentative side of his nature bore fruit for he was always ready and willing to engage them on every imaginable topic. He talked to, and at them, endlessly and from him they inherited a deeply-held social conscience. The most prominent feature of his legacy was that side by side with strong bonds of affection, he engendered in them enduring pride in their father's achievements.

Education was important. Ann and Christine attended Hutcheson's Girls' Grammar School, a fee-paying school with a high academic reputation. This did not strain the family budget unduly as Ann won a scholarship and by 1957 Peggy had returned to teaching. There was never any attempt to push them into any particular career, the emphasis being simply on 'doing well'. Nevertheless they were actively discouraged from going into the teaching profession. Macrae had little time for formal religion but Peggy believed the girls should sample both churches into which their parents were born. Following lengthy debates when Peggy prevailed, they were baptized in the Episcopal Cathedral in Glasgow but not until after Christine was born and Ann was already two. In Glasgow they went to Queens Park High Parish Church and during the holidays in Millport they were taken to the Episcopal cathedral. Macrae accompanied them only rarely, which spared the children the awkwardness of having a father who did not join in hymn singing. While he was interested in spiritual issues, he did not believe in the social function of the organized church, especially as he had a strong dislike of what he perceived to be hypocrisy. But regardless of his personal beliefs, he felt that regular church attendance was important for his children when they were young, and he never stood in their way or influenced them in matters of faith.

At home, he was not particularly domesticated. The pride of his achievement in the field of practical handiwork was the building of two small walls in the garden at Millport. Recreation, when there was time, was almost invariably walking. Exercise and healthy diet remained paramount amongst his concerns throughout his life. There were always rumours, possibly arising from a confusion in the public mind with the popular stereotype of the tipsy Scotsman, that he drank to excess, but these were quite unfounded. He was, however, a notorious tea drinker. But as is the way of the entertainment world, half-remembered stories become transformed into legend and Macrae's gastronomic preferences enjoyed distorted currency with the best of such generally harmless fabrications. His devotion to the latest fashion in healthy diets was nevertheless a byword. Nothing delighted him more than the discovery of pumpernickel bread.

In public and on formal occasions, Macrae presented a very dapper figure with a wardrobe of well-tailored suits. In private, his preference was for corduroy trousers, comfortable sweaters, hand-knitted socks and desert boots.

But the reality was that off-stage time was habitually occupied with the duties and responsibilities of his professional life. Long hours were devoted to Equity affairs. In 1956 he agreed to represent Scotland on the British Equity Council on condition that Scottish subjects were on the agenda. This meant more regular trips to London. Obligatory personal appearances and charity performances continued to encroach upon his private world. Peggy's constant support and the security of a settled, if unconventional family life gave him the luxury of taking risks in the full glare of publicity that goes with a successful career. Against this background he was ready to take advantage of the next opportunity as a freelance actor.

The 'Sherek Season' was an innovative idea, born of Stanley Baxter's restlessness over being gradually channelled, by 1955, onto the variety stage. His first preference was still for legitimate roles and he told Stuart Cruikshank, the Howard & Wyndham manager, that he planned to go south. When Cruikshank tried to persuade him to stay in Scotland to act in straight plays, Baxter, aware of the 'English' ethos at the Citizens', countered that no one was producing the kind of play that interested him. He wanted to act in Scottish plays by authors like Alexander Reid. Reluctant to let him join the ranks of expatriates in London, Cruikshank suggested that Baxter might undertake a season of plays at the Lyceum in Edinburgh. Baxter balked at the idea of weekly rep but said he would consider a two-weekly run of each play. Cruikshank then suggested that to run two companies might provide the solution; one to be headed by Baxter and, if possible, the other to be led by Macrae. Each company would play one week at the Lyceum in Edinburgh while the other played at the King's in Glasgow. Then they would alternate their plays between the two theatres, thus playing each production for two weeks. As an added temptation, Cruikshank told Baxter that he believed he could persuade the impresario, Henry Sherek, a formidable name in theatre at the time, to present the season. This would lend considerable cachet to the enterprise, especially in the eyes of Edinburgh theatre-goers who had a reputation for preferring more international fare than their Glasgow counterparts.

By November 1955, Baxter and Macrae had agreed to the idea in principle. They entered into negotiations with Sherek. Everyone connected with theatre knew about the enterprise and the lobbying for particular plays and playwrights to be included began in earnest. Amongst those who submitted scripts to Sherek was Macrae's old friend and associate from the early years at the Curtain, Donald McKenzie. McKenzie had written to the actor about a talk Macrae had recently given. Macrae replied without delay:

9 November [1955]

Dear Donald

Thanks for your letter. Alex Scott has asked me to write down for his 'Saltire Review' the gist of what I said and what you, no doubt, saw badly reported.

Hitherto I have not been one who trusted implicitly in the playwrights on whom to build our theatre in Scotland. I believed, and still do, that a pool of proficient acting is a prerequisite. We have, however indirect, something of the kind now. But without the additional incentive of suitable scripts on which to cut their teeth we are in a very weak position in expecting them not to fly off to London as all actors did up till recently.

You have not sent me a play as far as I remember, for some time. Now I have had the pleasure of reading your 'Rabbie Burns Slept Here' which I got from Henry Sherek, oddly enough. I have been fencing with him as a preliminary to setting up a company for the Royal Glasgow and the Lyceum Edinburgh next summer, and I have told him and Stuart Cruikshank that if I am in it, should like to do at least *one* new play and preferably more. He gave me also another of yours which I have not read yet.

Now what I need at present is a part more than a play. I'm to be engaged as an actor — not as an adviser or manager — and while I like 'Burns Bed' very much indeed I see no suitable part which they could justifiable bill me in. One crazy idea struck me. 'Aggie' is the best part and I have acquired some little reputation as a dame. There's a possible bit of novel publicity.

Do write again

Kind regards
John Macrae

Three days later, he returned to the topic of the Burns play:

You do not make any comment on my suggestion to play the Charwoman in 'Rabbie Burns Slept Here'. I make it again seriously. It's one way to sell the play.

McKenzie continued to press for his plays to be considered and Macrae replied with suggestions and advice. He pointed out that the plays for Sherek's season were still not chosen. When it was finally confirmed that *Rabbie Burns* was accepted, McKenzie tried to influence casting. Macrae made his position clear in a letter dated 26 January:

> Dear Donald
>
> Thanks for yours of 24th. Sorry not to see eye to eye, but I should not be happy with Iris [Russell] or Molly [Urquhart]. The best I can do is recommend. I have no authority.
>
> Cathy Muir is easy to cast, and I am still considering doing Aggie myself. To cast the American types is going to be beyond our resources up here. I think we must leave Sherek to get all three in London.
>
> *The Scots we can find.*

In the meantime, the companies went into rehearsals during the first week in April, accompanied by a rather acrimonious public exchange between Sherek and Richard Mathews, the current director at the Citizens'. Sherek opened the attack in a radio programme, broadcast in the Scottish Home Service on 4 April. He denounced the lamentable absence of Scottish actors who 'should have given up the fleshpots in television, radio and film to come back and stand by Bonnie Scotland' in the Scottish venture.

This provoked a response from Mathews in an open letter to Sherek in the *Scottish Daily Express*. Mathews pertly asked why Mr Sherek had left the security and eminence of the West End to come to Scotland. He catalogued the problems he believed Sherek would face, the main one being the difference in taste between Glasgow and Edinburgh audiences. Speaking from his own experience, he explained that while Glasgow's preferences were for Scottish and American plays, Edinburgh was very conscious of being the capital city and liked to think in terms of world theatre. Indeed, when the season with its essentially Scottish repertoire was announced, many subscription tickets were cancelled by the allegedly 'Anglophile' Lyceum audience.

Mathews meanwhile had been having his own problems. In May, he announced that the Citizens' was running into debt and that he would be leaving at the end of the season. He was quoted in the *Daily Express*:

> I believe that from the point of view of the theatre and myself the change would be a good thing... development takes time, and I feel I must make the change for the sake of my career.

Amidst the Board's strenuous denials of splits or bad feeling, four people — Mrs Rona Mavor, Norman Duthie, C.A. Oakley and George Singleton — resigned in July. Mathews was to be replaced by Peter Duguid.

Mathews's gloomy warnings were unfounded. Macrae had opened at the King's in Glasgow on 23 April in *Let Wives Tak Tent*, while Stanley Baxter launched the season at the Lyceum in Edinburgh. The two companies continued to alternate between the two cities for a twelve-week season until the middle of July. Macrae's six plays were *Let Wives Tak Tent, A Man Called Judas, Rabbie Burns Slept Here, Mr Bolfry, Tullycairn* and *Jamie the Saxt*. Baxter's were *Harvey, The Lass wi' the Muckle Mou, The Whiteheaded Boy, Festival Fever, Who Goes There* and *Voyage Ashore*. When the box-office returns were counted, Sherek's acumen was proved and Howard & Wyndham's business manager had no complaints.

Although the public had enjoyed the plays, it was quite another matter for Macrae personally who appeared to have been guilty of major artistic blunders. The leading role in *A Man Called Judas* was quite unsuited to his particular style, the decision to play Aggie in 'drag' in *Rabbie Burns* was looked on as ill-judged and in poor taste, and the cuts he chose to make in *Jamie the Saxt* were meaningless and Robert McLellan took strong objection to the way they had been imposed. Macrae had gone to see him in Arran, to discuss his own ideas for a necessary shortening of the script. Reluctantly, McLellan was persuaded to leave to Macrae's judgement, what he hoped would be judicious pruning. Curious about the results, he went to see a performance in Glasgow. He sat through the play in shocked silence. Macrae had taken many of the longer speeches and simply delivered the first and the last lines. The audiences were laughing although the mutilated speeches made little sense. In McLellan's opinion, Macrae's ability to draw comedy from his physical presence alone allowed him to disregard anything the author might have included as comic lines. He went round to see Macrae after the show and challenged him about the savagery of the deletions. Macrae's justification was that actors wanted to get home as quickly as other people. He was not, however, insensible to the barrage of criticism:

> Frankly, I have been disappointed. I feel I have given all I can to the parts I have played in a fortnight's rehearsal. I stick to my ideals about the Scottish theatre but I begin to think perhaps the time has come for me to turn my hand to producing plays.

Baxter had no such problems. He hoped to be asked to repeat his success the following year. Mamie Crichton, bluntly expressing her reservations about the trend in Macrae's performances, in particular the broadening of his straight acting technique since his participation in 'pantomime comicking', felt that he required direction 'as firm as his own personality is strong'. She was also critical of the choice of revivals of three of his previous successes, namely *Jamie the Saxt*, *Let Wives Tak Tent*, and *Mr Bolfry*. That Baxter had the better judgement was borne out consistently over the twelve weeks by the fact that his plays drew larger audiences than Macrae's in both Edinburgh and Glasgow. The errors in choice not withstanding, the Cruikshank and Sherek experiment was an excellent idea which could have become an annual date in the Scottish theatre calendar. The companies were superb in spite of Sherek's heated outburst about lack of solidarity. Macrae was supported by actors of the highest calibre including Iain Cuthbertson, James Gibson, Andrew Keir and Alex McAvoy, while Baxter was joined by Roddy McMillan and Lennox Milne. The financial success proved that the ingredients for entertainment were correctly mixed. Yet the experiment was never repeated.

Macrae went straight to London to go into rehearsals for Alastair Sim's production of *Mr Bolfry*. Since the earliest planning stages, Sim had been anxious to engage Macrae, whose talents he held in high esteem, to play Reverend McCrimmon opposite his own Mr Bolfry. The production, directed and partly financed by Alastair Sim himself, was to go on tour for four weeks to Eastbourne, Brighton, Manchester and Liverpool before coming in to London to open at the Aldwych on 30 August. Sim had assembled a very good supporting cast: George Cole as Cohen, Sophie Stewart as Mrs McCrimmon and Annette Crosbie as Morag, the maid. Fresh from her first job at the Old Vic — walking on and understudying — the twenty-two years-old Annette Crosbie felt 'very young, very Scottish and very frightened' in such illustrious company. The youthful actress, thoroughly intimidated by Sim's forbidding manner, was taken under Macrae's benevolent and sympathetic wing. On tour there was little to do during the day, so true to his fashion, Macrae took her for long walks in the countryside, talking intensely about everything under the sun. She was very impressed.

Sim turned out to be a very pedantic director and became intolerable to Macrae. When not on stage himself, Sim was given to peering through a window in the scenery, watching every move with eagle eye and at the interval he would go to Macrae's dressing room and make the mistake of commenting on an effective move or gesture. The move, of course, was never repeated. Working with Macrae was, for Annette Crosbie, an exhilarating experience. His unpredictability plumbed the resources of his fellow actors, coaxing from them performances beyond their wildest dreams.

The reviews were good. When the show came into the West End the critics generously proclaimed the revival 'long overdue'. The play closed in the first week in December and Macrae went home to Glasgow for the Christmas season, once again forsaking the traditional pantomime at the Alhambra.

Hoping to repeat the previous year's success at the Empire, Arnold teamed Macrae again with Chic Murray, Jack Anthony and Robert Wilson in *We're Joking*. The 'book' was the original Crazy Gang script for their show, *Joker's Wild*. It included the hilarious 'bell-ringing monks' sketch. On the whole, the material was a healthy mixture of wit and farce, laced with an acceptable dash of racy innuendo. Sketches, written in broad vernacular, were added to inject a more Scottish flavour to the Glasgow production. But 'Keep the Home Fires Burning' introduced an extra ingredient which offended many people. Macrae played a fireman, his costume complete in every detail from the top of his gleaming helmet to the toe of his big rubber boots. He was the very model of a modern fire fighting hero. The words of the sketch relied almost entirely on *double entendre*. The phallic implications of lines like 'my jet was oot in a flash' or 'och aye, I've been attached tae my hose for a guid number o' years noo' were obvious.The critics were quick to pounce. Macrae defended himself on classical grounds, claiming that his use of the prop was based on the best of authorities. The humour in the plays of the ancient Greek playwright, Aristophanes, frequently depended on just such sexual ambiguity. Despite the furore, the *Glasgow Herald*, while admitting the material was only adequate, described Macrae as 'a most elegant and polished comedian'.

The work pattern changed radically again in 1957 when the Empire show closed in the middle of February. The next nine months were taken up with a mixture of plays, radio broadcasts in Scotland and film and television in London. By 1957, television in Britain was an established part of everyday life. Its impact on live theatre was twofold. First, audiences were enjoying the novelty of staying at home for their entertainment and companies were playing to ever diminishing audiences as one by one, all over the country, theatres were closing. Second, television became a hungry mouth, able to consume a seemingly endless supply of actors, who in turn were only too willing to desert the stage for the financial advantages and national exposure on the seductive new medium. Provincial reps already struggling in straitened circumstances — the Citizens' no less than the others — were amongst the early casualties. The consequence was that many repertory companies, the training grounds for generations of young actors, were no longer able to survive. This compounded the exodus south of so much Scottish potential.

Macrae's new routine was very much in keeping with the times, namely a move away from live theatre into television and films. On the live stage, he played in variety and made rarer guest appearances with the Citizens' and the other Scottish companies at Perth and at the Gateway in Edinburgh. Relatively late in his life, he branched out into the wider circuit of commercial legitimate theatre which operated quite differently from provincial repertory, in that it was essential to work with the services of a good agent. In this respect, Macrae was fortunate to have Max Kester whom he had met during an Edinburgh Festival. Although he never achieved West End star billing — not something to be expected of a character actor in any case — after 1960 he began to attract the attention of directors of prestigious and controversial productions, in which he received very favourable notices. Had he not died at the age of 61, it is very likely that despite his nationalist instincts to stay in Scotland, he would have found a growing number of tempting offers from the south.

Nevertheless, he kept faith with all he had promised to do for Scottish theatre for a little longer. His belief that an actor who had established himself outside of the repertory circuit should enhance that circuit by regular reappearances was reaffirmed. When the Empire show closed in the middle of February 1957, he took a brief rest during which he recorded *A Surgeon for Lucinda* for BBC radio. This was James Sutherland's adaptation of Molière's *Le Médecin malgré lui*, a play with music by Arthur Blake. In April, he went to Perth Repertory Theatre to play a Perthshire farmer in Moray McLaren's farce about the Stone of Destiny, *Muckle Ado*, and in May he returned once again to the Citizens'.

The Board, very conscious of the dwindling audiences, were always anxious for Macrae to make guest appearances which guaranteed a welcome boost to box-office returns. They were equally aware, and privately admitted, that the company no longer had the drawing power of a Molly Urquhart or a Duncan Macrae. They also knew that in the face of the competitive offers he was receiving from many sources, apart from his genuine wish to play with the Citizens' on a regular basis, they would have to tempt Macrae, if not with money, at least with good plays. To this end there had been extensive debate about the best vehicle to offer him for his return. It was ultimately decided that *Dr Angelus* and *Romanoff and Juliet* would fit the bill. On this occasion, there was no carping about over-acting although there was the inevitable comparison with Peter Ustinov's original portrayal of the colonel in the latter play. As for the *Dr Angelus* production, Macrae crossed swords yet again with Mathews who found him more intractable and unpredictable than ever. When they were rehearsing, Mathews unwisely told Macrae how he had seen Alastair Sim play the final scene and suggested he might try it that way. Macrae listened to the idea with gruff mutterings. Macrae muffed the move and Mathews never found out whether it was deliberate or whether Macrae's concentration and creativity had been broken by the intrusion.

After some work in television, Macrae joined the Gateway Company in Edinburgh to play the Nabob in their production of McLellan's *The Flouers o' Edinburgh*, the role that had been originally created by Andrew Keir in the Citizens' première of the play in 1952. It had always been Macrae's preference to stay at home in Glasgow when working in Edinburgh, relying on the train service to deliver him on time. It was while working on *The Flouers* that the system failed him and he arrived one evening too late for his first entrance. The actors on-stage held their breath when, out of the corner of their eyes, they spotted Macrae's feathered turban moving stealthily round the scenery as he crawled, hopefully invisible to the audience, to his designated position. On a more sober note, he also took the lead in their *Dr Angelus* which was acclaimed as one of the Gateway's best ever productions.

He returned to the Citizens' in the autumn to play Malvolio in Peter Duguid's production of *Twelfth Night*. This was the third of Macrae's attempts at Shakespeare roles. The first, in *A Midsummer Night's Dream* was successful, the second, *Macbeth*, had been extremely fraught and short-lived. By all accounts, his interpretation of Malvolio was inhibited. Macrae was not comfortable in the role although, in theory, it was a perfect part for him. In short, his Malvolio disappointed. He had not risen to the occasion. The review in the *Evening Citizen* perceptively pinpointed the salient flaws, suggesting that Macrae was 'fighting the fun'. The reviewer described an unfamiliar Malvolio whose 'ever-so-chummy Glasgow voice and his gangling mannerisms' were redolent of pantomime at the Alhambra and slapstick at the Empire. It bore no trace of Mr Bolfry or Jamie the Saxt. He conceded that it was good pantomime and as long as the customers rolled in 'who are we to object?' Essentially, Macrae's performance lacked the necessary ability to examine what made Malvolio look ridiculous and, instead, turned him into a funny man. Macrae was aware of the problems he was having with the interpretation. *The Scotsman* reported that when he came off on the opening night, he mopped his brow saying, 'I hope it went all right. I feel ghastly. But I don't think I can get worse now.'

In an interview with the *Evening Citizen* on 19 October, he was praised for remaining true to his pet theory that stars should support repertory companies by making such guest appearances. He was quoted: 'It's an unlucrative way to spend my time compared to what I can get elsewhere.' It was a realistic appraisal of his own decisions.

The next day he set the cat amongst the pigeons at a conference held in the Citizens' Theatre. The conference was designed to foster the interest of civic, educational, industrial and social organizations in Glasgow and the west of Scotland, in the work of the Citizens' company. Speakers included Mr John Mack, a senior lecturer in citizenship at the University of Glasgow, Dr Tom Honeyman, Citizens' chairman, Colin Chandler, director of the College of Dramatic Art, Peter Duguid and Duncan Macrae. The first speakers, Mack, Honeyman and Duguid, were optimistic and agreed that the atmosphere and relationship between the city and the theatre had never been so good. All that was lacking was the right kind of support. Macrae then made his controversial statement, beginning with his belief that no one could claim that the Citizens' Theatre had so far fulfilled the intentions with which it had begun. The *Scottish Daily Express*, 21 October, reporting the proceedings quoted him:

> The stage is capable of far far more than frothy, frivolous stuff. Frothy plays will always bring in the mass of morons. People's tastes are incredibly shockingly low — tastes we don't pay much attention to. Responsible people must lead

the way. The others will follow in time. There is a point at which the mass of morons, the ordinary public, come in because other members of the public have told them they should come. They come in like sheep.

Colin Chandler bravely tried to soften the shock by telling the delegates that it was incumbent on the theatre to persuade audiences to come, 'not by pointing out the path of duty but by offering entertainment and excitement'.

The headline writers had a field day, seizing on Macrae's more startling and provocative vocabulary rather than examining any fundamental common sense underlying his blunt and admittedly tactless expression. The reports blurred the distinction between a blanket attack on audiences and what was essentially his defence of theatre.

Only the *Glasgow Herald* reported the speech in a calmer and more objective manner, scrupulously avoiding the more prominent reiteration of 'morons'. If Macrae had not been so outspoken and if the press had not, understandably, highlighted his forthright expression, the conference would doubtless have passed virtually unremarked. As it turned out, it sparked off a running debate in the press until December.

Forsaking the more dubious form of revue that the Empire had favoured for two previous Christmases, Macrae returned to the Alhambra for *Mother Goose.* It was to be his last, very welcome, appearance there in traditional pantomime. Playing opposite Stanley Baxter for the first time since they had appeared together as regular members of the Citizens' company, the critics described them as 'a partnership of obvious possibilities'. They had little material to work on but they were excellent foils for each other's individual brand of comedy. Like everyone else Baxter found working with Macrae at once challenging, frustrating and very rewarding. John Grierson wrote:

It is certainly as the living remembrancer of Lorne and Clydeside comedy that I myself admire Macrae most. He doesn't like me to say so — because he takes his acting a lot too seriously and doesn't agree with me that it is the clowning that is the miracle... Now even in this secondary comic part nothing could conceal the splendour of the tradition he carries in the wild lines of his face and the refined grotesqueries of his gaunt frame. Even when he is doing nothing or has nothing to do, he has only to move his hands — a look over his left shoulder and withdraw from the world to look what a clown should look like.

Baxter is an excellent mover — but Macrae's movement is different in kind. He moves to notation. His body doesn't work to music — it is a complete instrument in itself and Macrae knows every string to pluck. That's one of the true clown's capacities. Grock, Chaplin, Langdon, W.C. Fields, Cantinflas, Alberto Fratellini — you think to in this connection of German actors like Werner Krauss and Conrad Veidt — they all give this sense of being instruments in themselves — and so they isolate themselves and with that notion of loneliness which is a clown's prerogative.

The most remarkable feature of 1958 was that in the months between the Christmas shows, for the first time since the beginning of his professional career, Macrae's engagements were entirely divided between film and television. Equity continued to occupy him and to the credit of the organizers, by now three-quarters of all artists engaged in theatre, radio and television in Scotland were members. For some unknown reason, Alex McCrindle then tendered his resignation, but backed by Macrae and Baxter, the committee persuaded him to relent.

Keeping faith with his word, Macrae continued to earn the money in film that permitted him to return constantly to work in Scotland. He took on a contract that would have been impossible to resist. Michael Relph, the film director believed that it was 'perhaps foolhardy to attempt to follow *Whisky Galore'*. Despite his doubts, he decided that if Compton McKenzie had written a sequel, then the film makers should attempt one also. And so they did. A brilliant cast including Donald Sinden, Ronnie Corbett, Jeannie Carson, Gordon Jackson, Roland Culver and Macrae spent two months filming in the Outer Hebrides. The island of Barra once again became the scene of unaccustomed activities. Not quite so memorable as its predecessor, *Rockets Galore* is an agreeable, gentle comedy about the efforts of a group of Hebridean islanders to thwart the installation of a rocket range on their doorsteps. Macrae played Duncan Ban. It was a supporting role but Ban is one of the quaint assortment of locals, whose machinations and exploits to foil the strategies of the English army hold the plot together. His bizarre appearance and controlled performance contributed a great deal to the comedy perpetrated by the unlikeliest gang of saboteurs. The film proved to be much more amusing in the making than the result on screen.

Working in such a company was inevitably diverting, but the best entertainments were those the unit created for themselves when the day's shooting was over. The close proximity with one another for two months, dictated by living in such an isolated location, could have bred personal irritations. But there was a tremendous warmth of spirit and community. Most of the cast lived in cottages as guests of the local crofters who were delighted to have them. Ronnie Corbett, who shared 'digs' with Macrae, was both impressed and amused by his early morning 'Spartan rituals' of splashing with cold water and graceful exercising. Corbett and Macrae spent a great deal of time between shots, experimenting with ways of heaving great stones to one another. The unit's favourite spectator sport, however, was watching the regular hill race between Macrae and Donald Sinden, as they vied with each other to cut down the time it took to run from the hotel to the top of a nearby hill and back.

In the evenings, the company gathered for less strenuous recreations. Sometimes they met in the Castlebay Hotel for sessions of 'The Game' — a highly popular form of charades. On another occasion, inspired by the return of their host's daughter from a cookery course in Glasgow, Macrae and Corbett decided to organize a dinner party. Fillet steaks and strawberries flown in on the little plane which lands on the gleaming white Barra sands were augmented with freshly caught fish and, dressing for the occasion, the guests sat down in the stone walled cottage to a candlelit banquet fit for a king.

When filming was completed, before the crew left Barra, they produced a cabaret for the islanders as a gesture of thanks for the warmth of their hospitality. Macrae knew that Gordon Jackson was interested in German *Lieder*, as indeed he was himself. He suggested they might perform a 'wee Schubert song'. Jackson duly received the words of the song to study, written on a paper bag from the Hong Kong Hilton. It was in a wonderfully corrupt mixture of German and English and the opening line went, 'Mein hert's gebroken'! Accompanied by Jackson at the piano, Macrae performed with appropriate gestures, drinking props and great gusto.

Corbett and Macrae developed an affectionate respect for each other's work. Macrae constantly suggested to Corbett that they should do pantomime together. They never did, but the matching of the difference in their heights could have been magnificently exploited. In later years when Macrae was working in London, he invited Corbett to tea. Corbett had the impression that Macrae was never really happy working in London.

The film and television contracts continued to be a substantial boost to the Macrae finances. Four years after sampling of the holiday flat on Millport, in 1958 the Macraes bought a traditional Scottish house for £2,800. 'Dundonald' looked deceptively larger than it was as all the rooms faced to the front overlooking Kames Bay. The family spent all school holidays there apart from Christmas. Macrae travelled over to the island on as many weekends as his work schedule permitted, catching the ferry from Largs and returning on the 'dead' boat at the crack of dawn on Mondays. Life on Millport, when he had time to enjoy it, suited Macrae very well. The ideal restorative after the stresses of the theatre, he could walk, cycle and generally potter about in the open air. By chance there was quite a little community there with connections in show business. The broadcaster, Archie McCulloch, launched an unlikely venture for that part of the world. His night club, 'The Cumbrae', was an ambitious project which aspired to bring to the island something of the flavour of London night life, with imported cabaret artists and limited gambling in the form of fruit machines. Peggy became a member of the management committee. Macrae would offer to entertain, without fee, on Saturdays nights, trying out comedy routines on the audience which was very much attuned to his type of humour. Before long he was an instantly recognizable figure striding about the island, sporting an amazing assortment of hats. Friends from the entertainment world who were favoured with an invitation to 'Dundonald' bestowed on him the title of 'The Laird o' Millport'. But his argumentative nature surfaced even on holiday when he entered into a lengthy dispute with a neighbour about a partitioning fence. The Millport interludes acquired a certain mythical quality.

An innovation was introduced into the Scottish theatrical calendar in October 1958, when a charity show, *The Show of Shows*, produced by Equity members, was mounted at the Alhambra. It was so successful, with a revenue of £853 13s, that it was voted to become an annual event. Macrae, Stanley Baxter, Jimmy Logan and Kenneth McKellar were elected to handle the disbursement of the profit.

In swift succession, Macrae then did two plays for ATV, *You Never Can Tell* and *Death Hangs*, followed by another film, a lightweight Launder and Gilliat comedy *The Bridal Path*, adapted from Nigel Tranter's novel. Bill Travers headed the cast which included Roddy McMillan, Nell Ballantyne, Alexander McKenzie. Macrae had three impressive scenes as a police sergeant, further confirming his ability to give a well-controlled screen performance. When filming was over, the Macrae family set off for a holiday in London. There, the children enjoyed all the traditional sightseeing tours and a visit to the Victoria Palace Theatre to see the Crazy Gang — their father's favourite comedy team. More television with the BBC followed: a play, *Candlehaven*, and two weekly revue shows, *Better Late* and *Look Here*, which ran during November and December. The live theatre took its traditional break from legitimate drama and joined in the annual merrymaking.

Macrae now deserted the variety stage for the first time in eight years retracing his steps along the Bridie comedy route. For the first time, it was the Edinburgh audiences who savoured the delights of his comic acting in the Gateway's revival of *The Forrigan Reel*. The actor/director Tom Fleming once said that he would have done anything to have Macrae in a cast — he did in fact direct him in three plays, the first of which was this

Christmas show. It may have been a feather in Fleming's cap, but it could hardly be said that Macrae was breaking new ground.

The trend was similar in 1959. With the exception of appearing in a revival of *The Three Estates* at the Edinburgh Festival, after the Gateway show closed in February, the rest of the year was entirely devoted to film, some radio broadcasts and television. He appeared in *Lazarus* for BBC and *The Devil's Instrument* for ITV. Then he was cast as a Highlander in the Walt Disney film version of *Kidnapped*, with Peter Finch playing Alan Breck. The film crew, on location in Glen Nevis, was very impressed that swathed in rags, Macrae was the only actor prepared to brave five minutes shooting in torrential rain.

Moving from the wilds of Scotland to the urbane world of Graham Greene, he next made a brief appearance as MacDougal, a guest at a dinner seated beside Alec Guinness, in Carol Reed's *Our Man in Havana*. For the two weeks he worked on this scene, he earned £200. Then returning north, this time to a gentler Scotland, Macrae's next major milestone was in the first television adaptation of Neil Munro's *Para Handy*.

Sporting a wispy beard and a skipped sailor's bonnet, Macrae became Para Handy, the skipper of the shabby wee Clyde puffer, *The Vital Spark*, that steamed up and down the Firth of Clyde, straight into the hearts of all Scotland. For six weeks, a huge audience was captivated by the misadventures of the droll crew made up of Macrae, Roddy McMillan, John Grieve and Angus Lennie.

In the late 1950s it was not unusual for drama series to 'go out live.' It would have been impossible to do this on board ship, especially as camera and sound techniques were nothing like as sophisticated as they are nowadays. Brief sequences were filmed to establish location at places like Inverary, Tarbert on Loch Fyne and the Crinan Canal and these were alternated with interior shots, when the episode was transmitted. The series, directed by Pharic McLaren, was made at the Black Cat Film Studio in Springfield Road.

John Grieve found working with Macrae on *Para Handy* very trying as live transmission required meticulous rehearsal and total discipline during transmission. Macrae and Grieve had worked for several hours rehearsing a bar-room scene which involved moving a number of props around to different positions. On the day of the 'take' Macrae did something entirely different, destroying the scene's punch line, and driving Grieve to near distraction. The next morning Pharic McLaren, a gentle bear of a man who directed from his wheelchair, could contain himself no longer. In total silence Macrae received a display of fury totally uncharacteristic of McLaren — and they went on with the next episode. Some years later, when a second series was filmed, McLaren never discussed why he cast Roddy McMillan as the skipper. Macrae made no comment at the time either. John Grieve believed he was hurt at not being invited to repeat his popular success of the first series.

The fourteen-week contract ran until the second week in January which meant that he was unable to appear in any Christmas show in live theatre that year. It was no hardship as the *Para Handy* contract was for £105 a week. The days — and many evenings — before and after Christmas were devoted to filming, but Macrae was free to accept a momentous invitation to take part in the BBC Hogmanay Party. The New Year was ushered in on live television by artists from Scottish show business who entertained the nation in a series of solo spots and sketches, linked by nostalgic songs and a great deal of tartan-clad dancing. Hosted by the singer, Robert Wilson, the show was broadcast from the City Halls in Glasgow. With little time to plan or rehearse, Macrae resorted to the song he had first heard in the 1930s. 'The Wee Cock Sparra' made its television début to an audience who was quite entranced.

— 10 —

FROM SPARROW TO RHINOCEROS AND BACK

Working with Guinness, Mills and Olivier -
The first recordings - The White Heather Tours

The years that followed the extraordinary impact of that New Year broadcast were typical of the fragmented nature of the life of a freelance actor. The only certainty of working resided in being under contract in repertory. In England this meant companies like the National, the Royal Shakespeare Company, Bristol Old Vic, Birmingham or Liverpool and in Scotland companies like Dundee, Perth, the Royal Lyceum or the Citizens'. The alternative was to chase work wherever it was offered, or 'rest'. Some actors were in the fortunate position of being able to choose. Macrae had to reconcile his wish to remain in Scotland with the continuing need to earn his living in work that he did not necessarily find congenial or rewarding. The association with pantomime was reinforced by the image projected by 'The Wee Cock Sparra' song but it was balanced by the creation of the television Para Handy. His career now took on a pattern of fluctuation between the humdrum and the headlines.

In 1960, Macrae seemed to be on the threshold of a career as a national, leading character actor. For a brief spell he was working with actors of international standing which should have done his reputation nothing but good, moving into the charmed circle of the most distinguished actors in the profession, including Laurence Olivier, John Mills and Alec Guinness. This involved no more than two films and one play. While not in any sense diminishing the worth of the best of Scottish actors that he had worked with hitherto, it cannot be denied that, in the company of some of the biggest names in theatre, Macrae had 'arrived' —

183

that is, if playing in London's West End or in major films is reckoned to be the pinnacle of achievement. He took part in films that are acknowledged amongst the classics, films that are shown again and again on television and in a small way contribute to keeping alive the image of Macrae.

Macrae's first real taste of television fame was timely. It was reported that for the first time in their history, repertory theatres were suffering an appreciable decline in audiences as a result of the small screen's popularity. But in February, he moved away from the glare of publicity that still lingered after 'the Sparra' interlude, and went to London to work on *Tunes of Glory*, under Ronald Neame's expert direction.

Macrae made a lasting impression in that film, delivering a much praised portrayal of the stern Scots pipe-major in the Stirling Castle garrison. Alec Guinness said of working with him, 'I had a great admiration for Duncan Macrae and enjoyed working with him. He brought great simplicity and truth to whatever he touched and a very appealing amusement.' John Mills who worked with him only on this film said that he admired Macrae 'immensely as an actor' and thought that he was 'superlative'. Susannah Yorke, cast as his daughter, found him 'a splendidly eccentric, humorous, charming and cranky old(ish) man, very kind to me as a newcomer'. Macrae could so easily have been submerged in the company of the cream of British actors who, as well as Guinness and Mills, included Gordon Jackson, Kay Walsh and John Fraser. Once again, he was judged to be a very fine film actor. The momentum continued and Macrae moved on to his next prestigious engagement, this time on the stage.

George Devine, the artistic director of the Royal Court Theatre in London, had sent Max Kester, Macrae's agent, a copy of *Rhinoceros*, by Eugène Ionesco, the leading French exponent of the genre of absurd drama. The critic, Kenneth Tynan, wrote in a study of the English stage that *Rhinoceros* was subject to as many interpretations as there were people in an audience, with the rhinoceros symbolizing any regime 'that appears to threaten one's self-hood'. The plot revolves round the gradual transformation of each character into a rhinoceros, in a series of ever increasingly surreal scenes. The play had recently opened in Paris, produced by Jean-Louis Barrault at the Odéon on 25 January 1960. Kester, without reading it properly, passed it to Macrae who said he could make neither head nor tail of it. From the outset, the London production was conceived under a set of conditions. Olivier would do it if Welles would direct and Welles would direct if Olivier would play Bérenger. Agreement was eventually reached and casting began. Kester then re-read it and was convinced that Macrae could tackle the major role of Jean. After considerable persuasion, Macrae agreed to audition, influenced to some extent by the prospect of being directed by Orson Welles.

Macrae duly turned up at the Royal Court. Welles and Olivier were in the stalls. Olivier was sceptical about the unknown Scot, but Welles knew something of Macrae's work. When he finished reading, a discussion about Ionesco, absurd drama and surrealism ensued. Apart from Macrae's obvious grasp of the grotesque, Olivier was clearly impressed by his intellectual approach to the script. The part was his. The production went into rehearsal with Olivier as Bérenger, Macrae as Jean and Joan Plowright as Daisy. The cast was made up of a formidable array of experience and talent — Alan Webb, Geoffrey Dunn, Monica Evans (who understudied Plowright), Hazel Hughes, Michael Bates, Gladys Henson, Peter Sallis and Miles Malleson.

It seemed however that even in that eminent company, Macrae could not escape from the 'dame' image. Welles wanted to convey a sense of continuity with the past in the design. Macrae readily agreed to dress in period costume, men's and women's, and posed for photographs. These photographs were then used as the models for the paintings of 'Jean's ancestors', which decorated the set.

Some time after the production opened, Tynan described the direction as, 'dashingly and unmistakably by Orson Welles'. The truth was that Welles had been impossible to work with although it was generally agreed by the cast that his technique of overlapping the dialogue from one scene to the next, added another dimension to the text. He was, according to Peter Sallis, 'an extraordinary man, gifted with imagination and flair'. But when it came down to the basics Welles was constantly changing everything and trying to impose his will on the actors who found this inhibiting. The result was that when Welles went to Spain for a few days to see about financing his project for *Don Quixote*, Olivier took over the direction and some coherence was at last achieved. Welles came back in time for a run through before the full dress rehearsal. He was delighted and absolutely convinced that his actors had taken to heart everything he had tried to instil in them. Olivier and Macrae, who by this time had established an enormous mutual respect for each other as well as a magical working rapport, could scarcely conceal their amusement.

The play opened on 28 April. At the interval, Welles stormed into the dressing room shared by Peter Sallis, Miles Malleson, Alan Webb and Macrae, shouting that there were only three people doing as he directed, Olivier, Plowright and Sallis. When the curtain came down, Noel Coward breezed into their dressing room, proclaiming how perfectly ghastly he thought the play — and introduced the author, Ionesco, who was hard on his heels.

The reviews were generous although the cast were thought to be having to fight Olivier. Macrae's big scene, when he transforms into a rhinoceros was 'played without a false note' and was described in the *Daily Mail* as 'one of the greatest *coups* of twentieth-century drama'. Macrae was proud to have worked in such celebrated company. Nevertheless, he told Molly Weir, whom he met after she came to one of the performances, that working with Welles made him feel as if both his feet had been nailed to the floor! Such a restriction must have been intolerable to the man who relied so much on freedom to improvise his way across a stage. At a party given in his honour by the actor Leo Maguire, who later married Monica Evans, Macrae was quite open in his dislike of Welles and equally forthright in his admiration and affection for Olivier.

The whole production had been fraught with crises. Quite apart from the antagonism Welles had clearly engendered in the company, there were other undercurrents to cope with. At the time Olivier, separated from Vivien Leigh, was in the middle of a widely publicized affair with Joan Plowright. When the news broke, to avoid embarrassment to audiences, Olivier persuaded

George Devine that Joan Plowright should leave the cast. Monica Evans took over for the remainder of the run at the Royal Court. After six weeks there, the play transferred to the Strand Theatre with some changes in the cast which included Maggie Smith taking over Daisy and Michael Gough replacing Alan Webb. It ran there for a further eight weeks, playing to packed houses.

The glamorous social background that was part and parcel of such a prestigious production was light-years away from touring the Scottish provinces. Welles threw a glittering party for the company and Peggy, thrilled to be invited, went to London. Each member of the cast was presented with a small bronze cast of a rhinoceros which had been sculpted by Welles's wife. The play ran until the end of July and the Macraes took their daughters for six memorable days to Paris, the only time the family ever went abroad together.

Macrae's next moves were planned and booked well in advance of the end of the *Rhinoceros* run. Keeping the film profile alive, he played a police sergeant in the Disney film, *Greyfriars Bobby*, earning £1,250 over a period of three weeks. Then he joined a Scottish variety touring company, The White Heather Show, and set off on a gruelling nine-weeks tour of North America.

Macrae first met the singer Kenneth McKellar in 1947, when *The Gentle Shepherd* was broadcast on BBC radio. The next time they worked together was in the 1954-5 Alhambra pantomime. During the run of that show McKellar took ill and the Macraes, with their usual unobtrusive kindness, invited Kenneth and his wife, Heidi, to recuperate at Millport. From that time the two couples became firm friends and in 1960, McKellar who was heading the White Heather company, invited Macrae to join him on tour.

BBC television's *The White Heather Club* and the White Heather Tours were two distinct and separate shows. 'White Heather' was the name originally coined by the singer, Robert Wilson, for the annual American concert for expatriate Scots. Under an arrangement with Neil Kirk, a New York 'Scot', he supplied the artists for the enterprise which was funded by Scottish societies throughout North America. Kirk gradually took over the organization as it evolved into an extended tour lasting between ten and twelve weeks. Conceived as a concert party, the show became something of an institution over several years from the late fifties to the early sixties. Each show was advertised as the show of a particular star, for instance, when Kenneth McKellar led the company, it was 'The Kenneth McKellar Show'. Many of the most prominent Scottish variety artists headed the bills, with performers like Alec Finlay, Jack Radcliffe, Stanley Baxter and Andy Stewart, each taking his turn at entertaining the Scots abroad. When the shows toured in Australia and New Zealand they were co-ordinated by a group, run by Sir Robert Kerridge, which owned most of New Zealand's cinemas.

Macrae was again entering unfamiliar territory — not just geographically. He had been initially reluctant to accept the invitation, uncertain as to what kind of act he could offer in the very specific medium of a show which consisted of a series of solo spots. Finally persuaded by McKellar that he could handle it, he contracted to join the company for ten weeks from September. His contribution was a twelve-minute spot in each half. This required immense concentration and effort. But the Macrae name was a reliable enough box-office draw in North America as he was already well-known to the expatriate Scots for *The Kidnappers* and his face was familiar from *Whisky Galore*.

In the beginning, Macrae's choice of material was ill judged. Excerpts from Bridie plays, no matter how brilliantly performed, were not what the nostalgia-seeking audiences, many with fond memories of the stand-up comedy routines of the good old days at the Metropole, the Empire and the Alhambra, were flocking to hear. Before long, however, he mastered the microphone technique and, armed with different material — some of it hastily written for him by McKellar — he enjoyed the tour immensely.

In 1960, the company travelled from coast to coast, including Los Angeles in one of the concert stops. Kenneth McKellar insisted that when they reached the west coast the company would take a week's break, making a trip to Las Vegas, sightseeing along the Pacific coast, resting and relaxing. When they reached Hollywood, they were invited by Roger Moore to tea on the set of the television serial film, *Maverick*.

The schedule of one-night stops was exacting. The company would land at an airport and be whisked off to fulfil a social engagement prior to the evening concert. The moment their feet touched the ground, they were 'on duty'. The journey from Los Angeles to Chicago was very bumpy. When they landed the entire company was feeling thoroughly sick. They had no choice but to overcome their fatigue as they were rushed directly to a reception given in their honour by the society ladies of the town. Macrae was singularly adept at holding court at these gatherings, graciously answering questions and making erudite-sounding pronouncements. True to character, his capacity to charm was equally matched by his capacity to shock. He was perfectly capable of abruptly cutting short an exposition on the state of world theatre, inquiring the whereabouts of the toilet facilities, and then marching off, leaving his adoring audience flabbergasted.

The tired but satisfied troupe flew home in the second week of November. Macrae's first White Heather tour was voted a success. He enjoyed one month's rest before going into rehearsals for *Skerryvore*, a musical version of Bridie's *What Say They?* produced by the Falcon Theatre Organization at the former Empress Theatre, in St George's Road. He was to repeat the role of the janitor he had taken in the 1951 film version.

The Falcon project was a short-lived attempt made by a group of Glasgow business men to establish new forms of Scottish theatre. Macrae was not greatly involved in the experiment, but his appearance at the theatre lent a certain credibility to the enterprise, with the added bonus of his attraction at the box office. He was the latest in a line of internationally recognized performers such as Tom Lehrer, Donald Wolfit, Joyce Grenfell and Michael MacLiammoir who had been booked to boost the project's funds. The reviews agreed that the production was not up to standard but Macrae's presence was welcomed. The show ran for four weeks over Christmas and New Year.

Macrae revealed in an interview with Gordon Hislop of the *Sunday Express* that he was not taking singing lessons, but there were 'a few numbers' which he would 'just have to umpity-umpity-ump' and spoke of his growing disenchantment with the

189

Scottish theatre. He admitted that, while he would prefer to work in Scotland, there was no place for him there. It was his belief that the lack of investment by Scottish commerce had plunged Scottish theatre into a rut. Then, in a surprising flash of realistic honesty, which implied a measure of compromise, he agreed that he had been luckier than most, in the sense that in recent years he had earned enough to continue living in Glasgow while working away from home. Hislop asked why he stopped doing pantomime. Macrae's answer was equally revealing: 'I don't know if I stopped doing it or if they stopped wanting me. Anyway, I carried on till my contract ran out.'

In the meantime, pragmatism, to say nothing of popular demand taking precedence over preference, 'The Wee Cock Sparra' was trotted out again to be paraded on television on New Year's Eve. This time there was a bonus.

In the back shop, behind the tiny rural post office in Brig o'Turk in Stirlingshire, there lies an impressive array of sophisticated recording equipment. It is the operational centre of Scottish Records, a small company, run by the postmaster Douglas Gray, devoted to recording and marketing early and traditional Scottish music.

When Douglas Gray saw the 'Sparra's second outing on the 1961 Hogmanay show, he was very impressed. He contacted Macrae. To Gray's surprise, Macrae told him that his only venture into the recording field to date had been the narration on a recording of Burns songs for EMI. Gray, believing that it would be commercially viable to latch on to the evident popularity of Macrae's brief New Year television spot, proposed they 'do something together' — perhaps beginning with a recording of 'The Wee Cock Sparra'. He would make all arrangements and handle all the publicity. The idea appealed to Macrae. The partnership proved highly successful and the two men conducted their business most congenially. No formal contract was ever signed or even discussed. There was no talk of money other than an agreement on royalties.

The first recording was made at Park Film Studios in Kirkintilloch. It was disappointing. In contrast to the impact of the visual image of Macrae's singular delivery, on sound only, without any kind of backing, it was rather flat and uninteresting. Gray had a flash of inspiration. Some time before, he had made a film, with background music scored by Francis Collinson — a versatile musician who had been musical director in Drury Lane in the days of the Cochrane reviews. Collinson was a passionate folk song collector. As a diversion on his forays into the countryside, he had recorded specific bird song, which he identified as soprano, tenor, bass, and so on. He analysed the melodies and produced a kind of 'bird quartet', each bird being represented as an instrument. Gray believed that this might be the ideal backing for Macrae's voice. It worked.

'The Wee Cock Sparra' was first released as an E.P. record. An engaging mixture of fifteen poetry readings and simple songs included 'The Frog and the Mouse', 'Three Craws', 'The Paddo', 'The Laird o'Cock Pen' and 'The Wee Cooper o'Fife'. All the musical settings were by Collinson. The musicians were drawn from the ranks of the BBC Scottish Symphony Orchestra. Not every track had music, but Gray had compiled an ingenious programme, cleverly choosing those pieces which stood up well as unaccompanied narrative. The record turned out to be something more culturally aesthetic than a commercial exploitation of the notorious recitation, for the other items had been carefully selected from Chambers *Rhymes of Scotland*.

It was quite obvious to Gray that Macrae considered the Sparra trivial — a sentiment he, Gray, heartily shared. So, almost as if wishing to reaffirm their seriousness of purpose, they made another record. *The Real Macrae* consisted of excerpts from *Gog and Magog, The Three Estates, The Warld's Wonder* and *Let Wives Tak Tent*. These were reconstructions of theatrical performances, recorded before specially invited audiences. John Grieve and Alex McAvoy also took part.

Macrae's singing was pleasing and tuneful. The true quality of his compelling voice, with all the vocal nuances at his command, from the plaintive whimsical in the upper tones to the sonorous resonances of the lower register, was captured on record for posterity. Eight of these items were included in the compilation,

A Tribute to Duncan Macrae, which Gray released after Macrae's death.

Nobody except Douglas Gray believed that his next idea would work. Neil Munro's Para Handy stories had proved their lasting popularity when they were first televised with Macrae in the title role early in 1960. Recorded readings could not hope to compete. Gray's idea was to record a collection of songs linked by narrative — nothing more complex than the journey of a puffer steaming up and down the Clyde, going nowhere in particular. Gray was friendly with the actor Alex Mackenzie, the Engineer in the series, who in his younger years had been a schoolmaster on Skye. Mackenzie was very familiar with the character and sense of humour of the Highlander. Over the years, he had gathered a number of songs which, when adapted, were ideal for Gray's purpose. A team comprising Roddy McMillan, John Grieve, Mackenzie and Macrae built up excellent rapport as, bit by bit, *The Highland Voyage* was recorded. There was no song about the Crinan Canal, so a new one was created for John Grieve. The record turned out to be a great success both critically and commercially.

Some time after the record was on release, Gray approached Macrae and John Grieve, in December 1962, when they were working in the Citizens' Christmas show. He suggested that, if he could get McMillan and Mackenzie to agree, they should make a short film of the puffer journey to accompany the songs. They did. The film was never properly edited and was virtually forgotten by everyone except Douglas Gray. After many years he offered it to the BBC. In 1990, it was transmitted as the forerunner to a series of Scottish comedy. In a short introduction which began with a black and white clip of Macrae's recitation of 'The Wee Cock Sparra' John Grieve, blissfully nostalgic, was interviewed about 'the legendary Duncan Macrae' and the making of the film. *The Highland Voyage*, while being in itself of no great artistic merit, is intrinsically valuable as a rare record of these four Scottish actors appearing together as the crew of the *Vital Spark*. None of the original *Para Handy* television series has survived in the BBC archives. When Macrae died, the record royalties passed to the Macrae Memorial Trust.

The two months following *Skerryvore* were spent 'resting', apart from two weeks work in a play for ITV, *The Conscientious Ganger*, in February 1961, which earned him £337. This was a sufficient cushion against eight weeks without salary. But, typical of the work pattern of the freelance actor, the next three months were devoted to filming in Israel and Italy which was more than ample financial compensation for the leaner times.

Macrae was cast as a Scottish sergeant-major in the comedy, *The Best of Enemies*, a Dino de Laurentiis production for Columbia Pictures, directed by Guy Hamilton. It was a joint Anglo-Italian venture. The plot centres on the adventures and misadventures of a small troop of British soldiers, captained by David Niven. The soldiers, played by Bernard Cribbins, Ronald Fraser, Harry Andrews and Macrae, are captured by Italian soldiers after crashing in the Ethiopian desert in 1941. The comedy is derived from the various deals struck over the capture, freeing and recapture of each other.

The company flew out to Tel Aviv in April, and travelled south to Eilat, where the unit set up on location in the Negev desert. The intensity of the heat combined with the quality of the afternoon light, dictated that filming started at five o'clock in the morning and finished by lunch-time. One evening, despite the heat, Macrae, with his usual irrepressible energy, set off on one his famous walks, striking out along the beach at top speed. Even though he had not returned by bedtime, there was no panic as everyone assumed he was safe. Then, to everyone's astonishment, he was marched on to the set at 5 a.m. by an Israeli soldier! His excursion had taken him right out of Israel into Egyptian territory. Fortunately, he had been picked up by an Israeli patrol. Satisfied that he was not an Egyptian spy, the Israelis returned him to the film unit.

The combination of a half-British half-Italian company was not the easiest to work with. David Niven would sit quietly reading under a huge umbrella until he was cued — very orderly and very controlled. The Italian star, Alberto Sordi, on the other hand, would make a great business of being mopped with cold compresses and helped on to the set by his entourage. After five minutes of this kind of fussing, Niven would return to his seat and refuse to go on the set till the Italians were quite ready. It was after all too exhaustingly hot under the desert sun to stand about idly. The other British actors waited likewise, except for Macrae who would stand out in the blazing sun apparently oblivious to the furnace-like heat.

One of the first things Bernard Cribbins noted about Macrae, whom he met for the first time on the journey to Israel, was his excited interest in everything new and the immense pleasure he took in talking to people. There was ample leisure time and Eilat had compensations for the discomforts of the desert. Bernard Cribbins was a dedicated 'snorkeller'. Macrae enjoyed swimming and persuaded Cribbins to teach him the finer points of the snorkel. After a few breathless, water-filled mask attempts, and a great deal of Cribbins's patience, Macrae mastered the technique.

Seven weeks of working in these harsh conditions were followed by a spell in the relatively more agreeable Roman climate. For a time the cast stayed in a small *pensione*. In the evenings they usually ate together at a small restaurant, Crispi's, where Macrae kept everyone thoroughly entertained with tales about working in music hall and pantomime in Scotland. He was a great favourite with the company who found him a most accomplished actor to work with and a good companion.

The social life in Rome was unlike anything Macrae had ever experienced. Because of the Italian connection, the British actors were frequently included in the round of parties that seemed to be part and parcel of the Italian film industry. For many years, Peggy teased him about an alleged 'liaison' with a Roman Contessa. How this family lore came about is totally obscure but it probably arose from his accounts of the *dolce vita* when he came home. Peggy did go out to Rome for a short visit and later told her friend, Marion Blytheman, that it had been a most romantic interlude — almost like the honeymoon which they had never had. It was on this visit that Macrae bought Peggy a gold bracelet — one of the few pieces of jewellery he ever gave her.

On his return to Scotland, Macrae continued to grace the Scottish stage, however fleetingly. Resting for only three weeks, he joined the Gateway Company in Edinburgh, in their revival of Kemp's *Let Wives Tak Tent*, for part of its run during the Edinburgh Festival. He did not play the full three weeks as his second engagement with the White Heather tour, this time to Canada, had been a prior booking. Walter Carr was in the Gateway cast and took over Macrae's role for the remainder of the run. During rehearsals, the director, Tom Fleming, found that Macrae did not have his lines properly prepared. Giving him time to work on them, Fleming continued to rehearse without him, on the assumption that Macrae's apparently casual approach to rehearsals was because he had done the play before. Fleming then had occasion to pay a visit to the costumiers and found Macrae there having fittings for the Canadian tour instead of studying the script as agreed. Although this was just a small example of the kind of behaviour that earned Macrae a dubious reputation in some quarters, Fleming stood by his faith in him as an impressive actor. This was one of those occasions when Macrae was genuinely oblivious to the effect he had on other people. To his credit, he could behave with an innocent insouciance which made no pretentious attempts to impress. Laurence Olivier was in Edinburgh and came to a matinée at the Gateway. Fleming invited him round to see Macrae after the show. Olivier was more than delighted to go and talk to 'the wild genius'. Walter Carr was sharing Macrae's dressing room and to his vast amusement, Olivier was offered the hospitality of Macrae's current passion for Victoria plums. They all three sat in the dressing room, talking and eating the fruit from a paper bag, while Carr listened fascinated to Olivier and Macrae sharing reminiscences of playing in *Rhinoceros* the previous year.

The White Heather Company set out once again in the second week of September. This time, the destination was Canada. Macrae was prepared this time for the demands of the nightly performances and the flood of requests to attend teas, suppers and barbecues in their honour. The White Heather Show dates were marked on the calendars of every town on the route and the hard working company was amply rewarded by the warmth of their reception.

Peggy flew out with Heidi McKellar to join the company in Vancouver and travelled south through Portland and on to San Francisco with them. But three months on the road was a very long time to be parted from hearth and home, especially as there was absolutely no possibility of slipping home for an occasional weekend with the family as it was always possible to do from London or from some film locations. The tour finally ended. As the plane banked over the west coast of Scotland, coming in to land at Prestwick, Macrae thought he could pick out the island of Millport. Turning to McKellar, tears streaming down his face, he confessed he was glad to be home at last.

Two weeks later he was in rehearsal for *Aladdin* at the Empire, playing Widow Twankey to Johnny Beattie's Wishy-Washy. 'The Wee Cock Sparra' made its almost traditional appearance on Hogmanay television and pantomime ended in the middle of February. Macrae and Beattie had worked well together and in tribute to their happy association, Macrae gave Beattie a small silver dish inscribed

Johnny Beattie
'Aladdin'
'61-'62
J.D.G.M.

But there were less festive matters off-stage pressing for their attention and indeed for the attention of all members of the profession, in particular those with long-standing associations with the variety stage. In December 1961, the managing director of Moss Empires announced the proposed closure and demolition, in Spring 1963, of the Glasgow Empire to make way for office blocks. The next two years were to see constant concerted efforts to save the much loved hall. One of the famous Frank Matcham theatres, the Empire had opened in 1897 and had been the scene of countless theatrical triumphs and disasters, earning a reputation as the 'graveyard of English comics'. In a speech at a press conference, Macrae declared that the closure of theatres was not a matter for private speculators but a public issue. Supported by other Equity members, including Rikki Fulton and Johnny Beattie, his plan was to lobby the Secretary of

State and the local Corporation and to enlist as much public sympathy as possible. It was feared that the Pavilion and the King's Theatre in Glasgow as well as theatres in Dundee and Aberdeen were also in jeopardy. Their efforts for the Empire were to come to nothing.

After *Aladdin*, Macrae had no stage bookings until the middle of June 1962 when he was engaged to travel for the third and final time with the White Heather show. Taking advantage of the quiet period, he went into hospital in March, to have an operation to an injured knee. It was during this rare spell of no regular employment that Macrae made his one and only advert for television. Costumed in bonnet and plaid, he earned £400 for proclaiming the efficacy of Crofter's porridge oats. The advert became a firm favourite with viewers. With such occasional fees and the regular payments of £100 royalties on the Douglas Gray recordings, Macrae's earnings, combined with those of Peggy who now devoted her teaching to the needs of special education, could well sustain the family.

Unlike the trips to the States and Canada which had both been in autumn, the 1962 White Heather tour to Australia and New Zealand began in June to coincide with winter in the antipodes.

New Zealand and Australia welcomed the Scottish troupe with as much warmth and enthusiasm as North America. The company included Moira Anderson and a small section of the Jimmy Shand Scottish Country Dance Band. Macrae was now fully in control of his material and quite at home with the style of performance necessary for such venues as the stadium at Melbourne with its 7,000 audience capacity.

An incident occurred on this trip which could have been the result of extreme fatigue and the nightly stress of recreating rapport with different audiences, or, in retrospect it could have been one of the earliest warnings of illness. At Brisbane airport Macrae suddenly exploded in a fit of violent temper brought on by something very trivial, which in the normal course of events would have been dismissed. But Macrae's response was far in excess of reasonable behaviour. He shouted, gesticulated and was becoming an embarrassing public spectacle. Nothing quietened him until Kenneth McKellar physically seized him and warned him to calm down. The outburst vanished as suddenly as it had erupted and, contrite, Macrae apologized. McKellar began to notice that Macrae was increasingly subject to sudden swings of mood. Nevertheless, nothing in his demeanour was so extreme that it militated against his carrying on working as usual. If there were excesses, they were still attributable to his acknowledged eccentricity. The only more positive sign that there was something amiss was that he began to find the learning of lines more difficult, a skill with which, in spite of the fact that he would often ignore them in performance, he had hitherto had no problems. The company was back in Scotland by the middle of September. There was still time before the Christmas season for Macrae play the lead in *L'Avare* with the Dundee Repertory Company.

The White Heather tours were undeniably popular and successful. Becoming identified with them had diverse significances for Macrae. In the first instance they were financially attractive. Macrae had grossed nearly £1,000 on each of the North American tours and £3,600 on the Australian and New Zealand stint. It is essential not to underestimate the esteem attached to participating in these shows, within their own sphere. But no matter how excellent they were, in a wider artistic context, not only was Macrae sidelining himself from legitimate theatre but he was also making himself unavailable over prolonged periods for other work. Paradoxically, his decision to make these tours marked the beginning of a discernible drift away from the 'big-time hits' that had made him so famous.

He returned to Glasgow from Dundee at the beginning of December to go into rehearsals for the very last time at the Citizens'. Cliff Hanley had been commissioned to write the 1962-3 Christmas show. The actor, Graham Crowden, who was going to join the company later in the season to play in *The Birthday Party*, was invited to direct. Hanley created *Saturmacnalia* with Macrae in mind for the leading role of Duke McCash, 'the richest man in the world', but with no real expectation of securing him for the part. As it turned out Macrae was available and willing to do the show. He joined a very able company which included Phil McCall, Anne Kirsten, John Grieve and Alex McAvoy.

The rehearsal period was characterized by delay after delay, more often than not engendered by what seemed to the rest of the cast to be Macrae's increasing obstructiveness. The problem with lines resurfaced, only this time it was interpreted by Hanley as Macrae's innate 'persistent amateurism'. Making things extremely irksome for the other actors, as he gave no reliable cues, Macrae simply paraphrased the lines, only approaching something like accuracy during the actual run. Hanley had been extremely co-operative, both with the cast and with Crowden, attending most of the rehearsals, making cuts and alterations frequently demanded by Macrae himself. Ian Gourlay, who wrote the music, was equally accommodating. If Macrae was having difficulty with a song, an alternative one was written. Two songs were eventually included in the show. Macrae used one in a later radio broadcast and neglected to acknowledge the source, claiming it as his own. Hanley found Macrae to be isolated and unwilling to co-operate, behaving imperiously, even complaining on one occasion that he had not seen the playwright for two days. Part of the problem was attributed to the fact that Crowden, who hailed from Edinburgh, seemed unable to tune in to Hanley's fundamentally Glasgow type of humour. Additionally, Macrae and Alex McAvoy found that Crowden's notion of how comedy worked was very different from their own.

Advance publicity promised Glasgow that *Saturmacnalia* would be 'a riot of hilarity'. The current chairman of the Citizens', Michael Goldberg, determined to make a party of the opening, surprised the first night audience with champagne in the foyer. The next morning, however, the majority of critics, not quite so festive, expressed disappointment, finding the promised 'orgy' to be rather restrained. But regardless of their opinions, the audiences were treated to a spectacle that was 'sparkling and blazing through the fog like a bonfire'. Although the critics had reservations about how well Hanley's esoteric brand of satiric humour had been adapted to the stage, Macrae's return to the scene of his earlier triumphs was warmly welcomed. From the moment he swaggered on stage, with the lines:

Sell Millport
Make an offer for Pan American Airlines
Buy one Queen Mary
Cancel my subscription to the *Beano*

he had the audience in the palm of his hand with a first-class, witty, character study of the richest man in the world that had little of the pantomime dame about it. Macrae gave his last ever performance at the Citizens' with all his accustomed flair. His interest in the Citizens' activities was maintained when the company opened the Close Theatre Club in premises next door to the theatre. Macrae was one of the founder members although he never performed there.

When *Saturmacnalia* closed at the beginning of February, for the first time and only time in his career, Macrae had no immediate live theatre contracts, either to capitalize on or to advance his reputation on the legitimate stage.

Two events saddened the theatre community. The Empire closed at the end of March, but not before the Scottish Federation of Theatrical Unions gave it a rousing send off on Sunday 31 March with a gala variety performance directed by Johnny Beattie. Macrae's contribution to the evening was an appearance with Albert Finney and John Mulvanney as demolition men. Finney was working at that time in Glasgow with the Citizens'. At the end of their sketch they attacked the stage with their pick-axes, signalling the end of a glorious era of music hall. In April Macrae's old friend and partner, Tim Watson, died.

The major portion of Macrae's earnings in 1963 derived from filming. He had a small part in a thriller, *Girl in the Headlines*, made at Twickenham Studios, with a cast which included Ronald Fraser, Ian Hendry, Jeremy Brett and Jane Asher. In July, he played a doctor in *A Jolly Bad Fellow* which was made at Shepperton Studios. This was a typically British comic romp directed by Don Chaffey with an all star cast which included Maxine Audley, Leo McKern, Dennis Price, Leonard Rossiter, Alan Wheatley and Dinsdale Landon. Macrae continued to earn the admiration of his fellow film actors for his superb comedy timing. Film was a medium that clearly suited him.

Later that year, Macrae was reunited with Bernard Cribbins in television. The BBC ran a series of plays in Comedy Playhouse, as pilots for projected series. *Impasse*, written by the Galton and Simpson team which had been so successful with the Steptoe comedies, did not make the grade. Macrae played the trouble-shooting RAC man in the lightweight piece about a confrontation between motorists in a narrow country lane. Also in the cast were Leslie Phillips and Yootha Joyce. However, for Macrae it was a first step towards establishing himself in television comedy.

Television occupied the rest of the year with roles in *Kidnapped* and in *It's All Lovely*, as well as appearances in Scottish chat shows and on the BBC arts programme *Monitor*. There was more time again to pay active attention to the state of the arts in Scotland and at a very successful conference on 'The Lively Arts' held at the Citizens' Theatre, Macrae made a brilliant statement on conditions in Scotland. There was time also for a brief and pleasant interlude when Equity decided to mark the seventieth birthday of its oldest member in Scotland, James Gibson. Presenting him with a table lighter, suitably inscribed, Macrae, in all sincerity, paid his old friend and adversary handsome tribute.

On television, 'The Wee Cock Sparra' brought in the New Year for the third time and despite Macrae's growing distaste for the public's insistence on associating him with the hapless bird, it continued to bring him a small regular income in the form of record royalties.

— 11 —

NEITHER UP NOR DOWN

Re-enter Bachelors are Bold - Loot
The Scottish Arts Pamphlet

The most promising contracts in 1964 came from television. Macrae seemed to be keeping abreast of the increasing scramble for work in that medium, appearing in the BBC's networked series, *The Avengers* and *Dr Finlay's Casebook*. As for extending his range on the live stage, 1964 could be said to find Macrae in the artistic doldrums.

Although there were no contracts that year in the more rarefied realms of London theatre or in prestige film, it now began to look as if he was becoming an attractive prospect in the world of popular entertainment both in Scotland and England making guest appearances in the Andy Stewart show on stage and television and on the Ken Dodd radio show. If that was how he saw his career developing, then three months in variety at Sheffield and Blackpool was a good booking. The more fashionable seaside resort summer shows had always attracted the cream of variety artists. *What a Joy Ride* with Hylda Baker, who was at the height of her popularity on national television, was surely a good way to introduce himself to the English audiences with tastes similar to his faithful Scottish pantomime following. If on the other hand the highly-paid engagement was intended to subsidize the promised returns to work in Scotland, then that too would be understandable. Whatever the reason, it was an experience that Macrae did not enjoy.

A remarkable chain of events then brought Macrae to work with Jimmy Logan for the first time since they had appeared together in pantomime at the Alhambra, ten years before. It began when the failure of the Falcon Theatre enterprise in 1962 left the Empress vacant. Unfortunate as this collapse was for the investors, it was timely for Alex Frutin, whose Metropole in Stockwell Street, had recently been destroyed by fire — a fate common to so many older theatre buildings. Frutin transferred his activities to St George's Road, and the Empress, renamed the New Metropole, reverted to being the home of traditional Scottish variety.

Two years later, the Frutin family decided to sell out and the property was bought by Jimmy Logan. He set up Logan Theatres Ltd, with his parents — the famous Short and Dalziel comedy team — and his wife as co-directors. He had the twin ambition to make his theatre the base for the best in Scottish comedy and to develop gradually a sophisticated complex of bars and night club entertainments, by acquiring adjacent properties. The idea was that each area would help subsidize the activities of the others. Gordon Irving described Logan's brave new enterprise as 'history in the making... an occasion for celebration'.

As far as plays were concerned, Jimmy Logan knew exactly what his audience wanted. He planned a repertoire of well-tried, well-loved Scottish comedies, opening with Sam Cree's *Wedding Fever*. It was a runaway hit. The second production had to be as cunningly chosen. Confident that in 1964 there was still mileage in Tim Watson's brand of humour, Logan opted for *Bachelors Are Bold*. Although his own name topping the bill, would more than ensure good returns at the box office, Logan was astute enough to take the smaller role of the grocer and to invite Duncan Macrae to recreate the star part of the undertaker. While the fee Macrae could command from independent commercial companies such as Logan's was far in excess of the average repertory salary, taking on the familiar Gilbert Dalgleish role did not offer any new acting challenges.

Macrae joined a cast whose very names guaranteed the best in old-fashioned entertainment; Jean Faulds, Marillyn Gray, Morag Hood, Bill Henderson and Marjorie Dalziell. In Logan's own words it was to be a 'blockbuster'. His judgement was accurate. The audiences flocked in and it was packed houses for five weeks. Competition in the Glasgow theatres at that time was very equal. The Citizens' was running *A Sleeping Clergyman* as its twenty-first birthday production, the Alhambra had *My Fair Lady*, the King's, *Half Past Eight* with Rikki Fulton and Jack Milroy and at the Pavilion, Lex McLean's variety show enjoyed 'House Full' notices.

Idol of the audiences though he may have been, Macrae could and did infuriate his fellow actors. One of his worst ploys, conscious or unconscious, was to kill someone else's laughs by cutting across their lines. Jimmy Logan had been exposed to this kind of experience working with him in pantomime. Macrae would produce one of his irresistible gestures or vocalize in his singular fashion which diverted the audience away from the previous laugh line. Unable to tolerate this night after night, Logan challenged him. Macrae's answer was to analyse the move, or sound, intellectually, asserting it was justifiable as an impromptu response to audience reaction. The explanation was, in itself, reasonable enough. But it was just as likely that he was as unaware of his instinctive reactions as he was unable to account for how he raised laughs. Nevertheless, many of the actors working in that production vowed they would never play with him again. On the other hand, the younger members of the company, Paul Young and Bill Henderson, declared he was unfailingly kind and helpful. Logan, who was after all responsible for harmony in the company, was often driven to distraction. But he, like everyone else, was prepared to tolerate Macrae's shortcomings and admire him as a genuine eccentric with a blazing original talent.

The Macraes were able to enjoy the rare pleasure of a family Christmas that year, one of only three they had together since the professional career began. Money was still coming in from the porridge advert and record royalties and the BBC Hogmanay show brought another £85.

The most striking feature in Macrae's 1965 diary were four play dates in live theatre and a return to traditional pantomime. Three of these plays were in Scotland. Over the previous eight years the number of plays he appeared in had dwindled to one or two a year. For a time, it looked as if he had come to terms with a routine which would maintain his ideal way of life. He had proved he could subsidize living and working on the legitimate stage in Scotland by the occasional foray south, working in variety, or in film and television.

In 1965, he became involved with one of theatre's most notoriously controversial productions, Joe Orton's *Loot*. Michael Codron had agreed to produce the play which Orton had been writing during 1964. Having met Kenneth Williams, Orton told him that he would write the play with Williams in mind for the part of Truscott. All plays in those days had to be submitted to the office of the Lord Chamberlain to obtain a licence for performance. Orton's original title, *Funeral Games*, or alternatively, *Comedy of Horrors*, served due notice of the content which was the socially taboo subject, death. It was not at all surprising that the script was returned, dappled with the censor's blue pencil. The plot revolved round the farcical situation arising from the bundling into a cupboard of a naked corpse, some dubious stage business with a false eye and a text full of innuendo and expletives. With the offensive elements cut or rewritten, it was eventually licensed under its new title, *Loot*. To be fair, underlying the comical parody of the traditional gimmicks of detective fiction, was an essentially serious exploration of public attitudes.

By December 1964, in spite of Orton's scepticism about casting Macrae as McLeavy, a scepticism vigorously opposed by Williams, Macrae's name was added to the impressive cast list of Kenneth Williams, Geraldine McEwan, Ian McShane and David Batley. Peter Wood was to direct. According to John Lahr, in his biography of Orton, *Prick Up Your Ears*, the success or failure of the play rested with Kenneth Williams, who, like Macrae, 'was a celebrated theatrical exotic cast in a role that demanded a veneer of normality'.

The play went into rehearsal in January and the troubles, which the initial difficulties with the Lord Chamberlain had signalled, began in earnest. Peter Wood was also directing a production of *The Master Builder* at the National Theatre, and commuting back and forth to New York where he was directing *Poor Richard* on Broadway. Orton was feverishly rewriting the script causing mounting stress in the actors. Wood was constantly at loggerheads with Williams over his interpretation of Truscott. Williams seemed to have moved it from its original concept to the more familiar 'Carry On' character with all the farcical innuendo of which he was master. Williams was so lacking in confidence that on the opening night, he appeared in Nazi uniform and on the second night, he attempted to characterize Truscott as a Sherlock Holmes figure, complete with deer stalker hat. Macrae, McShane and McEwan contrived to go through their lines, although the metronome Wood introduced into the wings, allegedly to impose a rhythm to their speech, was summarily dismissed.

After three chaotic weeks of rehearsals, the play opened to a howl of disgust and disapproval at the Cambridge Arts Theatre. Kenneth Williams recorded his total demoralization and regret at having anything to do with the 'rotten mess'. The cast was effectively forced to work on two plays. During the day they were still being asked to rehearse rewrites, while at night they struggled with the stubborn original. In his autobiography, *Just Williams*, Williams expands on the atmosphere and tensions behind the scenes and describes how on the train journey back to London, after that first week at Cambridge, Macrae made a supreme effort to bolster the flagging spirits of the traumatized cast. With all his familiar abandoned accompanying gesture, he expounded on a variety of subjects ranging from the paved terrace he had recently laid by himself at the Millport house, to the virtues of the balletic quality of the Moscow Art Theatre actors he had seen in Glasgow in the twenties.

Justifiably apprehensive, the company set out on tour. At Brighton, Orton was still churning out rewrites. The audiences were no less hostile than at Cambridge. When they arrived at Oxford they still had to work late into Sunday night to perfect the new moves that went with the new version. The mounting hysteria was palpable. Macrae would come off-stage muttering to himself. Geraldine McEwan, constantly near to tears, would have preferred to be left alone to get on with the business of going to the theatre in the evenings for the performance instead of prolonged rehearsals which seemed never to solve the problems. Ian McShane was involved in a scrap with Orton and

Williams was becoming increasingly morose about the whole enterprise. Everyone in the profession from Laurence Olivier to Gordon Jackson who came to see the play, either condoled with the cast at having to work on that play, or loyally supported their efforts in the face of hostility. Audiences stalked out or stayed to cries of 'filth'. Some laughed.

From Oxford they moved into Golders Green Hippodrome where, half way through the week, there was a sudden reversal of fortunes. The more sophisticated audiences in the London suburb were receptive and appreciative. Everyone's spirit lifted. Macrae went out to dinner with Ruari McNeill, the Scottish Equity organizer, and told him he was enjoying the part which was quite different from the stereotype he felt had been trapped by in Scotland.

The company then moved on to Bournemouth. Christine received an encouraging letter about her School Certificate results from her father written in the Pavilion Theatre on the Sunday before they opened. He made passing reference to the uncertainty of the production's future and referred to the relative success at Golders Green :

> Easter creeps on apace, and I'm hoping to see you all then, either in London or elsewhere... We did a better-than-normal week at Golders Green and came on Saturday rather proud of ourselves, after a packed house and eight curtain calls.

Rising above the miseries of the first weeks with his usual good humour, he had settled into the routine he usually adopted while away from home, taking keen interest in every new surrounding. From Bournemouth he wrote:

> This is a lovely town. Unlike Blackpool, where the land stays flat for miles landward from the beach, this is built on a pretty steep hilly slope, cut into little glens which are called CHINES. All the roads curve and turn and rise. There are no rectangles. There are little burns running into the sea, quite clean and clear, and the houses are all nice big ones, like miles and miles of Taylors' house at Kilmacolm. I'm in a thing larger than theirs — a kind of

boarding-house with a big garden. I can walk to the
theatre in fifteen minutes. It was a cold clear day and I
walked along the front and through the 'Gardens', which
are quite lovely. The Theatre is pleasant — about 1400 but
we may not do so well as last week.

Bournemouth's anticipated negative reaction to the play was not
helped by bitterly cold and snowy weather which did little to
coax reluctant audiences into the theatre to find out for
themselves. The Bournemouth chill was nothing compared to the
attempted freeze-out at Manchester. According to Kenneth
Williams, there was a sharp division in the audience, with half
the house laughing and the other half silently disapproving. But
the local Watch Committee took to the high moral ground.
Because there had been so many rewrites no complete script had
earned the Lord Chamberlain's seal of approval and certain
lines, in particular those heavy with innuendo, were not going to
be permitted. Amongst the casualties were some of Ian
McShane's lines. The Watch Committee had even gone to the
length of posting policemen in the wings with instructions to
remove any actors who offended. After one performance,
Macrae told Williams about the barrage of criticism he had faced
in 1956 following his Aristophanic antics with a fire hose.

Over the frenzied weeks, Macrae and Orton developed a
liking and respect for each other. Macrae persuaded Orton that
the play should be revived with an entirely rewritten script.
Later, when the play was indeed revived, Orton told Ruari
McNeill he would have liked to have had Macrae in the second
production.

Time to arrange a West End opening was running out. On the
first night at Wimbledon, Michael Codron told the cast the only
available theatre, the Phoenix, declined to have them. If they
were willing to wait for a few weeks — without work — he
believed he could make an arrangement for the production to go
into the Lyric, Hammersmith. But the cast, glad to see the back of
the play, were unanimous in their refusal. With considerable
relief they disbanded and Macrae returned to Glasgow.

Before his only major working association with Rikki Fulton, Macrae made a brief celebrity appearance in his television show in April. Then Fulton was to direct him in the leading role in the Howard and Wyndham production of Philip King's farce, *See How They Run*, in May. Macrae looked forward to the partnership with pleasure. He told Peggy how much he enjoyed working with Fulton during rehearsals, particularly as they practised a similar approach to the creative side of comedy, based on a free interpretation of the physical context of the script. For one rare occasion in his career, Macrae was working with a director who was himself, as an actor, equally adept at exploiting the comedy in a given situation, as the opportunities presented.

See How They Run derives much of its humour from the perennially favourite spectacle of clerics in varying states of undress and, as the Reverend Toop, Macrae was described as 'grotesquely agile in combinations'. The relationship unfortunately soured when, during the run, Macrae's behaviour to certain members of the cast became so disruptive that Fulton threatened to sack him unless he exercized some self-discipline. The play opened at the King's in Glasgow in June and after seven weeks, it transferred briefly to the Lyceum in Edinburgh. It was extremely popular with audiences. The backstage atmosphere assumed a lighter, friendlier tone when Macrae invited members of the cast which included Una MacLean, Maurice Roeves, Jan Wilson, Anna Welsh and John Inman to spend a Sunday on Millport. On a more congenial note, on the morning of the opening day in Edinburgh, the entire company assembled in St Giles Cathedral to celebrate the wedding of Maurice Roeves and Jan Wilson. By all accounts, after the champagne breakfast, the performance that night was a memorable one, with the wedding guests in the audience noisily proclaiming their presence.

The summer's work was punctuated by visits to Millport and to Arran where Christine was working. Macrae's practice of copious letter writing, keeping in touch with his daughters, was carried on in the usual way, recording the daily round, noting the reactions of specific audiences, reporting his off-stage activities and exhorting and encouraging them to persevere in their chosen tasks. A brief holiday was proposed when the family might be together before Ann went to St Andrews University. As he was signed to play the Porter in *Macbeth* at the Assembly Hall during the Edinburgh Festival from 23 August to 11 September, Macrae suggested that the family might come to Edinburgh and for a few days indulge in the luxury of a hotel. He wrote to Christine that 'as the Porter is only in Act II for a few minutes', he would have plenty of time with them. These few minutes were more than telling. In an echo of his triumphs in *The Three Estates*, Macrae devil-portered with all the pithy wit he could wring from the script, pushing his lean body and mobile features into fantastical postures matching the innuendo in his voice.

During the rest of August he made a guest appearance on Roy Kinnear's television show and appeared in a revue, *This Is Friday*, for STV. Then in October he went to Aberdeen for three weeks to appear in two plays, produced by H.M. Tennent: Peter Whitbread's *Foursome Reel* with Robert Davies, Victor Carin and Brigit Forsyth, and Bridie's *Meeting at Night* with a cast that included James Gibson and Diana Chapell. Bridie's play came into Glasgow for a week at the King's. In certain circles, even though Macrae enjoyed star billing, it was held that to play in Bridie in Aberdeen was a decline in fortune, especially for an actor of Macrae's status in the mainstream of Scottish theatre, which is inevitably centred on Glasgow and Edinburgh. It was in marked contrast to the kudos of appearing in film or on the London stage with the lions of the profession. But common sense and opportunity, or indeed the lack of it, necessarily governed the choices Macrae made. He was certainly fulfilling his promise to continue to play in Scotland. For eight years he had been living a whirlwind of a life, tours, locations, hotels, planes and trains, interviews, controversies, commitment to Equity — perhaps he was becoming weary of the long separations from home.

It was while in Aberdeen that he was invited to supper by James Scotland who had written many of his comedy sketches for pantomime and the White Heather tours. James Scotland had the distinct impression that Macrae was a saddened man who felt that his career had 'drained away into the sand, after a start — more than one start — of limitless promise'. In spite of the adulation *The Wee Cock Sparra* had brought, he continued to feel haunted by the spectre of the Hogmanay bird and it grieved him for he began to believe that his audiences neither wanted nor expected anything more.

Then almost as if circumstances were conspiring against him, his chairmanship of Equity was placed in an ambiguous position. There was a hitch in the election procedure when the same person seconded both Macrae's and McCrindle's nomination. On ballot, there were eighty votes for each of the two nominees. The meeting agreed to have joint chairmen if Macrae would agree. But the matter was referred to the Council in London who suggested that the matter be resolved on the toss of a coin. The committee agreed and Macrae was elected.

But if it seemed to him that his artistic prowess was no longer commanding the attention he had become accustomed to, his efforts on behalf of the profession received singular recognition. He was requested, by the Federation of Theatre Unions in Scotland which was made up of the Musicians Union, the National Association of Theatrical and Kine Employees, the Variety Artists Federation and British Actors Equity Association (Scottish Committee), to draft a memorandum on the state of the arts in Scotland. In late November, his pamphlet, *Be Not Too Tame Neither* was published. The recommendations incorporated most of Macrae's own ideals, many of which were subsequently adopted and some remain to be fulfilled. It covered topics ranging from patronage to the role of the arts in education. The demand for the pamphlet was so great that extra copies were printed. This must surely have lifted his spirits.

— 12 —

LAST EXITS

The final illness

Christmas 1966. Macrae did not commit himself to any of the long running pantomimes as he was due to start work on another film in January. So once again he found himself in Aberdeen at the turn of the year to play a short engagement in the pantomime, *A Wish for Jamie*, at His Majesty's. While he was there he received notice that he had been elected Honorary Member of the Irvine Burns Club. This was no small honour as the constitution confined such membership to men who were distinguished poets, men of national eminence, or special benefactors of the Club. Macrae was in famous company, for amongst the Club's treasured holographs, are those of Walter Scott, Charles Dickens, Lord Tennyson, Garibaldi, Gladstone, Theodore Roosevelt, Marshall Foch, Churchill, Eisenhower and Bridie.

There was little cause to have negative thoughts as ten months of 1966 were already booked with contracts that promised to be artistically and financially rewarding. The first engagement was to play yet another policeman, Inspector Mathis, in the blockbuster James Bond film, *Casino Royale*. It was a small part but the film was crammed with stars from both sides of the Atlantic, Peter Sellers, David Niven, Orson Welles, Deborah Kerr, Charles Boyer, Woody Allan, all making guest appearances in supporting roles. Work of that kind meant that in Macrae's case 'resting' could certainly not be equated with lean days as he earned £2,500 filming for two months. During that time he made only fleeting returns to Glasgow. 9 Queen's Park Avenue was now very much the pied-à-terre he and Peggy had jokingly labelled the Glasgow flat when they bought 'Dundonald' on Millport.

The future on the live stage again looked bright with the first booking of the year at the Mermaid Theatre. By the end of March, Macrae was back in London rehearsing a cut version of Molière's *The Miser*, one half of a double bill (with *The Imaginary Invalid*). The plays, adapted by Max Loding, were directed by Julius Gellner. Macrae headed a cast which included Patsy Rowlands, Bernard Spear, Douglas Milvain, Mikel Lambert, Mark Rose and Tracey Lloyd. Bernard Miles played the lead in *The Imaginary Invalid*, supported by Russell Hunter, Eric Alan and Patsy Rowlands.

During rehearsals, Macrae sent his younger daughter the most poignant of letters written in the form of a blank verse poem. A depth of sadness, self-awareness and regret cast an unwonted shadow, compared to the habitually optimistic and jocular notes that enlivened the longer family separations.

Darling
Christine

I must apologize for forgetting your birthday today.
I hope you will forgive me. I forget so much
Oh, darling, you will never be 17 again, or 16, or 10, or
5, or even 1.
Nor shall I ever be 50 again. So there is some reason —
to shut one's eyes to the implacable march of time — for
forgetting.
Next year when I get my diary, you must insist that I
enter 14th April as a special date. It is. Our wedding day,
Ann's birthday, your birthday, and Mum's and my own
birthdays — I'm apt to forget them all, except the last.

Can selfishness go further?
I don't want to be reminded of mine.
It's now, at my time of life, a sort
of guilty secret.
Not so with you; the whole world
before you.
I'm sorry,
You can recall in the future that on

213

14th April 1966 your dad sat down and
wrote of sincere regret, coloured with the autumn
tones of his own age, and
gleaming with the light of spring.

Love
x Dad

The following week, after opening night, he wrote again. This time he seemed to have recovered his spirits and the letter returned to the familiar news and chit-chat that he always relayed when he was working out of Glasgow.

Darling Christine

I got Mum's wire with your and Ann's name too. Thank you. I'm writing this after the show. I don't know yet how it's gone. If I see any notices, I'll send them.
Not so many laughs as I would like. The producer wants me to do it with absolute sincerity — not the best way to get laughs. Bernard gave me a book about Shaw. Tracy gave me a wee bag of gold covered coins. I gave the girls violets and primroses. We had wine on the stage at the end, not too late because we did only one performance tonight. The other nights, we do two.
Hope you're getting time and peace of mind to study. The time seems so short. I'll be on this play until the end of May, but I'll be able to get a weekend, because we don't play on Mondays.
Michael Goldberg sent a wire, and Anna Welsh, who was in 'See How They Run' last summer.
I wrote to Ann. She'll be up to the nostrils in Anglo-Saxon.
The rain here's been terrible. As much in four days as the average for a month. So no walks. I do more jerks. Still get up at 8. Sometimes I lie down in the afternoon. I eat with great discrimination — half of what you ate here.
Hope you're all right now. Try fasting, and any exercise that makes you breathe deeply. In any case, write to me.

Love
x Dad

In light of the problems the cast met during rehearsals, the reviews exceeded everyone's expectations. The notices, as far as the play and the production were concerned, were lukewarm. But Macrae's interpretation of the miser, Harpagon, was something of a small, yet significant personal triumph. *The Times* critic was impressed with neither Max Loding's cuts — each play was reduced to one hour's playing time — nor his adaptation:

> The result of this enterprise is ham-fisted muddle. Molière's two masterpieces are comic diagnoses of human obsessions presented with the inspired finality of parables. In Mr Julius Gellner's production they unfold like music hall acts.

This comment looked suspiciously like the beginning of an all too familiar attack on Macrae's tendency to succumb to the techniques of pantomime, but in fact it was the prelude to a good notice:

> Of the two, *The Miser* turns out rather better. It is true that Mr Duncan Macrae, as Harpagon, bestrides the stage with a dance-like step; a rampant gleeful gnome, not harassed by money so much as simply going on about it. Still, he has an unmistakable comic presence and a fine sense of timing, and he saves the play from disaster.

The critics were less generous to Bernard Miles: 'There is no obsession in this performance and little for that matter of comedy.' Bernard Spear was in the cast of *The Miser*. He claimed that Gelling gave the actors little direction and each performer was left to his own devices. This would have accounted for the impression that the plays were composed of individual comedy turns.

Martin Esslin, one of the foremost contemporary authorities on drama, reviewed the productions for *Plays and Players*. Without superlatives, he gave Macrae the kind of notice he must have cherished. After asserting that Bernard Miles was miscast in *The Imaginary Invalid*, Esslin continued:

> Duncan Macrae, on the other hand, is really splendid as Harpagon, the Miser. He is a grotesque figure, very unlike one's usual conception of Harpagon, but convincing in his almost ballet-like dance step of a man besotted not only by love of money but also love of self, a macabre dandy. There is also, in this performance a sort of Brechtian quality. Duncan Macrae plays not only the Miser, but also his, Macrae's reaction to the idea of the Miser: he *demonstrates* Harpagon's folly with all the lightness and elegance that Brecht wanted to see in an actor who has mastered the alienation effect. A rare gem of a performance this! All the greater the pity that it is surrounded by no more than mediocrity.

Macrae had at last received recognition for the intellectual approach to acting he had so valued since his days with the Torch Theatre Club.

Production photographs revealed the strained and lined features of a man who, unbeknown to anyone, was already in the advanced stages of a grave illness. Yet as Harpagon, he gave what was probably one of the most sensitive — and unsung — performances of his career.

Back in Glasgow, Macrae had nearly two months to rest before returning to the exhausting regime of the Edinburgh Festival. During that time he worked for only one week on a BBC film, *Ransom for a Pretty Girl*, and earned £209.

Macrae's appearance at the Assembly Hall in 1966, turned out to be the last he was ever to make on the stage. *The Burdies* failed to bring him anything but the most modest of notices. The recently established Edinburgh Royal Lyceum Theatre Company was making its first contribution to the Festival and as such, the very Scottishness of the enterprise matched what Macrae had always believed: that the Festival should be a showcase for Scottish theatre. Douglas Young had translated *The Birds*, by Aristophanes, and transferred the action from fifth-century Athens to contemporary Edinburgh, complete with local allusions in broadest Scots. The material was ideally suited to Macrae's Aristophanic brand of exaggerated physicality. Under Tom Fleming's brisk direction, the powerful cast, which also included Callum Mill, Harry Walker, Lennox Milne, Martin

Heller, Morag Forsyth and Fulton Mackay, turned in 'sound enough' performances. *The Scotsman* found that, cast in the double roles of the Hoopoe Bird and a McGonnegal kind of poet, Macrae's performance disappointed. Fulton Mackay gathered the acting honours as the leader of the chorus of birds. On the whole, the adaptation was reckoned to be a clever idea. But the main thrust of the criticism, that the influence of pantomime was too intrusive, was unusually, not aimed at Macrae alone but at the entire production concept. The laurels were reserved for the ingenious and beautiful sets and costumes designed by Abdelkader Farrah. These proved to be the visual compensation for the obscurity of the language.

The Hoopoe Bird's first entrance was theatrically spectacular. A giant egg revolved to reveal Macrae splendidly arrayed in gaudy plumage and a fine head-dress, complete with beak. But thereafter, he was submerged in the production that Ronald Bryden described, in the *Observer*, as, 'a disastrous compromise between the demands of internationalism and the home market'. On that low note, Macrae gave his stage swan song.

John and Freddie Young drove the Macraes home from Edinburgh after one performance. Macrae looked tired, unwell and seemed to the Youngs, who had not seen him for some time, to be forgetful and strangely different in personality. The exhaustion was understandable. Every night when the lights went down at the Assembly Hall, he and Fulton Mackay rushed down the Mound and cut across to the Lyceum where, with Martin Heller and Eileen McCallum, they appeared in a late night revue, devised by George Bruce, *10.45 and a' that..*

As soon as the Festival was over he went to London, earning £750 for three weeks work on a film, *Thirty Is a Dangerous Age Cynthia*. He stayed on for post-synching on *Casino Royale* and came back to Glasgow in October for a welcome respite from the hectic travelling before embarking on the heavy schedule planned for the coming year. He went back to London briefly to take part in the cult television series, *The Prisoner*, which brought him £541. There was no doubt that in 1966 the earnings from film and television was excellent.

The next engagement was scheduled for November in another BBC television play, *A Black Candle for Mrs Gogarty*, with Phil McCall, Walter Carr and Peggy Marshall. Before rehearsals started, Walter Carr received an invitation to discuss Macrae's latest idea: to revive his greatest successes. Carr assumed that he was going to be offered the supporting roles in plays like *Jamie the Saxt* or *Gog and Magog*. To his surprise, he discovered that Macrae wanted not to act but to direct. Carr was to take all the old Macrae roles. They had worked well together on several occasions and it had been frequently remarked how physically similar they were. This always amused them, for they could see no resemblance beyond their tall angularity. Directing had been Macrae's first real satisfaction in his days in amateur theatre. Carr never discovered if this move was to be the fulfilment of an early ambition or if Macrae was too weary to go on playing.

Filming on *Black Candle* was almost completed by the end of November. Only the long shots remained to be done. At the same time as he was working on the television play, Macrae was preparing to be Long John Silver in Edinburgh Civic Theatre's production of *Treasure Island* at the Lyceum. Slipping comfortably into the familiar routine of dark evenings by the fireside, with Peggy 'hearing his lines', he was looking forward with some relish to this role. Presiding over the proceedings, perched in a cage on the piano, was a borrowed live parrot. But bearing in mind the old adage 'never act with children or animals', Macrae had decided that a 'stand-by' parrot of the stuffed variety would be more reliable on-stage if necessary. He would work with both birds.

On 1 December, Christine was dispatched on a trek round Glasgow to search for a likely matching candidate: the Art Gallery turned up trumps. The girl came home triumphantly bearing the prize bird which was duly installed on the piano beside its 'mate' while her parents continued with Long John Silver's lines. But when, at half past ten, Macrae announced he was going to the kitchen to make his usual cup of tea, he collapsed.

The family doctor first diagnosed brain haemorrhage and Macrae was rushed to the nearby Victoria Infirmary. He left 9

Queen's Park Avenue for the last time, leaving behind a frightened Christine with two parrots on the piano.

The following morning, with all the solemnity due to a celebrity, the hospital issued the first of a series of press bulletins :

> Duncan Macrae, the Scottish actor, was taken to the Victoria Infirmary late last night after collapsing at his home at 9 Queen's Park Avenue, Glasgow. It was stated at the Infirmary early today, that Mr Macrae was unconscious and 'very ill'.

After consultation it was decided that he would be best cared for in the eminent neurological unit at Killearn Hospital in Stirlingshire. Not far away in Kippen, the Macraes' friend, the Reverend Robert Begg, heard the news and rushed to the hospital. No visitors were allowed. Peggy was told that the minsiter had arrived and she felt that it was in answer to her prayer. She came out to talk with him in a corridor filled with well-wishers' flowers, too numerous to be accommodated in the confined space of the ward. Robert Begg promised to do all he could to support and help Peggy in her 'hour of need'.

On 5 December, the hospital announced: 'Mr Duncan Macrae continues to improve.' It was believed that he was out of immediate danger. He was able to get out of bed occasionally and walk with the aid of a Zimmer frame. His destination was often to the next room where he spent hours telling tales of magic and wonder to an enraptured small boy who was recovering from head injuries.

Ann returned home from St Andrews University and talk optimistically turned to recovery. The family was greatly heartened by the prospect of convalescence at Millport. Christine told her father that she intended to devote her life to the Scottish National Party. But, perhaps demoralized by a feeling that all the efforts he had made to encourage Scottish theatre had come to nought, he told her that he did not think it was worth the trouble.

In lighter vein, the press reported that Russell Hunter had volunteered to replace Macrae as Long John Silver and that to take the role, he had been released by the BBC from his contract in a television *Dr Who* series. Macrae was still sufficiently aware of his surroundings to be concerned about his replacement, but Peggy told him only that someone would be found. When she eventually announced that Russell Hunter was to step in, his reaction was simply 'Oh!'

The euphoria did not last long. To everyone's deep shock, further investigations revealed that Macrae was in the terminal stages of cancer. His particular kind of malignant brain tumour could take up to fifteen years to develop before the signs would become obvious in the everyday health and behaviour of a sufferer. The symptoms might include forgetfulness, lapses of memory, mood swings and uncharacteristic or irrational behaviour. Perhaps much that had puzzled those who had worked with him could now be explained. The sudden onset of the acute stage of the illness was all the crueller for being so unexpected. But with hindsight, there had been many hints which were all too often dismissed as Macrae's eccentricities.

It was agreed that the flat no longer had any purpose as there was no prospect of his ever working again. Peggy acted swiftly. It was sold within a week. For a while, it seemed that he might be able to come home to 'Dundonald' and, as temporary measure, Peggy moved to her brother's home in Mount Florida.

Loyal in crisis, the Macraes' friends rallied round. Marion Blytheman and Anna Taylor were always available to drive Peggy back and forth to the hospital. Macrae was comforted to hear that old friends were being so attentive, happy that Peggy would get 'a good meal at Jock and Anna Frew's at Newton Mearns', or that she spent many nights with the Littlejohns at Bridge of Allan.

By New Year's Eve, the hospital bulletin stated that while still seriously ill, there was little change and he was 'comfortable'. Gradually his condition deteriorated, and as he lost control of his body, his mind began to wander. He was irrationally beset, for a time, with the fear that Peggy might leave him.

On 22 January 1967, the Equity Committee received Peggy Macrae's letter thanking them for their good wishes and tendering her husband's resignation. The committee suggested he should be offered Honorary Membership. After some discussion, Alex McCrindle proposed that Macrae should be made Honorary President. It was agreed. The formal resolution read:

> In recognition of the work of Duncan Macrae as Chairman of the Scottish Committee since 1953, the Annual General Meeting of members working in Scotland request the Council to appoint Duncan Macrae, already an Honorary Member of Equity, to the post of honorary President of the Scottish Committee for so long as he may wish to hold it and to amend the Constitution of the Scottish Committee accordingly.

In February, it was unanimously approved that now that the illness had become critical, the Scottish Fund would pay Mrs Macrae's travelling expenses to Killearn Hospital. Peggy declined, declaring that it would be more appropriate to use such money at a later date to set up a scholarship or other appropriate foundation. The matter was discreetly put aside. She did not have to make the journey for long as it was soon evident that nothing more could be done at Killearn. Macrae was transferred to the Victoria. Gifts, flowers and a tide of good wishes flooded into the hospital.

The 1966 Report of the Scottish Committee informed the membership that Macrae had resigned from the Chairmanship as a result of suffering a stoke. It went on to pay tribute:

> John Macrae is the outstanding Scottish actor of his generation. Nobody who saw him in 'Let Wives tak tent', 'Gog and Magog', or 'The Three Estates', can forget the grace, the pathos or the humour with which he invested his characters. In his person he epitomizes the hopes and aspiration of a Scottish theatre.

There were good days and bad days. Sometimes he was lucid and cheerful and at other times he was withdrawn and depressed. There were days when he refused visitors, even close relatives, who were convinced that Peggy was over-dramatizing the illness. There were days when he welcomed gladly old friends like Alex McCrindle who left grieved at the extent of his suffering. Fulton Mackay telephoned Peggy from London every evening, anxiously hoping for some better news.

The winter sparkle of the distant pantomimes seemed so much dimmer that year as the months of waiting passed. John Duncan Macrae was never to see gleaming again the light of spring that he had so movingly written about to Christine on her birthday nearly one year before. By 23 March it was clear that he was going to live at most for another day. Peggy and Ann were continually at his bedside. Before Christine could reach the hospital, he had died.

Ann made a positive decision — 'no black clothes' for the funeral, although Peggy and Christine wore black. Years later, looking back at the press photographs, she doubted the wisdom of her choice. But perhaps her instinctive judgement was correct, one which her father himself would have applauded. He was to be cremated in Glasgow, and his ashes, according his wish, were to be buried at Kippen.

The streets on the route to Linn Crematorium were lined with people. Arms raised, half waving, half saluting, it seemed to Christine that they greeted the cortège, reaching out as if to make symbolic contact with someone who had briefly touched their lives. From poet to politician they came by the score, crowding into the chapel to the dramatically haunting lament played on the bagpipes by Sandy McNeil, the piper who had accompanied the first Citizens' European tour so many years before. It was standing room only — a fitting tribute to a man of the theatre. Robert Begg, the minister of the parish church at Kippen, described Peggy's invitation to conduct the funeral service, 'An unspeakable honour'. With dignified simplicity, he gave thanks for the joy Macrae had given to untold numbers, paying tribute to him as the great Scotsman, the great actor and above all the great and good man. At the committal, he read lines from the George MacDonald poem, 'Ane by ane they gang awa'.

Two weeks later, Peggy, en route to Kippen, arrived at Doris and Robert Littlejohn's house in Bridge of Allan, clutching a bag. Inside was the urn containing the ashes which she would entrust to no one until she reached the little graveyard. Once there, in contrast to the public thanksgiving of the cremation service, quietly and privately, the ashes were buried beneath a simple granite stone on which, crowned with a golden laurel wreath, were inscribed lines from Dunbar's poem, 'Lament for the Makaris':

> I se that Makaris amang the laif,
> Playis heir ther pageant syne gois to graif.*

Full circle to his youth, in the countryside he so loved, John Duncan Macrae finally rested on the hill overlooking the sweeping landscape to the North.

---

*   I see that poets, among other people,
   Play here their pageants, then go to the grave.

— EPILOGUE —

HONOUR, TROOPS OF FRIENDS

Peggy's tentative suggestion in February that a scholarship might be founded was not forgotten. In May, a working party was set up by Equity to organize an appeal to establish some form of memorial. Peggy offered the proceeds of her husband's endowment policies, a sum of between £4,000 and £5,000, as the basis of the fund.

Timed to coincide with the transmission of *A Black Candle for Mrs Gogarty*, the appeal was officially launched. In a brochure, with a reproduction of the William Crosbie portrait of Macrae on the cover, the committee declared it aimed at 'the creation of a permanent company to carry on where Duncan Macrae left off'. It included most eloquent and moving tributes from Hugh MacDiarmid, Ivor Brown, Andrew Cruikshank, Cliff Hanley, Robert Kemp, and Alex McCrindle. The Duncan Macrae Memorial Trust was established with The Lord Provost, John Johnston, as chairman, and Peggy Macrae, Michael Goldberg, The Hon. Lord Birsay and Alex McCrindle as the first trustees.

Alex McCrindle was able to report by October that the appeal had raised nearly £26,000. The money had been gathered in many ingenious ways. Students from the College of Drama sang Christmas Carols in the streets of Glasgow; children in Lenzie performed their own plays; the workers in a cigarette factory took a collection. Trade Unions, local authorities, commercial concerns and private individuals contributed anything from one shilling to £1,000. All theatre managements in Scotland had played a part. The biggest contributions predictably came from Macrae's friends and colleagues in the acting profession who gave their services free for shows that were put on from London to Dumbarton.

In London, a branch committee of the Trust mustered a formidable cast to put on a show, *Great Scot!*, at the Victoria Palace. The programme printed glowing tributes from each member of the cast. The Citizens' Company, in conjunction with the Close Theatre, designated the proceeds of a gala performance of *The Anatomist* to the appeal and the annual Alhambra *Show of Shows*, billed 'A Tribute to the late Duncan Macrae by his friends', reserved the entire box-office takings for the Trust.

But a more immediately tangible memorial was established in an annual Scots verse speaking competition for students at the Royal Scottish Academy of Music and Drama. An impressive plaque in the foyer of the Academy bears the names of the winners. Until the Trust's original aim to form a youth theatre could be realized, the Trustees decided to give the annual interest on the capital to groups already experimenting in this field. However, at Peggy's request, the first bequest of £1,500 was given in 1968 to the Citizens' Theatre even though they were not concerned in any major way with theatre for youth in Scotland. As it was the company's twenty-fifth anniversary, it was a fitting conclusion to that chapter of the Macrae story.

As for Macrae himself, Jock, John or Duncan, it does not seem to matter. Each of the masks created by these names allowed him to express the differing aspects of the essential Macrae who is recalled with much affection by all who knew him as a man of integrity.

As an actor he was judged by colleagues and peers to be possessed of natural instinct and the matchless timing essential to comedy. But he lacked the technical skill, usually associated with formal training, to recreate in performance something that had been fixed in rehearsal. He was a notorious 'up-stager'. Some say it was calculated, others claim it was artlessly unconscious. Whatever the reason, when he was on stage, it was Macrae that the audience watched, often to the detriment of the rest of the action. A favourite story is told of the occasion during rehearsals when he was asked by another actor where he, Macrae, would be at a given moment when he had no lines. Quick as flash came the answer that passed instantly into the treasury of stage lore:

'Don't you worry about me. I'll just be up at the back, picking up flowers.' Only the unwary would not know that this was the cue for all eyes to be riveted on Macrae's upstage business to the annoyance and discomfort of the actors whose concentration would be broken and whose lines would be disrupted by gales of unexpected laughter. Some who suffered from his waywardness never forgave him. Most did. The essential Macrae, despite his many infuriating characteristics, was an actor acknowledged and esteemed by other actors as a comic genius. But the cherished memories are of the jutting chin and the piercing eye which challenged an audience to watch only him, of the haunting musicality of the voice which could transform the most banal of lines into purest poetry, and of the eccentric charisma which bestowed dignity on the most trivial of roles.

The final word goes to Robert Cartland, the actor who played opposite him in *Gog and Magog* :

> If you were prepared to follow him through the highways and byways, night after night, you could scale the heights.

APPENDICES

— I —

A Memory of the First Production
of
Jamie the Saxt, 1937

In the winter of 1936-7 The Curtain Theatre was given the play *Jamie the Saxt* by its author Robert McLellan and it didn't take us long to find out that we had received something most special.

Parts were handed out and, with such a large cast, nearly all of us got something. I being given that of Jamie's Queen, Anne of Denmark — and she turned out to be one of the loves of my life.

We read it through several times and then Grace Ballantine, our producer, got us on our feet and started taking us through the moves and wonderful to behold, McLellan's king began, in the form of J.D.G. Macrae to take shape before our eyes. I cannot think that playwright and actor have ever served each other better.

Here was Bob's sharp, funny and most human monarch and here was Macrae with what, in the end, was to be the perfect interpretation, with every expression of face and voice and, above all, every movement of a long, gangling body, Macrae became, indeed, McLellan's royal Jamie.

Meeting most nights of the week we all worked with love and excitement on the play. The word 'love' is important because I think this first production of Jamie had a quality about it that was never re-captured in any subsequent staging of the play.

It wasn't easy. Having such a large cast and being a period play, costumes and sets strained a not very big budget and Norman Bruce, our chairman, was driven to going around his business friends winkling out fivers from this one and that.

As we, most of us, worked during the day rehearsals would go on into the night and it would be cold. The boys would rush down to the Grand Hotel at Charing Cross and come back with 'a small Drambuie' for our producer, who sitting through most of it wrapped in an assortment of rugs probably was freezing to death.

We worked on and finally — the dress rehearsal — everyone knows what they're like. In one scene I had a very pretty if somewhat low cut brocade dress to wear — Grace Ballantine took one look at me and said, 'Not enough bosom', and stuffed bits of Glasgow's beloved and defunct newspaper, 'The Bulletin', down my front, which I extracted after her back was turned, not wishing to be covered in printer's ink.

Word got around and we had a full house in Glasgow's Lyric Theatre — and they liked the play and were warm and appreciative and, I think, everyone was overcome with Macrae's performance. He was so entrancing in the part, I used to stand in the wings when I was off-stage watching his every move. I mentioned the word 'love' earlier and that is what shone out, all of us had put all our hearts into this play and it showed.

Waiting off-stage for the final curtain I found I was crying and I can still remember saying, 'What are you doing this for?' But after all this time I understand. I had taken part in a wonderful play and had watched a superb performance by John Macrae of His Grace Jamie of Scotland.

I saw the first of John's portrayals of the part for the Citizens'. John could never be other than great as the king, but in my small opinion, he was not as superb as he had been in the very first production by The Curtain Theatre.

As a post-script thirty years on — yes thirty years — a man, a stranger, stopped me on the road and said, 'I remember Macrae and you in *Jamie the Saxt* — my word, but it was wonderful.'

So, maybe I wasn't the only one to have been moved by the magic.

Pearl Brooks (Colquhoun)
Arran, 1988

'Cranks never make good democrats'

In Memoriam Duncan Macrae
by
Hugh MacDiarmid

Every movement of the lanky lean
Don Quixote-like figure
Was a revelation that made one smile
But never inclined to snigger.

For there was keen intellect in the fun,
A great comedian but no fool,
Measuring everything precisely
With movements like opening a joiner's rule.

His voice, the faces he made,
Every least antic, like a surgeon's knife
Intent on removing the ramifying tumour
That was poisoning Scotland's life.

The brainless clowning, the sheer fatuity,
of the 'Scotch coamics' whose psyche
In all its vulgar ignorance he laid bare
With masterly skill, by Crikey!

Duncan Macrae was a true Scot, a great Scot
And as such must not be forgot.
But whether we'll ever see his like again
on that, alas! I'd not wager a groat.

A wonderful operator, every gesture
An accurate, if perilous cut,
Deflating the foul complacency,
The Philistine idiocy and chortlin' 'wut.'

He made the matière d'Écosse
A little less impervious to sense
Than for several centuries, a single-handed
Triumph, against huge odds, for intelligence.

All the ubiquitous false Scottishness
He alone, it seems, could expose
With one thrust of an elbow or knee,
Turn of a bony wrist or poke of his nose.

If just ten men sufficed
To save a city long ago
We may well to Duncan Macrae alone
The salvation of the Scots genius owe.

Most theatregoers are morons, you said,
But why did you, dear Duncan, limit it
To theatregoers - it's true of all here.
There's no replacement now for your wit.

— III —

ROLES WITH THE CITIZENS' THEATRE COMPANY

AT THE ATHENAEUM THEATRE:
1943
Friar Innocence, in *The Holy Isle* by Bridie; **Sir William Heywood,** *The Good Natured Man*, Goldsmith; **Father Corr,** *Shadow and Substance*, Carroll; **Makarov,** *Distant Point*, Afinogenev; **The Man,** *Noah* , Obey

1944
First Policeman, *Liliom*, Molnar; **Hector de la Mare,** *Is Life Worth Living?*, Robinson; **Elder Daniels,** *The Shewing up of Blanco Posnet*, Shaw; **Sir Rufus Garnett,** *Bull Market*, Priestley; **Mr McCrimmon,** *Mr Bolfry*, Bridie; **Francis MacElroy,** *The Wise Have Not Spoken*, Carroll; **Scraggy Evans the Post,** *A Comedy of Good and Evil*, Hughes; **MacLaren,** *The Treasure Ship*, Brandane; **Justice Greedy,** *A New Way to Pay Old Debts*, Massinger; **Sir Charles Farwaters,** *The Simpleton of the Unexpected Isles*, Shaw; **Andrew Craigie,** *A Master of Men*, Corrie; **Donald MacAlpin,** *The Forrigan Reel*, Bridie

1945
John Duffy, *The Whiteheaded Boy*, Robinson; **Waiter,** *The Government Inspector, Gogol;* **Lovborg,** *Hedda Gabbler*, Ibsen

AT THE ROYAL PRINCESS'S THEATRE:
Israel Hands, *The Pyrates' Den*, Christmas Show

1946
Dr Levallois,*Victory Square*, Kemp; **Count O'Dowda,** *Fanny's First Play*, Shaw; **McCarthey,** *A Babble of Green Fields*, Romoff; **Father Shaugnessy,** *The White Steed*, Carroll; **Thomas Robertson,** *Day In Day Out*, Millar; **Bishop of St Andrews,** *Kate Kennedy*, Bottomley; **A Doctor,** *One Traveller Returns*, Murray McLaren; **Uncle James,** *It Look Like Change*, Donald McLaren; **His Excellency, Wang Yun,** *Lady Precious Stream*, Christmas show

1947
John Hananh, *A Sleeping Clergyman*, Bridie; **Michael Garaty,** *The Righteous are Bold*, Carney; **James VI,** *Jamie the Saxt*, McLellan; **The Bellman,** *Polonaise*, Kemp; **Johnny the Priest,** *Anna Christie*, O'Neill; **Finch McComus,** *You Never Can Tell*, Shaw; **Lord James Stewart,** *John Knox*, Bridie; **Inspector Goole,** *An Inspector Calls*, Priestley; **James Christie,** *The Christies*, St. John Ervine; **Angus Skinner,** *Weep for Tomorrow*, Carroll; **Tammas Biggar,** *Bunty Pulls the Strings*, Moffat; **Hugo,** *The Scuddievaigs*, Wallentein & Kennedy

1948
Mr Oliphant, *Let Wives Tak Tent*, Molière ad. Kemp; **Mortimer Neff**, *Double Door*, McFadden; **Quince**, *A Midsummer Night's Dream*, Shakespeare; **A Serious Person**, *The Black Eye*, Bridie; **Gaev**, *The Cherry Orchard*, Chekhov; **Flatterie & The Pardoner**, *The Three Estates*, Lindsay; **Donald MacAlpin**, *The Forrigan Reel*, Bridie (revival)

1949
Macbeth, [did not complete run of play, accident]; **Philip Ophid**, *The Devil was an Irishman*, Galloway; **Peter Stockman**, *An Enemy of the People*, Ibsen; **Bauldy**, *The Gentle Shepherd*, Ramsay; **Parmenion**, *Adventure Story*, Rattigan; **Moses MacIsaac**, *Vineyard Street*, Munro; **Harry Magog**, *Gog and Magog*, Bridie; **Sir Lucius O'Trigger**, *The Rivals*, Sheridan; **The Dame**, *The Tintock Cup*, Christmas Show

1950
Thomas the Rhymer, *The Lass wi' the Muckle Mou*, Reid; **Vulcan**, *The Queen's Comedy*, Bridie; **Dr Mortimer**, *The Atom Doctor*, Linklater

1951
Alex MacMillan, *Spindrift*, Mitchison and Macintosh; **Maitland**, *Mary Stuart*, McLellan; **Tartuffe**, *Tartuffe*, Molière

1952
Stage-manager, *Our Town*, Wilder; **Harry Magog**, *Gog and Magog*, Bridie (revival)

1953
James VI, *Jamie the Saxt*, McLellan (revival)

1954
King Dod III, *Right Royal*, Scott; **George Triple**, *Meeting at Night*, Bridie

1955
Sandiman Petrie, *The Sell Out*, Millar

1957
Dr Angelus, *Dr Angelus*, Bridie; **The General**, *Romanoff and Juliet*, Ustinov

1962
Duke McCash, *Saturmacnalia*, Hanley

INDEPENDENT PRODUCTIONS

1946
Pastor Manders, *Ghosts*, Ibsen - Unity; **Reverend Joshua McDowall**, *Torwatletie* - Unity

1952

Harry Magog, *Gog and Magog,* Bridie - Dundee Repertory Company; **Gilbert Dalgleish,** *Bachelors are Bold,* Watson - Scottishows

1953

Sir George Elphinstone, *Johnny Jouk the Gibbet,* Watson - Scottishows

1954

Harry Magog, *Gog and Magog,* Bridie - Scottishows

1955

Michael Scott, *The Warld's Wonder,* Scott - Scottishows

1956

Reverend McCrimmon, *Mr Bolfry,* Bridie - for Alastair Sim

1957

Angus McNaughton, *Muckle Ado,* McLaren - Perth Repertory Theatre; **The Nabob,** *The Flouers o' Edinburgh,* McLellan - Edinburgh Gateway Theatre; **Dr Angelus,** *Dr Angelus,* Bridie - Edinburgh Gateway Theatre

1959

Donald McAlpin, *The Forrigan Reel,* Bridie - Edinburgh Gateway; **The Pardoner/Flatterie,** *The Three Estates,* Lindsay - Edinburgh Festival production

1960

Jean, *Rhinoceros,* Ionesco - Royal Court Theatre, London

1961

Mr Oliphant, *Let Wives Tak Tent,* Molière, ad. Kemp - Edinburgh Gateway

1962

Harpagon, *The Miser,* Molière - Dundee Repertory Theatre

1964

Gilbert Dalgleish, *Bachelors are Bold,* Watson - Jimmy Logan's Metropole, Glasgow

1965

McLeavy, *Loot,* Orton - Tour (produced by Michael Codron); **The Porter,** *Macbeth,* Shakespeare - Edinburgh Festival production; **Mathew Bellows,** *Foursome Reel,* Whitbread and **George Triple,** *Meeting at Night,* Bridie - His Majesty's Aberdeen

1966

Harpagon, *L'Avare,* Molière - Mermaid Theatre, London

PLAYS IN THE SHEREK SEASON
1956

Let Wives Tak Tent (Molière, ad. Kemp); *A Man Named Judas* (Ronald Duncan); *Rabbie Burns Slept Here* (Donald McKenzie);*Tullycairn* (Joe Corrie); *Mr Bolfry* (Bridie); *Jamie the Saxt* (McLellan)

PANTOMIME AND REVUE

1950-1
Cinderella; Alhambra
1951-2
Aladdin; Alhambra
1952-3
Jack and the Beanstalk; Alhamabra
1953-4
Babes in the Wood; Alhambra
1954-5
Goldilocks and the Three Bears; Alhambra
1955-6
Just Daft; Empire
1956-7
We're Joking; Empire
1957-8
Mother Goose; Alhambra
1960-1
Skerryvore; Falcon
1961-2
Aladdin; Empire
1962-3
Satumacnalia; Citizens'
1965-6
A Wish for Jamie, His Majesty's; Aberdeen
1966
1045 and 'a that; Lyceum, Edinburgh - Revue
1966-7
Rehearsing for *Treasure Island*; Lyceum, Edinburgh

RADIO, FILM AND TELEVISION

RADIO PLAYS INCLUDE:
1945
Kidnapped; Julius Caesar; Master of Ballantrae; The 'Forty Five
1946
Too Late by Forty Years; Who Fought Alone; On the Mountain; The Man from the Sea; The Trial of J.S. of the Glen

1948
Disaster at Darien
1949
Storm in a Teacup
1951
Excerpts from *The Three Estates*
1952
The Lass wi' the Muckle Mou'; Hangman's Noose
1954
The Sell Out
1955
The Fortunes of Nigel
1958
Right Royal
1959
The Warld's Wonder
1962
Bachelors are Bold

OTHER BROADCASTS INCLUDE:

1948
Panel game *Catchwords; Chapbook;* overseas talk and poetry reading
1949
Short story readings
1950
Schools broadcasts and talks
1964
Ken Dodd Radio Show; short story
1965
Roy Kinnear Show

TELEVISION PLAYS INCLUDE:

1958
Candlehaven; You Never Can Tell; Death Hangs
1959
Lazarus; Para Handy; The Devil's Instrument
1961
Rory Aforesaid; The Conscientous Ganger
1962
Johnny Jouk the Gibbet
1963
Impasse
1964
It's All Lovely; Dr Finlay's Casebook; The Avengers;
1966
Green Pastures; Ransome for a Pretty Girl; A Black Candle for Mrs Gogarty; The Prisoner

OTHER TELEVISION APPEARANCES INCLUDE:

1958
Better Late
1959
BBC Hogmanay Party
1962
Crofter television advert
1963
Scottish revues and chat show
1964
Andy Stewart Show
1965
Rikki Fulton Show; *This is Friday*

FILM ROLES

[Year in which films were made, not year of release. American titles in brackets]

1946
John Macrae, *The Brothers*
1948
Angus McCormac, *Whisky Galore (Tight Little Island)*
1950
Superintendant Lodge, *The Woman in Question (Five Angles on Murder)*
Janitor, *What Say They?*
1953
Grandaddy, *The Kidnappers (The Little Kidnappers)*
1954
Schoolmaster, *Geordie*
1958
Duncan Ban, *Rockets Galore (Mad Little Island)*
Police Sergeant, *The Bridal Path*
1959
Highlander, *Kidnapped*
MacDougal, *Our Man in Havana*
1960
Pipe Major MacLean, *Tunes of Glory*
Sergeant MacLean, *Greyfriars Bobby*
1961
Trevethan, *The Best of Enemies*
1963
Barney, *The Girl in the Headlines (The Model Girl Murder Case)*
Dr Brass, *A Jolly Bad Fellow*
1966
Inspector Mathis, *Casino Royale*

— IV —

ARTISTS APPEARING IN THE DUNCAN MACRAE MEMORIAL APPEAL FUND-RAISING SHOWS.

Great Scot!

Victoria Palace, London
26 November 1967

Andrew Cruikshank, Andy Stewart, Dixie Ingram with Brian Sievewright and Girls, Jimmy Logan, The Corries, Ronnie Corbett, George Chisholm, Barbara Mullen, Ian Wallace, Joe Brady, Margo Henderson, Tom Fleming, the Alexander Brothers, Bill Simpson, Robin Hall and Jimmie MacGregor, Bill McGuffie, Gordon Jackson, Bernard Miles, Bernadette, Stanley Baxter, Moira Anderson, John Cairney, The Pipes and Drums of the London Scottish Regiment, John Laurie.

The Metropolitan Orchestra directed by Ivan Dozin
Prologue and Epilogue by Eddie Boyd
Directed by Eddie Fraser

The Anatomist

Citizens' Theatre, Glasgow
13 February 1968

Directed by Tyrone Guthrie
Designed by Robin Pidcock

Tom Fleming, Louise Breslin, Edith McArthur, Jean Taylor Smith, Gary Hope, James Gibson, Anne Kidd, Jean Hastings, David Blake Kelly, Roddy McMillan.

Show of Shows

A tribute to the late Duncan Macrae by his friends

Alhambra Theatre, Glasgow
17 March 1968

Seamus MacNeil, The City of Glasgow Police Pipe Band, Johnny Beattie, Sheila Lessels, Larry Marshall, Jimmy Shand and his Band, Kenneth McKellar, The David Wood Latin-American Formation Team, Tom Fleming, The Freemen, Rikki Fulton, Clem Ashby, Glen Michael, Chris Melville, Una McLean, Roddy McMillan, John Grieve, Walter Carr, Alex McAvoy, Jack Milroy, Josephine McQueen.

Directed by Rikki Fulton

— SHORT BIBLIOGRAPHY —

Winifred Bannister, *James Bridie and his Theatre* (London: Rockcliff, 1955)

Gourlay and Saunders, eds., *The Story of Glasgow Citizens' Theatre, 1943-48* (Glasgow: Glasgow Stage & Screen Press,1948)

Jack House, *Music Hall Memories* (Glasgow: Richard Drew, 1986)

David Hutchison, *The Modern Scottish Theatre* (Glasgow: The Molendinar Press, 1977)

J.H. Littlejohn, *The Scottish Music Hall 1880-1990* (Wigtown: G.C. Book Publishers, Ltd, 1990)

Ronald Mavor, *Dr Mavor and Mr Bridie* (Edinburgh: Canongate and The National Library of Scotland, 1988)

John Moore, *Ayr Gaiety: The Theatre Made Famous by the Popplewells* (Edinburgh: The Albyn Press Ltd, 1976)

Albert D. Mackie, *The Scotch Comedians: From the Music Hall to Television* Edinburgh: The Ramsay Head Press, 1973)

Helen Murdoch, *Travelling Hopefully : The Story of Molly Urquhart* (Edinburgh: Paul Harris Publishing, 1981)

Play Texts

Jamie the Saxt, by Robert McLellan (London: Calder & Boyars Ltd, 1970)

A Satire of The Three Estates, by Sir David Lindsay; adapted, Robert Kemp, ed. Matthew McDiarmid (London: Heinemann Educational Books Ltd, 1967)

Bridie's Plays:

TheAnatomist (London: Constable, 1932)
A Sleeping Clegyman (London: Constable, 1933)
What Say They? (London: Constable, 1939)
Plays for Plain People (The Holy Isle), (London: Constable, 1944)
Dr Angelus (London: Constable, 1950)
The Queen's Comedy (London: Constable, 1950)
Meeting at Night (London: Constable, 1956)
Mr Bolfry (London: Constable, 1978)

INDEX

Index

Index

Index

Index

249